Conversations with Ulrich Beck

CONVERSATIONS

Published

Bauman & Tester, *Conversations with Zygmunt Bauman*
Beck & Willms, *Conversations with Ulrich Beck*
Castells & Ince, *Conversations with Manuel Castells*
Giddens & Pierson, *Conversations with Anthony Giddens*
Žižek & Daly, *Conversations with Žižek*

Forthcoming

Eagleton & Milne, *Conversations with Terry Eagleton*
Hall & Schwarz, *Conversations with Stuart Hall*
Sennett & Klinenberg, *Conversations with Richard Sennett*

Conversations with Ulrich Beck

Ulrich Beck and
Johannes Willms

Translated by Michael Pollak

polity

Based on a revised version of *Freiheit oder Kapitalismus,*
© Suhrkamp Verlag, Frankfurt am Main 2000.

First published in 2004 by Polity Press in association with
Blackwell Publishing Ltd.

Reprinted 2008

Polity Press
65 Bridge Street
Cambridge CB2 1UR, UK

A catalogue record for this book is available from the British
Library.

Library of Congress Cataloging-in-Publication Data
Beck, Ulrich, 1944–
[Freiheit oder Kapitalismus. English]
Conversations with Ulrich Beck / Ulrich Beck and Johannes Willms;
translated by Michael Pollak.
    p. cm.
Includes bibliographical references and index. ISBN 978-0-7456-2823-3
(hb : alk. paper) – ISBN 978-0-7456-2824-0 (pb : alk. paper)
1. Liberty. 2. Sociology. 3. Social groups. 4. Capitalism.
I. Willms, Johannes, 1948– II. Title.
HM1266.B42513 2004
301–dc21
    2003008590

Typeset in 10.5 on 12 pt Berling
by SNP Best-set Typesetter Ltd., Hong Kong

For further information on Polity, visit our website: *www.polity.co.uk*

Contents

This book is based on the translation by Michael Pollak of *Freiheit oder Kapitalismus* published by Suhrkamp Verlag. It has been revised for the English edition.

Introduction: Thinking Society Anew

John Urry

Department of Sociology, Lancaster University

Every now and then a new way of thinking about the social world appears. And once that happens it is difficult to imagine how sociology had managed without that new way of thinking. It simply seems so obvious. Further, it is often difficult to see why it had taken so long to get to that novel way of thinking; once "discovered" it is hard to imagine what all the fuss was about. The new theory or concept or method rapidly becomes part of the academic furniture, one prop that supports or holds up sociological thinking. The distinctiveness of the innovation may thus be hard to see even just a few years later. It is normalized, making possible some understanding of the extraordinarily opaque and hard to fathom social world.

Teaching students can be difficult since some of the time one is trying to explain just why a particular theory or concept or method was such an innovation although it has now become part of the furniture. The teacher has to recreate the disciplinary world before that new way of thinking and this is something that contemporary, cool students may find hard to see the point of. I was struck by this issue while reading obituaries of Robert K. Merton who recently died aged 92 and who was responsible for probably more enduring innovations than any other sociologist during the second half of the twentieth century. But explaining the nature of Merton's contribution to those young people who at least as teenagers will soon only know the twenty-first century will not be easy.

It is also not easy to convey the sheer difficulties involved in generating really productive new ways of thinking. They are not simple to achieve. Indeed most innovations have a very short shelf life; they never survive more than a few outings within various books, articles, and papers. Like new start-up companies new ways of thinking die rather rapidly and the author's innovation remains at best a small footnote in the history of the discipline. Not that small footnotes are unimportant since building on the "small footnotes" of others is how all disciplines make even faltering progress. Merton incidentally emphasized the importance of developing intellectual work that builds "on the shoulders of giants."

Intermittently, however, something more than a small footnote does occur and the new way of thinking becomes part of the furniture. Indeed to become part of the furniture is the best measure of success and scholarly achievement. Within sociology there are relatively few such bits of furniture. This is in part because the social world is so opaque, social systems are incredibly open, and there are extraordinarily diverse processes affecting human practices moving through time and across space.

Ulrich Beck's concept of *risk society* is one such innovation that has become part of the furniture of modern sociology, an innovation nicely simple to grasp but which conveys a profoundly illuminating argument that deals with how the results of social activities powerfully and unpredictably move through time and space.

Beck argues that there is an epochal shift from industrial to risk societies. The former were based upon industry and social class, upon welfare states and upon the distribution of various *goods* organized and distributed through the state, especially of good health, extensive education, and equitable forms of social welfare. There were organized societies, there was a national community of fate, and there were large-scale political movements especially based upon industrial class divisions that fought over the distribution of these various "goods." In the postwar period in western Europe there was a welfare state settlement in such industrial societies based upon achieving a fairer distribution of such goods.

By contrast the concept of risk society is based on the importance of bads. Risk societies involve the distribution of bads that flow within and across various territories and are not confined within the borders of a single society. Nuclear radiation is the key example of this, something few sociologists had ever examined. The risks of nuclear radiation are "deterritorialized." They cannot be confined into any specific space nor into any current sector of time. Such risks thus cannot be insured against. They are uncontrolled and the consequences incalculable. The unpredictable consequences of radiation stemming from nuclear energy will last into the unimaginable future.

These risks have largely resulted from the actions of people – of state officials, scientists, technologists, and corporations – treating the world as a laboratory. These risks are thus not simply physical effects although they have profound physical consequences. Such risks are difficult to see or even more broadly to sense and yet they can enter and transform the body from within; they are not external to humans.

This concept of the risk society of Beck was a kind of revelation. It provided for sociology a way of speaking of the physical world and of its risks that brought in a striking array of new topics. In effect it enabled people to speak of things, indeed in a way to "see" things, that they had been trying to speak of and to see, but where the concepts had been chronically lacking.

First, then, the notion of risk society puts onto the sociological agenda the very nature of the physical world and of the need to create a sociology of-and-with the environment. No longer is it possible to believe that there is a pure sociology confined and limited to exploring the social in-and-of itself. The distinction of society and nature dissolves. The thesis of risk society brings out that most important phenomena within the world are social-and-physical, such as global warming, extreme weather events, global health risks such as AIDS, biological warfare, BSE, nuclear terrorism, worldwide automobility, nuclear accidents, and so on. None of these is purely social but nor are they simply physical either.

Risk society brings out how important aspects of people's lives are structured not through social processes alone such as the distribution of goods in a welfare state society. Rather major aspects of human welfare stem from the movement and potential impact of these "person-made" risks. So people's lives, we have come to understand, are affected by the global spread of AIDS, by global warming, by the ubiquitous spreading of the motorcar, by acid rain, and so on. Welfare is a matter of bads as well as of goods.

Second, the risk society brings out the importance of human bodies within sociological analysis. In going about their lives humans sensuously encounter other people and physical realities. There are different senses – and indeed sensescapes – that organize how social arrangements are structured and persist. Moreover, some such realities can in effect get inside the body. In the case of nuclear radiation generated by the 1985 explosion at the Chernobyl nuclear power plant (in what is now the Ukraine) people right across northern Europe had their lives transformed by something that could not be directly sensed (in the UK sheep farmers in Wales and Cumbria, for example).

Only experts with specialized recording equipment could monitor such direct exposure, while some effects of Chernobyl are still being generated decades later as children are being born with multiple deformities resulting from the explosion nearly twenty years ago. The naked senses are insufficient – so humans have to depend upon experts and systems of expertise to monitor whether they are subject to risks that may get "inside" their bodies. So bodies are subject to expert intrusions, as with the monitoring of HIV/AIDS, as risks pass in and through humans. And this in turn generates complex relationships between expert knowledge and lay forms of knowledge and especially with how the latter in a "risk-expert" society are often treated as inferior, subordinate, and replaceable by expertise.

Third, these risks know no boundaries. Rich and poor people, rich and poor countries are all subject to the nuclear radiation that emanated from Chernobyl. Such radiation does not stop at national borders nor at the homes of the rich, although there are big inequalities in the distribution of expert resources to remedy the unintended consequences of such risks.

This risk society results from the changing nature of science. Once upon a time science was confined to the laboratory – a spatially and temporally confined site of "science." Although there are examples of science escaping – most famously in Mary Shelley's story of the monster created by Frankenstein – generally this does not happen. But nuclear energy and weapons change this equation. Suddenly the whole earth is the laboratory – the monster has escaped and risks now flow in, through, over, and under national and indeed other borders. The mobility of GM (genetically modified) crops is a more recent example that shows the difficulties of trying to limit the location and impact of testing GM crops within a confined area (in so-called field trials). Modern science according to Beck increasingly treats the whole world as its laboratory and this spreads risks across the globe. In recent formulations Beck emphasizes the global nature of risks; that there is not so much a risk society as a global risk culture.

This argument about the "borderlessness" of the risk society has, together with the writings of many others, developed the analysis of "globalization" and of the implications of this for sociology. Beck has especially shown the nature and limitations of what he calls "methodological nationalism." What does this mean and what is wrong with it?

He means that sociology has been historically concerned with the analysis of societies, with each society being based upon a distinct national state (or nation-state). So there is a system of nation-states and sociologists study their particular society defined in national state terms. The nation-state provides the container of society and hence the boundary of "sociology."

Moreover sociologists tended to generalize from "their" particular society to describe how "society" in general is organized. Especially American sociology developed in this way, presuming that all societies were more or less like that of the USA, just poorer! It was perfectly possible to study that particular society and then to generalize as though all, or at least most, other societies (at least those that mattered!) were much the same. This led to debate as to the general nature of order or of conflict within "society" based upon the particularly distinct US pattern. Order and conflict theories were to be "tested" within the USA and it was presumed that these conclusions could then be generalized to all societies or at least to all rich industrial societies.

It is not hard now to see many problems in this although it took Beck and various others to expose its limitations. For decades it was simply how sociology worked; it was a taken-for-granted way of doing sociology.

First, though, we now know that societies do differ a lot. The US and Scandinavian societies both have high levels of economic wealth. But the former has never had a welfare state while the latter countries have continued with a substantial welfare state (many "goods"). So generalizing from any particular society as though that tells one about all societies (or even all rich societies) is wrong.

Second, it is also clearly wrong to presume that all societies are on some kind of evolutionary scheme and that each will develop towards the "western model" (even if there were such a single western model). Beck and others have helped to subvert any sense of a single evolutionary scale of the development of society from the less to the more developed.

Third, global transformations represent a meta-change that makes us develop new concepts to displace what Beck rather provocatively calls *zombie* concepts. Zombie concepts are those that were appropriate to the period of methodological nationalism. They are not appropriate to the contemporary period.

One zombie concept is that of the "household" that operated within the time of the first modernity. But now there are so many different kinds of household. Because of the "normal chaos of love" there are very many "loving" and "living" relationships so no single notion of "the" household can remain. Beck uses the notion of "who washes their clothes together" as an illustrative indicator of the huge variety of now who counts as a household member and who does not.

Overall Beck seeks to capture the sense that late twentieth-century societies underwent an epochal shift. But he rejects the idea that this is a move from the modern to the postmodern, as was characteristically argued by analysts a decade or so ago. For Beck these are all "modern" societies; there is not a moving beyond the modern to its opposite. So rather helpfully he suggests there is a *second* modernity.

The first modernity was "nation-state centered," the second is "non-nation-state centered." In the second the indissoluble link of society and nation-state is fundamentally broken with the emergence of a logic of *flows* including of course the flows of risks discussed above. In such a situation modernity is radicalized, subjecting itself to reflexive processes. Second or reflexive modernization disenchants and dissolves its own taken-for-granted foundations. The normal family, career, and life history have all to be reassessed and renegotiated. The notion in, for example, Talcott Parsons's writings that each society is a closed and self-equilibriating system dissolves, albeit at uneven speed and impact.

This second modernity can be seen in many different aspects. Particularly what is emerging is a banal cosmopolitanism comparable with the banal nationalism characteristic of the first modernity (that is most shown in waving national flags). Banal cosmopolitanism is seen in the huge array of foodstuffs and cuisines routinely available in many towns and cities across the world. It is possible with enough money to "eat the world." What others have viewed as a "postmodern eclecticism" is seen by Beck as not against the modern but as rather a new reflexivity about that modernity, as cuisines (and most other cultural practices) are assembled, compared, juxtaposed, and reassembled out of diverse components from multiple countries around the world.

There is thus coming into being a new system in which everyday practices involve exceptional levels of cosmopolitan interdependence. This transforms people and places from within, especially with the proliferation of many new and extensive *transnational* forms of life. Probably the most extensive of these is that of the overseas Chinese, a transnational society with tens of millions of members around the world. In many ways this is a powerful society. It is simply that its members do not live within a single territory. We thus need ways of understanding the developments of transnational "societies" that have nothing to do with a single nation-state that acted as its container. This is the second modernity according to Beck.

And in this analysis Beck strongly emphasizes the distinction between globalism and globalization. These words may sound the same but there is a distinct difference of meaning.

Globalism involves the idea of the world market, of the virtues of neoliberal capitalist growth, and of the need to move capital, products, and people across a relatively borderless world. And this is what many business and other writers mean by globalization. They argue that globalism generated much economic growth over the past two decades, especially since Reagan and Thatcher inspired the general "deregulation" of markets in the 1980s. Many, of course, object to this neoliberal globalism but Beck emphasizes how opposition will not be able to resurrect the power of the nation-state since that institution and its powers stem from the first not the second modernity.

Globalization for Beck and indeed others is a much more multidimensional process of change that has irreversibly changed the very nature of the social world and of the place of states within that world. Globalization thus includes the proliferation of multiple cultures (as with cuisines from around the world), the growth of many transnational forms of life, the emergence of various non-state political actors (from Amnesty International to the World Trade Organization), the paradoxical generation of global protest movements (such as the WTO), the hesitant formation of international states (like the EU), and the general processes of cosmopolitan interdependence (earlier referred to as banal cosmopolitanism).

Roughly speaking Beck argues that globalism is bad (or at least very problematic in its neoliberal face), globalization is good and is in fact the only vaguely progressive show in town. There is simply no way of turning the clock back to a world of sovereign nation-states. That world has been lost in the second modernity. We have to go with the grain of contemporary globalization.

In terms of contemporary politics one might pose this as a conflict between the USA and the UN: the USA represents globalism, the UN a hesitant and flawed globalization/cosmopolitanism. These two visions of the second modernity haunt contemporary life, each vying to control and regulate an increasingly turbulent new world.

And one reason for this turbulence is that both globalism and globalization are associated with increased *individualization*. In the first modernity there was a clear sense of social structure, with many overlapping and intersecting institutions that formed or structured people's lives. People's experiences were contained, ordered, and regulated. Family life, work life, school life, and so on took place within the boundaries of each society that possessed a clear and constraining social structure. Such a social structure was based on distinct and regulated social roles. Sociology for most of the last century sought to describe and analyze such social structures that mostly held people in place. Sociology investigated social roles and how they fitted together to form social structures.

But, say Beck and other analysts, in the second modernity (at least in the rich countries of the "north") these structures have partially dissolved especially because of the very development of global processes. This forces or coerces everyone to live in more individualized ways. Lives are disembedded from family, households, careers, and so on. Social roles are less clear-cut and determined by an overarching social structure. There is a radicalization of individuals who are forced by social and cultural change to live more varied, flexible, and fluid lives. Beck shows how globalization coerces people to live less role-centered lives, lives that involve extensive negotiation and dialogue and where people have themselves to accept responsibility for their actions as they try to work them out with others in their network.

This shift might be characterized as the shift from social role in the first modernity to social network in the second. It also means that the key concepts for sociology change. So although we still study social inequality – and indeed across the globe inequalities seem to have increased – it is less clear that social class is the principal unit of analysis and investigation. Beck rather provocatively has helped to develop the argument that individualization is the social structure of the second modernity and this produces non-linear, open-ended, and ambivalent consequences. This is again a very different vision from most sociology focused around the zombie concepts of the first modernity, especially the idea that social class based on occupational division is the key element within social structures and that the object of class struggle is to transform the state.

Beck has helped to develop three strong points here. First, poverty is no longer a characteristic of those within the working class. It is something that many people will now experience, including especially young middle-class people undergoing higher education! Second, the world of a second modernity is a world of unbelievable contradictions and contrasts. There are "supermodern castles" or citadels constructed next to scenes from *Apocalypse Now* (as with the now destroyed World Trade Center in New York with thousands of beggars living in the subway below). Class hardly captures such shimmering inequality. Third, the major movements of change have little to do with class, even that responsible for the most stunning transformation of the past two decades, such as the dramatic and unpredicted bringing down of the Soviet empire by various rights-based social networks.

And the collapse of that empire is an interesting case of where changes took place almost overnight although the Soviet system had seemed so resolutely in place. Everything appeared unchanging. There was an apparently fixed social structure found throughout most societies of eastern Europe, including the German Democratic Republic (GDR, now part of a unified Germany). And yet that social structure crumbled away, like sand running through one's fingers. There was an avalanche, an explosive change, a dynamic that went out of control, to use some of Beck's terms.

Indeed in many processes in the second modernity there is a regressive uncertainty so that the more we know, the more uncertainty grows. In some ways this is an example of complexity thinking that is partially present within Beck's analyses. In the case of BSE in Britain in the 1980s, the attempts to limit uncertainty by providing new information had the very opposite effect. The information designed to re-establish equilibrium resulted in movement away from equilibrium. And this sad story of British beef unpredictably spread across much of Europe in ways that beef producers elsewhere were unable to control. There was a contagion that could not be resisted.

What this analysis is dealing with is how in the second modernity there are many out-of-control processes, systemic unintended side effects. Beck, for example, describes boomerang effects, that corporations or western science can generate consequences that return to haunt them. With the mobile nature of risks across the world, the generators of schemes can also suffer the consequences. Within complex systems everyone is inside and suffers the effects.

Beck's exemplary investigations of global risks and global cosmopolitanism have highlighted the implausibility of sociology of the first modernity based on the triad of nation-state/social structure/role. What his analyses are now doing is pointing beyond these zombie concepts to initiate new terms appropriate for the second modernity where there are complex mobile systems, not simply anarchic but on the edge of chaos. Beck has provided some analyses by which to begin to capture the unpredictable, dynamic, global complexity of the second modernity.

Conversation 1

Postmodernity or the Second Modernity?

JOHANNES WILLMS *Let's begin with what sociology means, and why it's useful. What is the task of sociology?*

ULRICH BECK The simplest answer is that sociology is the study of society. But that just regresses the question, because what is society? You can't see it, you can't smell it, you can't taste it, and you can't hold it in your hands.

What do you mean? Are you saying that society isn't sensuous? If I walk down a crowded sidewalk, or into a bar or football stadium, society seems to fill my senses, sometimes almost to the point of overwhelming me.

Yes, but that's not what sociology means by society. Society is certainly there where you sense it, but it goes beyond your senses. It is present where you find a lot of bodies, but it can't be reduced to them. It's something that manifests itself through them. The individual who reads a book quietly all alone in her room is still doing it within the force field of society. It is there in her origins and her education. It could be that she's writing a review. But whether she's making a living or fulfilling a duty or experiencing a pleasure, society is enabling and constraining her. Society is realizing itself through her actions.

Society's ethereality is only the first in a series of problems. We have then to deal with the fact that society is always disguising itself. It is covered over with a thick shell of its own interpretations. Society is composed of conscious agents, be they parties or unions, or less formally defined groups like the rich or the educated, and every one of them is constantly producing its own interpretations in order to explain and defend its position. This is the decisive difference between the social and the natural sciences. You can't just stick society in a test tube and analyze it scientifically. Unfortunately, these interpretations are not just nonsense that can be dismissed and swept away. They are important. They contain essential and indispensable knowledge that can only be gained by studying them in detail and analyzing out their truths.

What sociology does is to develop its idea of society out of these partial views and in contrast to them. For this reason, the sociological understanding of society necessarily entails at least a partial withdrawal from immediate perception. Society in the sociological sense is only graspable by means of a conceptual framework, one which has to seem abstract by comparison with the partial views that frame our everyday experience.

Then there is the question of power. By means of this process of abstraction and development, sociology necessarily undercuts the self-interpretations of society's actors. This necessarily brings it into collision with the lay sociologists who represent them. Some of these views have a great deal of power behind them. Others have less power but have the authority of expertise because they are propounded by social critics or cultural theorists.

What we get in the end is such a tangle that sociology often seems cursed. But this is also its attraction for an ambitious thinker: the challenge of making sense of it all, and beyond it of society.

Let's take up the question of power for a moment. What would you say to the view, to put it a bit polemically, that sociology is just the handmaiden of power? That it supplies the information that political decision makers need to do their job?

Many sociologists would deny that. But the fact is, there is a deep connection between the ideas of sociology and the reality of the nation-state that manifests itself even in denial.

To start with, it's worth pointing out that sociology doesn't usually analyze society. It analyzes *societies*. We talk, every day, without giving it a second thought, about German society, French society, American society, Iranian society, Japanese society, etc. But what this way of speaking implies is that there are as many societies as there are nation-states. In the common sense of sociology, societies are assumed to be organized in nation-state terms. The state is assumed to be the regulator and guarantor of society. The nation-state is conceived of as something that contains society within its borders. The state is conceived of as something that fixes society, that secures and stabilizes it.

This idea that fully realized societies are nation-state societies is sociology's fundamental postulate, and it has molded every one of its central concepts. This is what I mean when I say that sociology is dominated by *methodological nationalism*. Its key assumption is that humankind is split up into a large but finite number of nations, each of which supposedly develops its own unified culture, secure behind the dike of its state-container.

How does this affect sociological practice?

It structures our entire way of seeing. Methodological nationalism is the unquestioned framework which determines the limits of relevance. The social space that is bordered and administered by the nation-state is assumed to contain all the essential elements and dynamics necessary for a characterization of society. The nation-state has become the background against which society is perceived. And when the sociological gaze is attuned like this, it has enormous difficulty in perceiving society when it appears outside this framework. The result is that non-nation-state forms of society are overlooked, minimized, or distorted. They are literally difficult for sociologists to conceive of.

Historically speaking, what sociologists have done in practice is that they've analyzed one nation, the one they've lived in, and then drawn inferences about society in general. In the best of cases they dallied a bit in a middle stage where they compared their chosen society with a couple of others before leaping to universal conclusions. This is true of Marx, who built his picture of capitalism out of the experience of nineteenth-century Britain. It holds for Durkheim, who was thinking of France when he asked his question "What holds modern societies together?" (He famously answered of course by arguing that the new division of labor that divides society also produces a new kind of organic solidarity to hold it together.) And it's true of Weber. When Weber was constructing his theory of bureaucracy and instrumental rationality, the main picture before his eyes was turn-of-the-century Prussian administration. To make a mea culpa, it was originally also true of me. My first book, *Risk Society*, articulated a vision of how global risk consciousness would soon affect society. But society was assumed to be a welfare state much like Germany of the 1970s and 1980s.

But isn't this methodology a little questionable? To distill concepts out of the experience of your own society, and then make those the standards against which to measure all societies of the same period, no matter how different their historical formations?

It's extraordinarily questionable. And, as many people have pointed out, it also represents a kind of western conceptual imperialism.

Yet none of that should blind us to the paradoxical fact that this approach was extremely fruitful for a long time. No matter what school of social thought you subscribe to today, sociology had a major role in shaping it. And every sociological concept, whether developed by Marx or Durkheim or Comte or Simmel or Weber, grew out of this generalization of the European experience of the nineteenth and early twentieth centuries. Its genius and its limitations are inseparable.

This is also the mixture that allowed western thought to misrepresent imperialism as the process of "western rationalization." Sociology was contemporaneous with, and was one of the expressions of, the formative upsurge of European national consciousness. Within that framework of thought, colonial exploitation was firmly identified with progress. As an explicit assertion, this idea has now long been abandoned. But it still survives tenaciously in our assumptions. You can see it in the conceptual blindness that ascribes all improvement in developing countries to westernization, and ascribes all deterioration in their situation to not westernizing or not modernizing enough.

These conceptual blinders impose serious limitations on our ability to produce valid theories about the present world situation. They are also a political barrier, since, as a narrative of the history of the relations between the so-called center and the so-called periphery, this one is so opposed to the historical experience of the periphery's inhabitants that it poisons the attempts of the two sides to communicate. This is one of the main reasons why, for many non-Europeans, "globalization" looks like just a new euphemism for the same old imperialism and exploitation, only this time by a "world market" that flies no flag. For both the sake of a social science worth its salt, and a politics that is just and effective, it is urgent that both sides communicate. For that to happen, we need a historical and conceptual framework that makes sense of both sides' experience.

What you say of sociology's conceptual imperialism is clearly true in retrospect. But as you say, it was true of all nineteenth-century European thinking. It doesn't seem like something we can really condemn sociology's founding fathers for not transcending.

That's true. But the retrospective view highlights deficiencies that we still need to fix. What we today consider conceptualized description, most of their contemporaries regarded as prescription and prediction. We don't because we can easily see that the world they predicted didn't come to pass. But this means something was fundamentally wrong with their system of statements that we need to fix in order to understand the world as it actually exists.

The achievement of classical sociology was to grasp the internal dynamics of the industrial market society that was then just coming into existence. Sociologists distilled its basic principles out of their own contemporary experience. The concepts they developed spread out and conquered the intellectual world. They were extremely fruitful for empirical research and they had huge political effects. But the irony is that the power of these ideas, and their consequent success, was all founded on this questionable inference from each theorist's society to society in general. We could call it the universalist inference. It's false. Yet the perspective it made possible had an enormous amount of explanatory power.

Our job now is to rethink sociology so that it no longer presumes this inference in each and every one of its concepts. We have to change our perspective. This necessarily also means changing our sociological practice. No one knows better than sociologists that every perspective rests on a social foundation.

The reason this task has finally become urgent is that the explanatory power of the classical model has been steadily growing weaker. Globalization is creating a world very different from the nineteenth-century world in which this universalist inference took form. It presupposed a world of bounded and opposed societies, each in its own container, and each with its own culture, its own economy, its own identity, and control over the destiny of its own people.

What we need to do now is make the change from a *universal* perspective to a *cosmopolitan* perspective. When we infer from *a* society, usually our own society, to society in general, the result is naïve universalism. *Globality*, by contrast, is what results when sociologists from all countries of the world, having interpreted their own societies through the use of the same universal categories, then meet and confront each other with their different findings and try to reconcile them. It then becomes immediately clear that there is no longer a privileged standpoint from which society can be investigated. In order to deal with this problem, a global or cosmopolitan sociology has to introduce a radical change of view. It has to open itself up to *dialogic* imagination and research. In order to accomplish this, it has to rethink and rebuild both its conceptual and its organizational forms. It has to get away from using the nation-state as the underlying unity of its thought and observation. It has to get away from the North Atlantic, and from the myth that this region shows the rest of the world its future. It has to move out to embrace the social cosmos. What is happening is a mutual reorganization of the global and the local, destined to trouble the here/there cultural binaries for ever. Postcolonial voices from the so-called periphery have to play a weightier role, not only for understanding the periphery, but also for understanding the so-called center. The reason why sociologies and social theories of the center have traditionally been blind to power might well be because it's right in front of their face. The perspective of the other, sharpened to the reality of power through the experience of humiliation, has an essential role to play in understanding both sides of the power equation.

The transition from the classical to the cosmopolitan perspective in the social sciences will be analogous to the change from a Newtonian to a relativistic perspective in physics. The former has validity, but it will be shown to be a special case. However, in the case of the social sciences, this will take much longer, because a cosmopolitan viewpoint by definition cannot be the work of one man, even a genius, and it cannot be summed up in a few universal laws. It will be more like the change of perspective that accompanies the transition from a rural society to an urban one. Only this time it will accompany the transition from national perspective to a global one.

I see that many of the concepts we'll take up later at great length have already managed to sneak their way in. But I'd like to spend a little more time talking about the classics of sociology. How did they become the classics?

The most remarkable thing about the holy fathers of sociology is that their scriptures are still actively reverenced today. They haven't passed into history like their equivalents in all other sciences and most of the humanities. There is no other social science in which writers who wrote in the nineteenth and the turn of the twentieth century are still such a central, living presence. Weber, one of the greatest thinkers of his time a century ago, is still one of the most influential thinkers in sociology today.

There is not in sociology a set of theoretical models that define the discipline, as there is in the natural sciences or in economics. The classics are our replacement for theory. That's why they seem irreplaceable, and that's what makes them classics. Unfortunately, this privileged role they play (especially in German sociology) is what makes it so difficult to relativize the historical content they poured into categorical form 150 years ago when modern society was just beginning to take shape. To give them their due, these were thinkers who really knew how to forge a concept. However, the end result is that their system of mutually necessary truths is still the rail system on which sociology travels today.

This sounds to me like a paradox out of theology. Religious truths are developed under specific social conditions, from which they are then abstracted. The result is that they end up covertly dragging along social ideas that once made transparent sense (like lord and master) and translating them into completely different social contexts. There, though, the source of the problem is clear. The fathers of the church can never be murdered.

The object of the classical sociologists, the nation-state which they called society, has clearly gone through a lot of changes since they lived within its boundaries. It is not only that those bound-aries have become much blurrier. The nation-state has also lost the sacred meaning that it had in the nineteenth century, when nation-alism was widely considered a form of moral regeneration. It was already impossible to think that way about nationalism after World War I, and that was almost a century ago.

So now we live in a new era, and we need new categories to understand it. Isn't it obvious that sociology has to completely rein-vent itself if it's to meet the challenge of the changed situation?

I think so, and this is central to my diagnosis of what's wrong with sociology. I also think it is the key to many of the tensions, uncertainties and outbreaks of hatred we see in society at large. Many of them emanate from difficulties in coping with the same basic question: "How can we think, or even live, without the cherished ideas that make us who we are?" When sociology debates – or rather mainly resists – the question of its own rein-vention, it is reflecting many of these tensions in society at large.

My theory is that what we are dealing with here is a *meta-change*, a change in the coordinates of change. This meta-change is best understood as a new dynamic that was created when the process of modernization began to transform its own taken-for-granted foundations. Modernity then passed an inflection point and began to change into something qualitatively new.

Many of my colleagues react with panic to this interpreta-tion because they think it sounds the death knell of sociology. I think the opposite. I think it marks its rebirth. However, unlike when sociology first was born, this time it starts out already firmly established in the university system, socializing students from all over the world into its system of reference, and dis-posing of far-reaching research facilities. Now it suddenly falls into a situation where the framework of society is changing. This should be exciting. It means all the big questions have to be rolled out again, and all the small ones too. They all have to be posed anew, negotiated, and answered again – and not through universalistic arm-chair theory, or through the lost innocence of counting national flyspecks, but through truly transnational and comparative statistics that we have yet to develop. Sociology doesn't have to sacrifice the professionalism it has attained. But we have to have the courage to pose the big questions again, and not continue to assume that they've all been answered. So this should be the opposite of the death of sociology. On the contrary, opening these questions up again is exactly what is needed to give sociology back the ability it once had to fascinate everyone who came into contact with it.

You speak of a crisis, a conceptual and foundational crisis in the social sciences, as a source of renewal. Max Weber once said something similar. He said: sometimes the light changes, and it makes all central problems look different, and then the sciences have to re-equip their conceptual toolkit to make any progress. But how does one go about it practically?

Essentially there are two complementary ways of proceeding. The first is to unearth fundamental assumptions that are now shaky. The second is to treat new phenomena as if they were really new, and ask, "How can we understand this sociologically?" The way to renew sociology is to treat problems as starting points rather than ending points.

My own theory begins with this empirical curiosity, which is indispensable for a renewal of the social sciences. My own central concept of the "second modernity" is very much something that grew out of empirical analysis. Of course, that also made it a declaration of war on a petrified sociology that had repressed and forgotten the historicity of its object through its fascination with the classics.

My central contention is that sociology developed in the container of the nation-state. Its categories of perception, its self-understanding, and its central concepts were all molded to its contours. And because the concepts thus engendered refuse to die, the sociological imagination is now inhabited by zombie categories. They haunt our thinking. They focus our attention on realities that are steadily disappearing. And they haunt our empirical work, because even the subtlest empirical work, when framed in zombie categories, becomes blind empiricism. Zombie categories embody nineteenth-century horizons of experience, the horizons of the first modernity. And because these inappropriate horizons, distilled into *a priori* and analytic categories, still mold our perceptions, they are blinding us to the real experience and the ambiguities of the second modernity.

*That's a big claim. The proof, of course, is in the working out. Can
you give me a concrete example?*

Here's a good example. The household is a central unit of reference. It plays a key role in almost all our categories of social
analysis. In order to define classes, for example, we operationalize our definition of households. The income of households,
which is mostly identified with the male breadwinner, is used
as an indicator for the class position of all members of the
family. But what exactly counts as a household nowadays?
Pressed far enough, that simple question can throw your average
inhabitant of Europe into as much confusion as if you asked
him what New Labour stands for.

In the microcosm of the family, you can see taking place in
miniature all the changes that are taking place in society, and
you don't have to be a sociologist to be struck by them. There's
a little bit of everything in there. My children, your children,
our children; divorce, remarriage, living together, living apart, or
having more than one living space; juggling different careers,
permanent mobility, etc. Just take grandparents, for example. It's
not only that they are becoming more important, as a reserve
army of home care that stands ready to help manage the
turbulence of everyday family life. They are also multiplying,
through no effort of their own, and without any genetic mani-
pulation, simply through the divorce and remarriage of their
children.

All this only scratches the surface of the normal chaos of love.
Against this background, the question "What is a household?"
is like one of those little kid questions that seems simple but in
fact calls everything into question. But remember, if you can't
define a household, you can't tell us anything definitive about,
for example, class.

This is a perfect illustration of a zombie category. None
of what I've just said is news, least of all to sociologists. Yet
we still measure households like we always have. And we still
use numbers based on them because "they're the only reliable
numbers we've got." So all of our assertions about social reality
are built on something we know is a fiction, but which we continue to treat as a reality. So what keeps this dead idea walking
as if it were alive? The dauntingness of the alternative. We know
households don't correspond to the old model anymore, and

that in fact only a small minority now consist of a breadwinner, his wife, and two kids. What we don't know is where to begin to make a new model. Because if we admit it isn't a unity, how do we measure it at all? Furthermore, since the family reflects in miniature changes going on in society as a whole, redefining it necessarily involves other terms that are just as questionable, such as career, religion, ethnicity, and class. Pull this one thread, and the whole sweater starts to unravel. It seems impossible. Yet the alternative is that the heart of our social reality is dissolving and we're acting like it's not. Not only family sociology, but the sociology of classes, and sociology itself, rests on the household. And it doesn't exist anymore.

Now I'm beginning to understand the attitude of your colleagues. This is subtle sociology. But it also seems like sociology dissolving itself, no?

No, on the contrary, it's the beginning of the process forward. The critique of zombie concepts is the first step in the creation of a reflexive sociology. The renewal of sociology begins with the question, "To what extent are our fundamental categories based on assumptions that have become historically obsolete?" Each answer to that question begins the process of developing new and more historically sensitive categories. So first we uncover key generalizations that are no longer true. Then we develop new dichotomies and a new system of reference. And then, having opened up a new space for the imagination, a new way to think about society and politics, we color it in and fill it with life through empirical work, empirical work that this rethink has made possible. Once this process gets rolling, it will take on a dynamic of its own. It will continuously reveal the weaknesses of accepted ideas and suggest new ways to improve them.

Part of what we need is a willingness to try out alternatives. If we can't define the household or the family, then can we begin somewhere else? The French sociologist Jean-Claude Kaufmann starts out with the question, "What is a couple?" The immediate answer in that case is no more obvious than it is with the family. A couple is no longer defined by a marriage license or even by gender preference. So Kaufmann tries a different kind of answer: a couple exists when two people do one load of washing. In other words, he uses an empirical marker. But by fully explicating its meaning, he reveals much of what is new about everyday life: a whole tissue of entanglements, negotiations, excuses, and protestations that he sums up under the heading of "dirty laundry" (which is the title of his book).

The fact that nothing is obvious when you look closely is the key to understanding these negotiations. It's what generates them. To start with, what counts as dirty? Who washes for whom? When does it have to get done by, and is ironing really necessary? Most important of all, what happens when he answers yes to one of these questions and she says no? What makes everyday life second modern is that everything is in principle negotiable, because there are no pre-given norms from which we can derive answers; and yet *answers are continuously arrived at,* because the work has to get done, and it can't be divvied up without implicitly producing working principles.

It's not always a conscious or intellectual process. In fact, crucial parts of it probably can't be. There are always several key questions that a couple can't negotiate directly because it drives them nuts. In addition, the practical realities of living together mean that we can't question everything all the time. So we consciously set limits to our doubting. This is where the real problems of empirical analysis begin, because, as we all know, most arguments about dirty laundry aren't about dirty laundry. They're about mutual recognition and feelings of neglect. This is also true of society's "dirty laundry" in general. Almost all fights about everyday tasks are overlain with potentially explosive conflicts about recognition and identity. What does it *mean* that you won't do my laundry? It means that you have no respect for me as a person!

Behind the zombie category of the household lies a rich social reality. Reinventing sociology means conducting excavations on the unknown society in which we live. Society is reproducing itself, and transforming itself, behind the façade of our cherished descriptions. We have a lot of work to do before we can see what it really looks like.

"Zombie category" is a wonderfully nasty phrase, which is probably why I'm inclined to linger on it a bit. How do you recognize a zombie category when you see one? You've given us an example, with the household. Are there general principles?

There's no litmus test for it, of course. But I think we can say somewhat systematically that there are three principles on which our old conceptualizations rested that have now become questionable. And although it may not be immediately obvious, all of them ultimately derive from the national container perspective.

The first is the assumption that territory is essential to the nature of society. The conceptual world of sociology still bears the impress of the national container in which it was formed. It assumes any social action requires physical traction on the ground. It assumes that geographical closeness produces social closeness, even though we are faced with a growing number of situations in which people who live geographically close to each other are socially isolated from each other, while being intimately connected with people far away.

Almost all social and political theory still has this territorial bias. Today we occupy a world of transportation and communication networks in which social and physical space have diverged. Social and spatial borders now vary independently of each other. Both kinds of border still exist, both are still important, and both are being constantly redrawn and reinforced. But to understand them, we need to rethink their relation from the ground up.

The second shaky principle is the belief that to understand individuals sociologically, we have to subsume them under pre-existing social collectivities. Sociology understands the individual as largely determined by the situation in which she finds herself, and we mainly conceptualize this situation as assigned (rather than as chosen). This is how our concept of classes works, as well as our concepts of family and nation and many others.

This was a very important premise in the history of sociology. It was this assumption that justified abstracting from individual action to sociological concepts in the first place. Sociology considered individual self-understanding suspect on ideological grounds, precisely because the facts of the collective situation only receive partial expression there. But while this principle played a constitutive role in the creation of sociology, today it is obscuring new forms of individualization which we'll discuss in greater detail later on. (See chapter 2.)

The idea of society as being fundamentally made up of large constituent subgroups presumes that there are pre-given collective situations that make common sense to all members of those groups. New processes of individualization and differentiation are rendering this assumption less tenable. As each individual's relation to society's institutions becomes less like those of her fellows, correspondingly more in each individual situation has to be consciously chosen. Choice has become not only a more important but also a more constitutive element of the individual situation. We can no longer treat volition as an epiphenomenon.

Individuals are increasingly constructing their most important collectivities and doing it consciously, in the broadest sense of the word conscious. Consequently the self-definition and identity of individuals is increasingly independent of any single collective situation in which we might like to frame them. Rethinking sociology will require us to develop a new concept of individualization, and to place it in the foreground. We will also have to rethink the social basis of individualization. Society still enters deeply into the constitution of the individual, but in a different way, and not simply through constraint.

The third crumbling pillar of the classic perspective is the evolutionary principle. By this I mean the assumption that the West's is the best possible way to organize a society; that its pattern of differentiation is the one all other societies must develop toward if they want to develop at all; and that its future will necessarily be a continuation of its past. This is an article of faith rather than science, of the original faith in progress that gave birth to social science. It now stands in the way of that science's continued development because it blocks sociology off from the implications of contingency. Social development is open-ended. Its end cannot be foreseen, and that has to be incorporated in our conceptual framework. This same faith has also kept us from seriously considering the question of whether some aspects of the first modernization have not been outweighed by their dark sides, especially when those dark sides have been exported to the periphery, or to the future, and not therefore credited to the present account.

The uneasiness caused by these developments has been felt in many places and formulated in various ways. Some people talk

*about postmodernity, others about the second modernity. The
latter is your concept, of course. What is the second modernity?
How would you distinguish it from the concept of postmodernity?*

Well, there are as many postmodernisms as there are postmodernists. I've learned a lot from many of them, such as Zygmunt
Bauman, and even from French philosophers of postmodernism
like Lyotard. There could not have been a theory of reflexive
modernity without having engaged with the central ideas of
postmodernism.

However, that said, postmodernist theory only tells us what
is *not* the case. It doesn't say what *is* the case. I'm afraid I am
somewhat sick of the "post-ism," "de-ism," and "beyond-ism" of
our times. Individuals and institutions and social movements
need a reasonable picture of meta-change that they can use to
orient themselves, which requires empirical investigation and
conceptual hard work.

Modernity is a problem in need of a solution for which
Europe bears a special responsibility. Europe invented it, even
if it did borrow crucial bits from other cultures. Europe therefore has a special responsibility for its shortcomings. When a
manufacturer puts a faulty product on the market and it causes
trouble for the customers, the manufacturer announces a recall
and offers to fix it. In a certain sense, Europe needs to "recall"
modern society, which it sold to (or forced on) the world with
all its faults. What we need is a fundamental self-critique, a redefinition – we might even say a reformation – of modernity and
modern society. Modernity needs to be re-formed in the fullest
sense on a global level.

For this task, postmodern thought is inadequate. It explains
why the old ways of conceiving modernity are no longer valid,
and then it stops short. It explains why the old ways of drawing
boundaries rested on hidden and unjustifiable assumptions, and
then it stops, leaving it a complete mystery how social life continues on. It seems unconcerned with that. There seem to be
two obvious inferences to be drawn from this attitude. One is
that the ruling ideas must not matter much, because if you
destroy them, things carry on much as before. The second is that
there must not be a real crisis. It must only be a confusion of
ideas, because if there was a real crisis, a turning point in reality,
there would be some urgency about addressing it.

This finally is my real beef with postmodernism. Despite all the hubbub, when its stance is reasoned out to its ultimate conclusions, postmodernism finally seems to deny the newness and crisis nature of our situation. That is true even of the term itself. What seems to be an end, a breakdown, a "post" is, looked at from the other side, always a beginning and a restructuring. This has always been true in history, and history's not ending, not so long as there are humans left to interfere.

So to simply criticize normal sociology and then stop, to simply deconstruct and then stop, is not enough. We need to reconstruct and to restructure our concepts. If the old science of society is no longer adequate – and it is not – then we need to develop a new one.

This is exactly what we are doing in the research institute in Munich that I'm involved in. We are trying to redefine the basic concepts of social science. We are trying to make clear what distinguishes the first modernity from the second modernity, and to develop the pluralized perspectives necessary to comprehend it. The challenge of theorizing the second modernity is that the system of coordinates is changing. But we are not simply between two perspectives. We are involved in a transition from one perspective to several simultaneous perspectives. There is a pluralization of modernities in the making.

A fair starting point is to say that the difference between the first modernity and the second one is the difference between "nation-state centered" modernity and "non-nation-state centered" modernity. However, this is a much deeper change than it looks like at first sight. Every fundamental distinction and criterion that we have up until now identified with modern society takes as its premise that society and the nation-state are identical. If we remove this taken-for-granted premise, these distinctions no longer make sense.

It may not be immediately obvious that the nation-state is at the bottom of all our sociological and political concepts, but that is only a sign of how pervasive and naturalized this assumption has become. We literally find it difficult to imagine thinking without it. Therefore, we think, it *must* be true. But it isn't. And once we admit that it isn't, where do we begin? What can "modern society" mean if *not* the nation-state? What can modernization mean if it is *not* equated with westernization and Europeanization?

If the first modernity was predominantly a logic of structures, the second modernity is largely a logic of flows. But how can one research such a "liquid modernity" (to use Bauman's term for it)? As a practical matter, how can we make reasonable decisions about the future under conditions of radical uncertainty? Especially collective decisions? And how can reflexive social institutions grow and develop in a world that is, in some respects, literally fluid and boundless?

So these are the sorts of questions you are tackling at your research center?

Exactly. As well as trying to build the organizational structure of a cosmopolitan social science, where scholars bring different perspectives and evidence from various parts of the world into fruitful confrontation and collaboration.

Let's return to the postmodernists. Your main criticism is that they are interested in deconstruction without reconstruction, and that the social sciences need to construct new concepts.

Yes, and also, very importantly, that these new concepts have to be connected to the empirical world.

Are there ideas in postmodern theory that you think are useful for understanding the second modernity?

Oh, absolutely. There are many places where postmodernism has furnished our starting point. Take, for example, the idea that there has been a fundamental change in the nature of boundaries, including social and conceptual and even natural boundaries. This is central to the thinking of several postmodern thinkers, and it is central to the definition of the second modernity. There has been a pluralization of the boundaries: within and between societies; between society and nature; between us and the other; between life and death. This pluralization changes the inherent nature of boundaries. The more boundaries increase, the easier it becomes to draw new ones, for better and for worse. They become not so much boundaries as attempts at drawing them. Every boundary becomes in some sense optional, in some sense a choice, and in some sense arbitrary. This in turn changes the nature of the collectivities that are defined by them.

Postmodern and second modern theorists are in complete agreement up to this point, but then they diverge. Where postmodernism simply celebrates this multiplication and opening up of boundaries, the theory of second modernity starts with the problem this new reality poses for individual and collective decisions, and with the problem that the continued existence of such decisions poses for theory. People have to make decisions. Neither social nor individual life is possible without them, and every decision draws a line of inclusion and exclusion. So long as social life goes on, there must be a practical logic that allows us to draw boundaries on a daily basis, and it is the job of sociology to find out what that logic is.

Through empirical examination, we find out which boundaries are being created along with decisions. At the border between life and death, there are now multiple boundaries where there used to be one. For example, the brain can be dead while the heart is still beating. Here, exactly as theory posits, the more boundaries there are, the more each takes on an "as-if" character. But the result is not that it is impossible to determine a socially legitimate boundary. Instead what happens is that there is a heated debate, and an arbitrary and fictive boundary is designated, but one which thereafter is handled as if it were true.

Institutions that are capable of such conscious boundary drawing are enabled in a way that those of the first modernity were not. But this process also generates qualitatively new kinds of trouble and crises. To investigate those troubles is to unveil the emergence of the second modernity.

This is a different approach from that of a thinker like Donna Haraway, who celebrates cyborgs. She implies that we should celebrate that there are no borders anymore and that everything is combined with everything else. I think this is a challenging view, and in some respects it has validity in the realm of culture, but social institutions don't work that way. They have to construct and legitimate boundaries in an age of flows. That's what they do, that's what makes them social institutions. In the second modernity, they have to do it in a new way, they have to do it reflexively.

So how would you distinguish your view of contemporary society from that of postmodernity?

Modernity has not vanished, we are not post it. Radical social change has always been part of modernity. What is new is that modernity has begun to modernize its own foundations. This is what it means to say modernity has become reflexive. It has become directed at itself. This causes huge new problems both in reality and in theory. The first modernity depended, tacitly but crucially, on many non-modern structures for its clarity and stability. When modernization begins to transform those structures, and make them modern, they cease to be usable foundations. This is what distinguishes the second modernity.

This is not an intentional process. It is a process of cumulative unintended side effects that eventually produce a change in fundamental social principles. These are often effects that were originally intended to be more narrow in scope than they turned out to be. Market expansion, legal universalism, and technical revolution, after shattering the boundaries of traditional society, have gone on to revolutionize their own foundations. Marx once summed up this process in the phrase "all that is solid melts into air." It turned out to be even truer than he could have imagined.

Is this what you mean by "reflexive modernization?"

This is exactly it. Simple modernization becomes reflexive modernization to the extent that it disenchants and dissolves its own taken-for-granted premises. Eventually this leads to the undermining of every aspect of the modern nation-state: the welfare state; the power of the legal system; the national economy; the corporatist systems that connected one with the other; and the parliamentary democracy that governed the whole. A parallel process undermines the social institutions that buttressed this state and were supported by it in turn. The normal family, the normal career, and the normal life history are all radically called into question and subsequently have to be continually re-negotiated.

This is the new and complex reality we have to figure out on both a theoretical and an empirical level. It is not beyond modernity. The distinction between the first and the second modernities is an attempt to account for both the continuities and discontinuities that are involved in this change. The goal is to open up a space for redefining modernity as a global conflict.

So it is not a rupture but a mixture of continuities and discontinuities. Can you systematize your distinction between the first and the second modernity?

Yes. For the purposes of empirical research, it has been useful to identify a basic set of assumptions which underlie the first modernity, and which are called into question in the second through the process of reflexive modernization. They are as follows. In the framework of the first modernity, society is thought of as organized in terms of the nation-state. Secondly, it is conceived of as based on pre-given collective identities that are anchored in large collective groups. Thirdly, it is thought of as full-employment society. Paid labor is supposed to be available for all normal people, and people are defined as normal by participating in it. Fourthly, the first modernity rests on a clear distinction between society and nature. Nature is conceived of as the "outside" of society, and as a functionally infinite resource and sink. And lastly, the first modernity presupposes Weber's principle of technical rationality, which presumes that all the side effects of industrialization and rationalization are predictable and controllable.

These are the basic premises of the first modernity. When I say they are increasingly being called into question through the process of reflexive modernization, this is not something that happens all at once, but rather something that has been happening on several different time scales since the middle of the twentieth century. The presumption that society is something "contained" in nation-states has been undermined by globalization, which I don't mean only, or even mostly, in the economic sense, but even more as a social and cultural and political phenomenon. The idea of pre-given collective identities that are provided by a small number of large collective groups has less and less empirical relevance to a society that has been structurally transformed by the ongoing process of individualization. The paradigm of a full-employment society is increasingly inapplicable on account of the fragmentation of work and the increasing variety and predominance of non-normal forms of employment. The idea that nature is an infinite sink and resource has been called into question by the ecological crises that loom in every direction. The idea that that there is a clear distinction between society and nature has been called into question by things like gene technology, human genetics, and nano-technology, all of which blur the line between them.

These last technologies also bear on the premise of predictability and controllability, which has been undermined by the proliferation of global risks. Because such risks are systemic, they change the very concept of risk, from one of probability to one of radical uncertainty. The fact that they cross national borders also makes them impossible to capture in national statistics or to cope with through national action.

Global risks produce global risk society. (See chapter 3.) This brings us to the last point, which is that sociology's view of society as a closed and self-equilibriating system full of linear processes, a view most clearly embodied in the work of Talcott Parsons, is being historically superseded through reflexive modernization.

The concept of the second modernity is necessarily an open one. We can't describe it in terms of a closed arrangement of institutions. We can only describe it as a process of transformation of the first modernity. Since modernity was always a dynamic system of continual change, what we are thus describing is a change in the coordinates of change. This is why I've called it a meta-change.

The goal and direction of this change is completely nondeterminate. It can yield new institutions, but it can also yield new fundamentalisms that attempt to resurrect and reinforce the premises of the first modernity under changed conditions. So this is a very variable process which can give rise to a host of completely different scenarios. It can't be interpreted as a simple process of transformation from A to B. The second modernity is not an evolutionary concept.

Nor can the first and the second modernities be thought of as mutually exclusive in time or space. They exist simultaneously, and completely interpenetrate each other. This is what makes the analysis and understanding of this meta-change so difficult.

It was precisely to solve this analytical problem that I introduced the distinction between the first and second modernities.

It is purely a heuristic device. Its purpose is methodological and pragmatic. It enables us to pose the question of new categories of thought and a new frame of reference in the clearest possible terms. It allows us to conceive of frameworks in emergence, and of frameworks in overlap, and of both at the same time, which in the end is what we're actually dealing with. It should in no way be misunderstood as an evolutionary periodization.

You wrote a book about "reflexive modernization" with Scott Lash and Anthony Giddens. But Lash and Giddens both seem to mean the term differently than you do. Could you briefly sketch out the differences in your positions?

Well, of course a theory that values pluralism as highly as this one should be internally pluralistic, and in fact it's true that our common book contains three very different interpretations of reflexive modernization.

With Tony Giddens, it's actually *reflective* modernization that's his central concern, in the sense of self-reflection on the foundations and consequences of modernity. He sees this as anchored in systems of experts who are continually analyzing and then overthrowing their old conceptual foundations and thereby making new structures possible.

This overlaps, of course, a great deal with my own approach. I completely agree that self-reflection is an important motor of modernization. But there are also a few problems, from my point of view. In the first place, if we make this the central identifying feature, it becomes almost impossible to draw a distinction between reflexive modernity and normal modernity. I think this leads Giddens to interpret reflexive modernization as essentially a new stage in the same process. He emphasizes the continuity more than the discontinuity. I focus more on the unintended consequences of the modernization process, and on how they eventually coalesce into a qualitatively new dynamic, a transformation of society.

A key part of this has to do with the concept of uncontrollable and incalculable risk. The dominant view is still that all risks can be reduced to probabilities and thereby rationalized. This amounts to pretending that there is no such thing as the unknowable future. It denies in effect that such kinds of risk can exist and only makes them worse.

My work in this area began with my first book, *Risk Society*, which focused on the environment. This was clearly an area where dangers were being intensified through being denied because experts literally couldn't perceive them, never mind reflect on them. So when I speak of reflexive modernization, I specifically mean to include this kind of non-reflection. What I mean by reflexive modernization is the self-confrontation of modernity, its confrontation with the side effects of its own success.

For me, reflex is *action*, action directed backwards, a process of alteration that begins to alter itself, to progressively become a new process. One of the key effects of this is that it introduces turbulence into institutions. This is not only true whether experts register it or not, but in fact their initial obliviousness often plays an important contributing role.

How would you distinguish your view from that of Scott Lash?

Scott Lash developed a position in that book that contrasts with those of both Giddens and myself, and I think he made some very strong points. He accused us both of largely limiting our notion of understanding (at least in practice) to cognitive understanding, and of not giving enough emphasis to the noncognitive and emotional aspects of modernization. He claimed that while both of us focused on the importance of taken-for-granted backgrounds, we didn't fully appreciate that being noncognitive was essential to their nature, that it is what enables them to serve as backgrounds. He does a very good job of bringing the philosophical tradition to bear. He concentrated most of his fire on Giddens, because there the difference was more stark. Lash argued that neither emotional phenomena, nor violence, nor aesthetic symbols could be considered "reflexive" in the conscious sense that Giddens was using it. In Giddens's framework, they would have to be treated as non- or pre-reflexive. My use of the word reflexive is very different, as I've just discussed, and doesn't at all exclude unconscious phenomena. But Lash's larger philosophical points about the importance and nature of backgrounds could just as well have been raised against me. I took them very seriously, and I've attempted to meet them in later publications.

So, to return to my opening question, in the face of the second modernity, is the task of sociology no longer to describe the society before us, to illuminate it, to make an efficient model of how it functions, but rather to predict the future society that will result when all these side effects have run their course?

No. That's impossible, because the process is not determinate. The idea that we can predict the future is something we have to get over. Not only is the future indeterminate, but its indeterminacy is part of the meaning of the present. This is something we need to incorporate into the way we think.

The first thing we have to do is describe how society is reacting under the new conditions. Our starting hypothesis is that all everyday social relationships are changing and dissolving along the lines of our household example. Everywhere we look, our familiar black/white either/ors are becoming checkerboards of overlap. For example, the enormous split between the center and the periphery, the first and third world, is now being displaced to, and reproduced within, the metropoles themselves, where the super-rich and the globally excluded often occupy neighborhoods that are physically actually quite close. We still think in the orderly categories of the first modernity, but we live and act in the gray zones and turbulence of the second modernity.

This is by no means simply a negative process. Inside the container state and outside it as well, new social realities are taking shape that we can study as exemplars of how society is beginning to regenerate itself in deterritorialized forms. This is visible among the global elites, who already think of themselves as global players, as citizens of the world. They are aware of happenings all over the globe and they all speak the same language. At the other end of the economic spectrum, there is a vast body of transmigrants who are developing forms of life which are just as transnational. It is normal now for an Indian taxicab driver to live in Chicago but to be at the same time still intimately tied to his homeland. Modern technology makes it possible for him to be as much a part of an extended household as if he lived in another part of his home country. The money he sends home can arrive just as regularly, and cable television and cheap phone calls can keep him in daily contact with events. He is integrated into both societies, and a new form of society is being

integrated by people like him. He doesn't live in the either/or
reality of container societies, where you are either in the USA
or you are in India. He lives in the this-as-well-as-that reality of
transnational society. He exemplifies how this society is coming
into being.

Part of the work before us is to analyze exemplary phenomena like these from the perspective that they may symbolize the
future development of society. That's exactly what the classic
sociologists of the nineteenth century did, by the way; they
didn't just describe the society before them. But while we are
just as intent as they were to study society in transition, sociologists today have to completely give up the idea that we can
predict the future.

Comte dreamed that sociologists would become the priests
of society. That never happened and thank goodness. Real sociologists can't assume the status of experts, and shouldn't want
to. In the first place, it's anti-democratic, and in the second place,
it's anti-scientific. Experts who proclaim the dominant creed of
social development are expounding a dogma. Even if we could
make it less dogmatic, by incorporating contingency and contradictoriness, this mode of pope-like proclamation is in itself
inimical to the advance of knowledge.

Sociology's job is to take the trouble to make empirical obser-
vations, to document them clearly, and then, by means of these
results, and a heightened sensibility, and a methodical approach,
to make a developing reality clear and graspable.

*If we assume the second modernity as a given, how should soci-
ology react? And doesn't this necessarily launch you into a war
with all your colleagues? You seem intent on taking away all the
toys they've become fond of.*

The first step is to think seriously about what will happen if we
really remove the nation-state from the concepts and principles
that organize our research. What does it mean to *not* assume
the nation-state as the fundamental category before we even
begin? At that point we enter an amorphous zone, where we
have to try out new ways of measuring, perceiving, and distill-
ing reality into concepts. I think the starting point should be
what Martin Albrow calls "globality": the everyday and often
banal experience of living in a global world.

What does that mean, concretely speaking?

We could start with the feeling that we are facing a common threat, that we now live in a world that has the capacity to destroy itself. The interconnectedness of the world, and the extent to which it outruns our capacity to foresee or control it, is illustrated in things like Chernobyl or the Asian financial crisis. As the world gets more interconnected and more technologically advanced, it becomes more prone to systemic threats.

However, globality is experienced very differently depending on where you live. We all experience the global imperative, but we don't experience it equally. In the USA, the experience of globality and the experience of nationality overlap and confirm each other. Here the everyday experience is the indescribable lightness and self-forgetfulness of imperialism, which vanishes (for those who practice it) into its good intentions. For Europe, a shorthand for all other countries with solid democracies, globality is experienced as something which threatens their existence as nation-states. And for the vast majority of countries in the world, for example, those in Africa, South America, and Asia, globalization is primarily experienced as the de-democratization of democracies that were fragile to begin with. They experience the global imperative as a series of economic impositions whose executives are the IMF and the World Bank. Lastly, there are those regions of the world in which state structures have completely collapsed and which have become the no-go zones of the so-called world community. For them, globality is the experience of a new economic apartheid. We have to keep these divisions continually before our eyes if the idea of a "global conversation" is ever to become more than a literary phrase.

But there are also other very different ways in which globality has become part of everyday life. The British sociologist Michael Billig has developed a very suggestive argument about how everyday routines reflect and mold our political consciousness. He has dubbed this process "banal nationalism." He describes a wealth of ways in which we "show the flag" in everyday life in the course of our normal routines; how this marks off our political identity from those of others; and how such identities are reproduced and reinvigorated through this constant semi-conscious national rivalry.

I think Billig is spot on in his description of how political identity is anchored in the routines of everyday life. But I think he is selective to the point of distortion in his choice of routines, because there are obviously many cases of "banal cosmopolitanism." I think that in fact there are more of them, and that the disparity is growing. I think banal cosmopolitanism is hollowing out the everyday experience of nationalism, and filling us instead with the experience of globality, even if our conscious recognition is still lagging behind.

A simple example is food. If we are what we eat, none of us is national anymore. It simply isn't possible to eat locally. The labels may disguise the fact, but even yogurt, meat, and fruit involve us in global chains of production and consumption. And let's not even talk about the Germans' supposedly national dish, the wurst; it's a global mish-mash. The food of the world has already united, and we experience this unification every time we go to the supermarket. We are now all used to finding foodstuffs that used to be separated by continents and cultures freely available side-by-side as mass market commodities. This selection is both fostering and filling a new need. It is the basic ingredient of a culinary cosmopolitanism that many of us are just as viscerally attached to as local people were once attached to their local foods. Where the norm of food was once repetition and the perfection of traditional standards, now the norm for many of us, at a surprising number of class levels, is eclecticism. It is not something we do by accident and substitution. It is something we celebrate and revel in. World society is in some ways baking in the oven and broiling in the pan. The national dishes that Billig emphasizes are really islands in an overwhelming river of banal cosmopolitanism.

So if we accept Billig's argument about how political identity is reproduced through the routines of everyday life, and remove the blinders that make us think that the only kind of politics are nation-state politics, we are led inexorably to the conclusion that new cosmopolitan political identities are being formed through the experience of everyday life. When the phrase is unqualified, this is what I mean by the "experience of globality." The background of our national consciousness is changing. And as originally happened with nationalism, what is still a pre-political and pre-conscious identity today can become a political and conscious one tomorrow. But it needs concepts that suit it, and institutions to give it form. Without them, it often goes unnoticed and underestimated, just as the signs of national identity first did in the age of empires.

When the "German" firm BMW sold the "British" firm Rover, the workers in the affected regions mobilized against it. In this case, the flare-up of banal nationalism was quite visible. But it was also short-lived, and after their protest, the workers went down to the pub, drank "Dutch" or "German" beer, and cheered on their "home team," a soccer squad that combined players from completely different national cultures as if it were the most normal thing on earth. We are all of us more cosmopolitan than we think.

So how does sociology go about forging concepts that capture the experience of globality?

The first step is accepting globality as a reality, and accepting it in its full diversity and contradictoriness. That is easy to say, and in fact things like that are said every day. Unfortunately, however, once people start investigating, they almost always leave those proclamations on the shelf, and go back to operationally assuming the primacy of the nation-state and the evolutionary nature of modernity. To accept globality as a reality means to truly suspend both of those assumptions in our empirical work. I am using the term "empirical" broadly to include every activity in which we are collecting facts and using them to support our arguments.

A cosmopolitan sociology posits globality as the experience of a deterritorialized culture. Modernity is no longer conceived of as a phenomenon that has secured a large territory and is trying to spread out and secure more. We must start from the premise that there is more than one modernity; that there is more than one perspective on each of them; and that none of those viewpoints is inherently privileged, including the western one.

The question then is, "How we can operationalize this conception of the world as a collection of different cultures and divergent modernities?" It's not as difficult as it looks. We can't investigate globally; we can't investigate the whole world at once in all its aspects. But we don't need to if we follow out our basic insights about deterritorialization. The second modernity can be found right this moment in many widely scattered places. It is being born within the interstices of the first modernity, most of all within its cities, but by no means only there.

There are two different ways to understand globalization. The first one is *additive*, and the second one is *substitutive*. As long as one posits the nation-state as an unchanging reality, to which all social phenomena are subordinate, then globalization can only be conceived in the first sense, as an *external* relation, as something added on to the nation-state.

What your English friends have called "another dimension of analysis"?

Exactly. One is left analyzing what those English theorists have called the *interconnectedness* of nation-states, in which the framework of globalization is seen as simply an additional dimension of analysis. This perspective of globalization as an add-on never really puts the nation-state into question. In addition, the term "*inter*-connectedness" is at its heart euphemistic, because it implies symmetry where there are often in fact very asymmetrical relationships. It creates a bias towards glossing over the issue of dependence.

In my conception of the second modernity, by contrast, globalization is considered as a phenomenon *internal* to the nation-state, and *internal* to its citizens. It is something that is transforming them from within. Social networks are not being added on to the national container; they are changing its nature, both by making that container more permeable, and by introducing relationships that pass through it that are weightier than the relationships within it.

Transnational forms of life – transnational paths of work, transnational connections to homelands, transnational means of communication, and the transnational consciousness and identity that arise from experiencing them – are occurring at *all* levels of society. They can be seen at the national, the regional, and the local level. They can be seen in economics, in the workplace, in social networks, and in political organizations.

So I think globalization should be chiefly conceived of as globalization from *within*, as *internalized* globalization. This is how we can suspend the assumption of the nation-state, and this is how we can make the empirical investigation of local-global phenomena possible. We can frame our questions so as to illuminate the transnationality that is arising inside nation-states. This is what a cosmopolitan sociology looks like. Internalized globalization is its object of investigation.

The food analysis gives just one example of how this can be investigated within the container of the nation-state. Banal cosmopolitanism is only one aspect of internalized globalization, and food is only a tiny part of that. So there are no practical barriers to the empirical sociology of the second modernity. What we need is to forge a new set of concepts and build a new perspective. It isn't as hard as it seems because we don't have to do it all at once. In fact we can only build it bit by bit. That's not a shortcoming. It's integral to the nature of the enterprise.

The result is that globalization can only be investigated locally. This is not just a practical limitation. It also has theoretical importance. In a paradoxical sense, globalization can never be global, that is, homogeneous, precisely because it is divergent.

Furthermore, the essence of globalization lies in its transformation of locality. It produces a new definition of place, both geographically and socially. It also gives a new structure to "locality." As the mayor of New Orleans said recently, it's hard to be a mayor anymore without having your own foreign policy. Cities and metropolises are the nodal points of the second modernity, the main site of the global-localization that some people have dubbed "glocalization." In these newly transformed glocalities, first and third worlds are becoming mixed.

A cosmopolitan sociology is one that treats the transnational existence of its inhabitants as the emergent rule, rather than as the increasing exception. Transnational connections do not simply fuzz the barriers between nation-states. They weaken the container nature of the container-state. These new connections puncture and pass through it and develop out into transnational networks and institutions and patterns of life. In order to gain access to this new reality, all that is needed is to be open to it, which essentially means investigating it within a framework that treats it as central rather than marginal.

This idea of a world society existing locally is not new. In Nietzsche we already find the idea that we are entering an "age of comparison." What Nietzsche meant by an age of comparison is that cultures were no longer divided into territorial empires that were separate and distinct. Rather in each cultural space elements of every other culture were to some degree present. This seems to me to be one of the very first conceptions of global society existing locally. What really differs today is the degree. Now we can actually look at many localities and *see* global society existing locally. It sometimes looks as if they were settlements of a more plural world society that have been set down in the midst of (relatively more) homogeneous national societies.

Our mixing may differ in degree from that of Nietzsche's time, but his reflections on this question were quite deep, and may apply to our time even better than his own. He noted that a single element of a culture is easily absorbed, just like one person is easily absorbed into a culture. But a collection of elements, or a collection of people, brings with it its own cultural logic. And, as Nietzsche is most famous for arguing, cultural logics don't mix harmoniously right out of the box. On the contrary, what usually strikes us most forcefully at first is their incompatibility, their irreducibility, the ways in which they contradict each other. However, if contradictory cultural elements are forced to coexist, and forced to interact, they will over time evolve a *modus vivendi*.

An indispensable part of any such solution will be a learned ability to translate from one culture to another. Thus, when driven past a certain point, the age of comparison turns into the age of cultural translation. This is something that takes place inside our own lives as much as it takes place in zones of world culture. They are two sides of the same coin. In both cases, contradictions that have long been present in the world, but have previously only been put into intellectual relation to each other, now come into close proximity and real relation. They contradict each other inside individuals and localities. We live those contradictions and we are forced to come up with makeshift solutions to resolve them. Such solutions require creativity. They require non-algorithmic solutions. And the necessary precondition of such creativity is a *dialogic imagination*. But dialogic imagination is simply these new social relations, this new lived experience, made conscious. This new background is what makes new solutions visible, not only to the immediate problems of our own lives and identities, but also to the political, economic and scientific problems that face us collectively.

So unlike earlier eras, ours can't erect ghetto walls that will isolate these elements that contradict everything we believe in. As when people would sit back after an Easter dinner and give the fullness of their salvation an extra savor by reflecting on the terrible suffering of people far away.

That dinnertime utopia is now an empty incantation. The idea that one can lock the aliens out, send them back, localize them, or confine them so that the rest of society won't need to worry about them is simply untenable. The aliens are here. They are already integrated into our lives, even if they have not yet been integrated into our national political societies or our consciousness.

But isn't that exactly the big danger right now, if we can jump into current politics? Many people are clamoring that we should reinforce the walls of the nation-state container. They believe very much that the nation can still be defined in ethnic cultural terms and that only the will is lacking. They feel themselves threatened by the processes that we've sketched out here under the name of the second modernity. They feel threatened in their property, threatened in their feelings of social security, and threatened in their expectations for the future. And they react to this feeling of having everything endangered by circling the wagons in a hedgehog defense.

Yes, that's one reaction formation. I agree that the same conditions that are presenting us with *theoretical* challenges – the opening up of closed structures, the melting away of borders, the loss of clear dichotomies – are also producing the increased *polarization* that seems to mark the advent of the second modernity. This is what makes our task so pressing. It makes intellectual challenges into political and social ones. These attempts to build new and better walls, to draw new borders that re-exclude the others, and to enforce this with violence and terror – that's definitely one reaction.

On the other hand I'm convinced that there are also tendencies which are combining local consciousness and cultural rootedness with openness and a desire for cosmopolitan renewal. I think these tendencies have a strong foundation in the process we just described, where the global and the local are developing into something new, into a global sense of place. I also don't think this global sense of place is taking shape only in the world's metropolises. It's occurring in other places as well.

I think therefore we are standing before two alternatives. The globalization process will affect all local identities, there is no escaping that. The alternatives result from how each local culture responds. It can try to block itself off from these developments. But – and we have to be clear on this point – that is just as much an active process as opening up. It means a locality has to actively attempt to change its course of development, and in a sense to refound itself anew against resistance. The other option is that the duality that local inhabitants are already experiencing can become conscious of itself and find a way of expressing itself coherently. It can produce a new kind of plural culture, one that satisfies the desire to reach backward into local traditions without stopping local culture from opening up and letting more of the world in.

The second modernity emerges from this field of tensions. At the moment it's not clear what will be the final result of this clash of reaction formations. This is the fundamental misunderstanding I keep running into in discussions of the second modernity. People always want to know whether it's an optimistic scenario or a disaster scenario, when the whole point is that it's neither, it's a new frame of reference for interpreting new social structures. Within this new framework, we can sketch out various scenarios as a means of clarifying our thinking. But my attempt is to lay a new foundation for social interpretation. It has nothing to do with optimism.

If we look back at the nineteenth century, we might say that all the classical sociologists were optimists when compared with their contemporaries. The prevailing idea at the time was that all the values that held up society were dissolving into anomie, and that without the force that church and religion exercised over men's souls, society would no longer be possible. The classical sociologists by contrast said, "No, what's happening is the coming into being of a new order, an industrial order, which will bring with it class conflict, and revolution, and democracy, and what we need to do is forge a new way of thinking that comprehends it." To their contemporaries, this sounded completely absurd and Pollyannish. What they found hardest to swallow was the idea that economics and politics could hold society together without religion, never mind that society might be even more tightly integrated than it was before. Now, of course, we all agree that the economic interpretation was obviously right. On the other hand, from our new perspective, it doesn't seem all that optimistic. Nobody thinks of those gloomy Gusses as optimists nowadays. However, their claim that a new society was being born was undoubtedly true. Today we find ourselves in a similar situation. Foundations are being destroyed that we can't imagine society without.

This is why I think it's so important that we recognize the second modernity as a structure of possibilities, one that presents several different paths of development, several of which can at this point only be adumbrated. We have to do a lot of work in order to make ourselves conceptually sensitive to these new possibilities. But their existence as real possibilities doesn't rule out the equally real possibility of this reflex desire to enforce new borders, this mobilization of violence, this inscription of ethnicity with blood that we've seen in the Balkans and in other places as well. Both paths are possible. Both are realities.

Look at Europe, for example. There it's easy to see the opposition of two different projects in the same geographical space. On the one hand, there's the conservative idea of a Christian Europe, which excludes all other religions, and which intends to remain eternally frozen into nation-states, each bitterly defending its sovereignty. And then there's the completely opposed project of a cosmopolitan Europe. The latter is deeply bound up with the new civil religion of human rights, a doctrine which in principle can't stop at the borders of the nation-state, and can't be limited to those with whom we share a national identity. It is a creed which is diametrically opposed to the old ethnic reflexes. It's also one which seems without question to have grown by leaps and bounds over the last decade.

There are many parallels to this in the history of the first moder-
nity. Throughout its history, modernity was (and still is) marked by
extremes of uneven development that on occasion led to crises.
Some were overcome by great leaps forward in social organization,
and some led to enormous wars. The situation seems to be the
same in the second modernity. We have extremely uneven devel-
opment that is unleashing similar kinds of instability. Once again,
there is more than one way to react.

Do you have any specific parallels in mind?

Well, to start with, both transformations were driven by a revolu-
tion in communications in the largest sense of the word, including
transportation. In both cases, this was combined with a revolution
in manufacturing and a qualitative transformation of capital
markets. In the second half of the nineteenth century, it was the
expansion of the railroads that played a key role. In the late twen-
tieth century, it was the expansion of the internet. Where the first
industrial revolution was synonymous with a revolution in manu-
facturing, the analogous revolution in recent years was the inte-
gration of computers into the production process, which was at the
heart of the so-called "productivity revolution." Lastly, the nine-
teenth century saw the transformation of large banks into public
corporations that were able to mobilize the extensive savings of
the little people into large-scale investments. Today, innovations
have enabled the little people to speculate directly, daytrading in
stocks or futures or what have you, and the influx of their funds
has once again revolutionized the financial system.

Those are all excellent points. On the other hand, when we
leave the economy and turn to the political front, the parallel
only goes halfway. The first time around, these economic developments were accompanied by, and stimulated the development of, a national political democracy that was in many ways
the solution to the problems they caused. This time around, one
can't help but be struck by how the nation-state framework that
supported earlier developments is now being broken out of on
all sides. For the parallel between the first and second modernity to be complete, a world state should be coming into being
to play the role that the nation-state did before. That doesn't
seem to be happening. Instead of a transition from nation-state

to world state, we seem to be witnessing a transition from state to market. Instead of a transition to something different but equivalent, it looks like we're suffering a loss. It looks like the foundations of politics are being dismantled.

That last point is certainly true: the old foundations are being dismantled. But I think we err in thinking that world economy can only be matched by a world state. I think that's taking the historical parallel too far, acting as if the future can only be a rerun of the past, and that if it's not, we can only be headed for disaster.

The problem is that when we try to conceive of a world state, we think of a big nation-state, that is, a huge mass of territory. We think of the world economy in the same terms, even though we know it isn't true. A more fruitful way to frame the problem is to say that we have a deterritorialized, multi-centered economy, and we need a deterritorialized multi-centered state to go with it. And that, it turns out, is not only possible, it's in the process of evolving. Its eventual shape and extent is of course indeterminate, but not its possibility.

The raw material of politics is power, and there is no question that power is now being wielded most effectively by capital markets and transnational corporations. If we look closely, we will see they are wielding power in completely new ways. In a certain sense they are like Columbus, discovering a new country . . .

. . . or rather something beyond country. Like Columbus, a new world.

Right, a new world. They are putting down their flags in deterritorialized space and claiming it for themselves. This global space that they've begun to move about in is showing the rest of us what deterritorialized power looks like. This is what states have got to learn to emulate. I would argue that they are in the process of learning exactly that. They are evolving into the kind of states that can wield such power. They are not in the same league yet, but they can get there.

Global action exerts a qualitatively different kind of power than that exercised by the territorial nation-state. It is a soft and diffuse power that is more efficiently coercive than the military power that is the monopoly of states. We have seen it bring states to their knees. The advent of this kind of power is the decisive difference between the dawns of the first and the second modernity.

But can state power develop a counterweight to such power? Or will the state just crumble before it? Isn't it possible that the end of the national container will be the end of politics as we know it?

As we know it, sure. But I don't believe this is the end of the state, never mind the end of politics, or even the end of state-based politics. It's the end of a certain kind of state, and the end of a certain understanding of politics that went with it, namely the politics of the *territorial* nation-state. But the state hasn't come to an end. It is possible to have a deterritorialized state. And it is completely conceivable that a new kind of state and a new age of politics will emerge out the state's desire to hold power.

In order for states to counteract the power of transnational corporations and NGOs, they will have to evolve into what I call *transnational cooperation states*. In order to understand what that entails, we have to take a closer look at the nature of deterritorialized power that is currently being exercised by transnational corporations.

The power of the multinationals is not their power to invade. It's their power to withdraw, to exercise their exit option. To paraphrase Joan Robinson, in the age of globalization, the only thing worse than getting exploited by multinationals is not getting exploited by multinationals. It's this power to withdraw, to *not* enter countries and to *not* provide investment, that is their real coercive force. This is what forces states, against their will, to dismantle their systems of social protection and instantiate the neoliberal regime. This diffuse economic force is purposeful, and it is cooperative. Competing investors and companies all share the same basic demands, and they all refuse to enter a country until those basic demands are met. Together they wield what is proving to be an irresistible force.

Now, where is the state in all of this? The old power game between capital, labor, and the state took place within the container of the nation-state, and in that container, the state held all the trump cards, whether it used them or not. Capital has now escaped that game. It is playing a new, higher-level game, in which labor and the state are not only completely out-matched, they're not even in the game. It's as if they are using the same pieces to play checkers while the companies are playing chess. They make their moves just like they always have, and then they're checkmated, and there's no way to avoid it, because they don't know how to produce a checkmate of their own.

Historically, though, as you pointed out, they've been in this position before. The national corporations of a century ago had a similar power that transcended local boundaries, and it set off a similar tax competition, a similar competition for jobs. They were met by a national state and by national unions. The transnational corporation will have to be met by transnational unions and transnational states. But the key here is the concept of *transnational*. It is not just a bigger version of a national state. If it comes about, it will be qualitatively, fundamentally differ-ent. There will be transnational *states*, plural. They will evolve from the national states we see before us now, but they will be different in their individual nature and different as a systemic whole. To provide a counterweight to the power of the global economy, they will have to wield deterritorialized power them-selves. To do that, states will have to become themselves deter-ritorialized. The societies which they represent are already on the way to doing just that.

This is interesting, but I'm not sure I'm following you here. You say the power of the transnational corporations lies in their power to march out of countries rather than their power to march in. In other words, they can choose the location where they will set up pro-duction, and the locations have to compete for their favors.

Exactly. That's the decisive point. International economic agents choose their location on the basis of purely economic criteria. So when they compare states, they compare how far they can maximize the infrastructure that will be provided for them and how far they can minimize the tax and social contributions they will have to make in return. This power of withdrawal, this threat of packing up and moving elsewhere, has been qualita-tively increased in the last 25 years by the advance of informa-tion technology and the global organization of production.

But how can states imitate that power? During the first industrial revolution, where you made steel where the coal and iron was, and regions that were blessed with such resources, like the Ruhr Valley, had a certain inalienable power tied to the land. Now such districts are in crisis. Once power is deterritorialized, what can the state's counter-power be based on?

On cooperation and the denial of that cooperation, just like the power of transnational corporations.

The new element that is revolutionizing the nature of power is the change in the nature of cooperation that has been made possible by the digital revolution. It has allowed economic cooperation to evolve beyond the cooperation of localities in geographic space to an integrated cooperation based on function. A little while ago, we were talking about how the revolution in communications technology, through its effects on the transmission of money and packages and people, was making social distance independent of geographic distance, so that someone could be closer to a person on another continent than to their neighbor next door. Well, this is exactly what has allowed the multinational corporation to organize itself globally on functional lines. It is limited by cost, but the cost of such technology is now quite low. The result has been a deterritorialized organization of the relations of production and of the calculation of profit and loss. It is an organization which not only escapes the container of the nation-state, but which, through its joint cooperative action with its fellows, is contributing to the erosion of that container. (See below, p. 170.)

Now, as we've just said several times, when we inquire into the transnational corporation and the nature of its power, we find it is no longer the imperialism of marching in, but instead the imperialism of marching out. It is the *withdrawal of cooperation*, the banishment of a state from the cooperative economic network that is now essential to its existence, that is the terrible threat. This is a threat that each individual multinational can wield both as an element in, and as a representative of, that global economic network. The positive sanction of bringing in employment and tax revenues necessarily implies the negative sanction of taking them out. This negative power, this power of saying no, is the power of the economic network being wielded.

It is the *power of denial,* of the denial of the cooperation on which the state is now dependent.

This power of denial is almost exactly the reverse of what we normally understand as territorial power. The state's monopoly of the use of legitimate violence is bound up with its control of a clearly bounded territory and all the people in it. It is this combination of forces that equips it to win its position of power in the world. If it wants to exercise this power against another territorial state, it does so by marching into its territory, or by blackmailing it with the threat of it.

But where the power of the state is based on borders, the power of the transnational corporation is based on free capital flows. What "free" means is free with respect to borders, that is, free to flow across them in both directions, free to operate as if they didn't exist. In this world of flows that can rush across borders, the worst thing that can happen to a society is that the flow suddenly rushes out, leaving them high and dry. The state suffers a shock to its circulation system, that is, its tax revenues and its ability to provide jobs. On a day-to-day basis, this threat has given economic actors a power superior to the powers of the territorial state.

Now we come to the point. This is what people see and what makes them think, "This is the end of politics." But it's not. It's the end of first modern politics. It's the end of the primacy of the territorial state *vis-à-vis* the economic (and social) actors it "contains," precisely because it no longer "contains" them.

Every time a system of politics has passed away in history, people have thought it was the end of politics. It never has been. The question should be rather what will be the shape of the politics to come. In other words, it's a question of how politics can be globalized to match the globalization of the economy.

But what guarantee do we have that politics can be globalized? Maybe every loss of politics in the past has led to a new form in the future, but, as they say in the markets, "past practice is no guarantee of future results." More importantly, if the only politics we really care about is democratic politics; and democratic politics arose only with the modern nation-state; then isn't there a real possibility that democratic politics will vanish with that state? A democratic world government is difficult to conceive of. And even if we can conceive of it, it's hard to imagine it happening any time soon. So if by politics we mean democratic politics, why isn't the end of the territorial nation-state the end of politics for the fore-seeable future?

Because the state as we know it isn't ending. It is undergoing a transformation analogous to that of the transnational corporation. It is being transformed into a transnational state. It is undergoing this transformation as a reaction to the power of the corporations. It is one step behind them, just as it was during the rise of the first modernity. But there is every reason to think that when it finishes this transformation, it will be more than a match for the transnational corporation, just as the national state was more than a match for the national corporation. (At least in theory. Whether it exercised that power in any particular nation-state depended, of course, on politics. But the real possibility of exercising that power was always the basis of real national politics.)

The key point is that we don't need a world government to exercise power anymore than corporations need a world corporation. What we need is a cooperative network of governments. We need the kind of states that can take their place in a flexible network of power because they are internally connected. They will then be able to wield the power of political non-cooperation in a way analogous to the way corporations and investors now exercise the power of economic non-cooperation. A community of states would then wield the ultimate power in the international realm just as the national state wielded the ultimate power in the first modernity.

If we look at developments that are now going on, at transformations that state and society are presently undergoing, the possibility of an effective community of states, a flexible network of state power that is just as deterritorialized as the economic power of global corporations, is not inconceivable. States are already transforming, just like societies.

But you've talked about the territorial state becoming a zombie state.

And I mean it. But it is exactly where it's becoming a zombie state that the transnational state is being born. Remember, a zombie concept is one where the idea lives on even though the reality to which it corresponds is dead. But that doesn't mean reality is dead! It means exactly the opposite. It means that there is a lively new reality that we are not seeing because our minds are haunted and clouded by dead ideas that make us look in the wrong places and miss what's new.

In other words, every place where the nation-state is becoming a zombie state is a place where we can red-pencil that function and ask, "Why do individual states do that anymore?" This is especially clear in Europe. Why do we need state central bank systems when both macro- and micro-economic decisions are increasingly being made by the European central bank? Conceptually we can go one step further and ask whether all states really need their own ambassadors to every country in the world.

If we want to know the politics of the future, this is the key question. How far can political actors go in emulating economic actors in escaping the bonds of the territorial state and exercising their power extra-territorially? The same question goes for non-state actors that find themselves up against the power of transnational corporations. We are seeing the beginnings of this in the labor movement, which is trying to reorganize itself on a global scale, and to harness the same information technology that has changed the redistribution of work to change the organization of workers. This emerged into the public view in a big way with the coming together of various protest movements in Seattle. The process is also going forward in less spectacular ways that may in the end be farther reaching. The union at Volkswagen, for example, now has a transnationally organized works committee, where the various transnational parts of the enterprise are covered by a correspondingly transnational union representation.

It's also important to note that, while the transnational corporation disposes of a new form of power, it also seems to be afflicted with a new form of vulnerability (See p. 141ff.). It may even turn out in the end to be more vulnerable than the national corporation, because unlike it, it won't have a state to call its own in time of crisis. If political and social power eventually evolve into a network reality in the way economic power already has, the contest between them may be more than equal.

We have to realize, however, that this doesn't happen all at once. There won't be a constitutional convention where we'll all sit down and create transnational institutions. Instead, there is a transnational reality in which states and societies are all already participating. States are evolving into the kinds of states that can serve as the elements of a larger network through their participation in networks that already exist. If countries do someday give up their individual ambassadorships, it won't be something that comes out of the blue. Ministries and subdepartments are already linked horizontally into a network of ongoing and cooperative relationships. It is true that these links are still being broken and overridden at crucial junctures by the imperatives of the nation-state. But it is not far-fetched to think that these networks will continue to develop further, in a sort of two steps forward, one step back progression, and that the nature of the state will continue to be transformed by the process. Post-national cooperation-states are conceivable. And with them so is a counterweight to the power of transnational economic actors.

But couldn't Europe and the EU serve just as well as a counter-example, displaying how a process that could have happened in fact didn't? Arguably, this was on purpose. In many ways, from its original founding as the EEC, the European Union has been a project to rescue the nation-state from its embarrassments. Wasn't the European Coal and Steel Community a conscious attempt to deal with parts of the nation-state that were already by that time in crisis? And to solve them with solutions that traversed borders, but in such a way as to leave the political core of the nation-state untouched? The European Union often looks as if it were designed intentionally to preserve the old model of the nation-state by enabling nation-state cooperation in spheres like the economy without allowing the emergence of any corresponding transnational state institutions. Without such transnational state institutions, the EU never gains the legitimacy they would bestow. This seems to be the EU's great lack.

The EU is the biggest single challenge for state theory today. It doesn't have what Max Weber called the state's sine qua non, the monopoly over the legitimate use of violence within its territory. There isn't a European army or a European police. In addition, the EU has almost no power to levy taxes on its own, so it can't finance and control its own budget. On top of that, almost everything that constitutes the welfare state has been left to the individual members. So by the classical definition, when we look at the EU, there isn't any state there. The one feature that sort of looks state-like, the euro, was only accepted after being put to national votes, and was discussed by national publics in terms of national costs and benefits.

Yet at the same time there is all this talk of how states are losing their sovereignty, and of how the European community is exercising power over them. If those things are true – and they are – there can't be nothing there, even if the classical definition says there's nothing there. The solution is that what's there is a network. A dense, regulative network, a network of power. And each of the states in it is undergoing internal modifications so as to adapt to that network. Each state is being regulated, and each is contributing to the production of new regulations.

How far this regulative regime will extend in a political direction is still an open question. Monetary policy and health regulations already contain a lot of clearly political content. But the EU regulative regime also seems to be expanding by a process of trial and error into more explicitly political areas. For example, the control of immigration. Or, for that matter, the expansion of the union itself. These are issues of internal and external borders, of political inclusion or exclusion, that go to the very the core of what used to be called citizenship.

Recently there was an ad hoc reaction to the election of a coalition in Austria that was assumed to be hostile to immigrants and expansion. That was an excellent example of a case where inclusion seemed to get raised to a principle on a trial and error basis in a way that might get built on and institutionalized in the future. Even if it was something of a failure in the short term, it stirred passions and determination because it touched on core realities and interests. It is possible to imagine the political project of a cosmopolitan Europe crystallizing out of a string of events like this into something that is not a super nation-state, but a densely regulative network of transnational cooperation states. In the end, it is even possible to conceive of the EU itself as a form of cooperation state or regulation state, as a network of power that precipitates out of cooperative action. (See p. 214.)

It is thus quite possible to imagine the transnational political network taking on more and more of the powers and functions of the nation-state without becoming a nation-state itself. We have to be careful that we aren't blinded by our deep but hidden assumption that a territorial state is the only form that can wield these powers. Another buried assumption is that the nation-states we grew up with have an eternal nature that they can't change. The truth is that as the network evolves among them, they evolve too. They have the same borders, but those borders have different meanings, and are controlled differently. It is quite possible that nation-states will evolve into transnational cooperation states without any change happening on a map. But the meaning of their borders will change.

For me, the big question is not whether this process is happening, but to what extent it is developing its own independent dynamic. In order to be able to ask that question, it's important that we leave open the question of what form this independent dynamic will take. It's not that I'm not interested in whether the EU will evolve transnational political institutions. I'm vitally interested in that. If it happens, it will obviously raise the process to a whole new level. However, that doesn't mean that before it happens, the process isn't already underway. The transnational network, and the transformation of the states that make it up, is already building up through an accretion of side effects that only appear marginal because we continue to look at them through the lens of the nation-state. They seem to be giving rise to an independent dynamic over time. The question now is how strong this independent dynamic will be in relation to the power of the individual nation-states. It's an open-ended process and it varies. There is no predicting which way it may go, even in the short run, *especially* in the short run. It is endemic to this process that there be periodic and clamorous returns to the autonomy and sovereignty of the nation-state. Then at other times the independent dynamic is stronger, and everyone seems to think it's the only way forward. We'll see which way wins out. It's a question of politics, clearly. And, as you point out, a question of legitimacy. There is no question that building cooperative state structures would legitimate the idea of the transnational cooperation state. It would push the process forward and make it less reversible.

Perhaps. But the problem still seems to be the imbalance of power between politics and the economy. The dominant economic religion today is neoliberalism. Maybe this would be a good place for you to elaborate on the distinction between globalization and economic globalization. Many people equate the two, including both people who are for it and against it. You earlier used the term "globalism" to distinguish this infernal global market boosterism from the broader reality of globalization.

Globalization is a process of cumulative side effects. It's a multidimensional process that describes a general tendency of change in every aspect of society. It's not something that is just happening in the economy. It includes things as diverse as cultural multiplicity; the development by individuals of transnational forms of social life; and the growing importance and multiplication of non-state political actors, from Amnesty International to the WTO.

Globalism, on the other hand, is the naïve (but very forcefully imposed) idea that the world market is the patent medicine for all of society's ills. It's the idea that if only states stopped trying to regulate the market, and handed over all their functions to transnational capital, then everybody would become rich, and we'd all have jobs, and social justice would no longer be a question, because it would be produced spontaneously by the workings of the market. On this view, all the problems that have appeared, all the negative side effects, are always the result of deregulation not being carried far enough. If something goes wrong, the solution is always to go even farther, because eventually we're sure to reach the promised land of success.

Isn't that exactly the credo of the WTO? The power of neoliberalism stems from neoliberalism being in power.

Intellectual power and real power reinforce each other, there's no doubt about that. But that relation can also serve to mask weakness. Personally I think that while neoliberalism is still in power, intellectually it's largely a spent force. Many of the world's best economists have mounted sophisticated critiques of how its assumptions don't hold true and its models don't correspond to reality. Its political opponents have indisputably grown stronger in the last few years. And lastly, there is the balkiness of reality itself. The failures of this approach can't be indefinitely attributed to not going far enough when one is confronted with catastrophes like Russia in the 1990s, and with growing inequality, and with whole areas of the world, like Africa, that have been completely decoupled from development.

I think intellectual opposition, political opposition, and these policy failures all work to reinforce each other. I expect the opposition to neoliberalism on all fronts to become more forceful in the future.

What do you think about the prospects of an economic crash? More specifically, what effect do you think such a crash might have on neoliberalism and globalization? Many people fear that such a thing could come to pass when this bubble economy finally bursts. They say that behind this turbo- or casino-capitalism there isn't any real production or provision of services but just pure speculation.

I share those fears. I'm not an economist, but it seems to me that if you take the underlying model of neoliberalism seriously – the idea that the world's various markets are and should be merging and approximating the reality of a single market – then, if we haven't in fact overcome the business cycle (which we haven't), it seems only a matter of time before we get a globally synchronized downturn, which we haven't seen since the Great Depression. In lesser form, the phenomenon of economic "contagion" is well established, where events in Russia can instantly affect Brazil. There seems no avoiding the fact that system-threatening crises seem to be occurring with a drumbeat regularity: the EMU crisis, the peso crisis, the Asian crisis, the Russian crisis, the latest Argentine or Brazilian or Turkish crisis. All of them have so far been contained at various levels of unraveling. But the image of a system under repeated threat is hard to avoid. If multibillion dollar crisis interventions are constantly necessary, as the IMF claims, to keep preventing system meltdown, then the system is as fragile as the will for such continued intervention.

I think world economic society is developing into a subspecies of what I have called global risk society, where increasing technical control leads us paradoxically into a world of increasing systemic risk. But, as I have argued since my first book, *Risk Society*, I don't think this is simply a path to inevitable disaster. I think the spectre of disaster, the growth in significance of border-spanning risks (like global warming or mad cow disease), is one of the key factors forcing global society to become conscious of itself, to become conscious of the fact that it is a global community of fate, and that it needs to evolve a global approach if it is ever to become capable of dealing with such problems. I think the same is true of the spectre of global economic breakdown. It tends to stimulate international coordination. If that becomes impossible within the current framework, it is possible that the powers that be will be forced to generate a more legitimate global framework.

This then brings us back to the distinction between globalism and globalization. If neoliberalism, both as an ideology and as a policy regime, collapses because it reaches its limits, that will not mean the end of globalization.

That is an extremely important point. Globalism is a particular ideology, which many people, from different motives and perspectives, see as something they have to defend themselves against. But whether or not we have globalism, this won't change the underlying reality of what Martin Albrow and myself have called globality: the fact that we live in a world where borders are of decreasing importance, and where the reality of our everyday lives, of our patterns of work and politics and social relationships, can no longer be properly understood through the image of being enclosed in a national container. We have to adjust ourselves to this new reality and develop a way of thinking suited to it.

For me, one of the great intellectual dangers is that people will equate globalism with globalization, and from the justified critique of the one, draw the conclusion that the other can be shooed away. This is an enormous and dangerous illusion, and one found among left, right, and green. The illusion is that if we conquer globalism, we can then return to the old order of the nation-state – that we can somehow restore the potency of its democracy, and its power to guarantee our welfare and security.

The underlying premise of this equation of globalization with globalism is that there is no alternative way to structure society than the nation-state. This is why I see this view as unconsciously carrying water for the Jörg Haiders of this world, even though many of its proponents couldn't have more opposite motives. The fundamental rejection of globalism has at the same time to present an alternative global future. Otherwise it just leads back into the snail-shell house of the ethnic nation.

But is such a retreat possible? People like Haider might talk about it, or even try it, but can he pull it off? Haider is an opportunist. The most important thing for him is to take Austrians' fears for their future and remint them into electoral success. Maybe he'll turn around and amaze us, and betray everyone who voted for him, and turn into Austria's modernizing globalizer. I'm convinced that if modern fascism ever comes to power in the second modernity, it will accelerate the re-modernization process just as the original fascism accelerated modernization. Classical fascism used the language of blood and soil, but in fact it gave an enormous boost to modernization.

The reverse is also true. Fascism didn't hinder modernization. But modernization didn't hinder fascism, either. This is important to keep in mind. Some people think that because fascism failed in its aims, and had to fail in its aims, it can't happen again. But being objectively impossible doesn't stop things from happening. The original fascism only lasted a short while, a tiny conjuncture in historical time. But what a conjuncture! It redrew the map of the world. The whole world lived out the consequences of that conjuncture for the next half-century.

Fascism was a manufactured modernity, a modernized anti-modernity. That is definitely a danger we still have to take seriously as we enter the twenty-first century. Angry, hate-filled citizens don't appear in our classical theories of democracy. But watch the political news and you can see them on the march everywhere. The erosion of the nation-state, of the national economy, and of national identity has produced a very complex and dangerous moment in history. The structures of power are most dangerous when they are collapsing and when they are coming into being. It's difficult to say which period is worse.

We have seen several times how denationalization can lead to the reconstruction and embrace of exclusive ethnic identities that lead to horrible civil wars. However, there is no theoretical reason why such newly re-produced ethnicity has to stay at the level of subgroups within nation-states. It is quite conceivable that social movements could arise that are ethnic, and exclusive, but transnational, and which avail themselves of the modern means of communication and organization now at their disposal. They wouldn't be fighting to preserve the nation-state, but rather to fight cosmopolitanization in all its forms, with a much diffuser but just as serious goal of taking power. There is definitely a large spectrum of possible alternatives here. To take another scenario, it is quite conceivable that if there were a world economic collapse, there could be a drive to reinforce the state's domestic power with new forms of discipline and control.

To return to your original question, it is certainly true that one possible answer to the challenges of the second modernity could take the form of a new authoritarianism, one that combined traditional elements of authoritarianism with elements of the second modernity it purports to be combating. We have to realize that, while the economy has taken a large bite out of the authority of the nation-state, it has also placed before it, in the form of information technology, the tools of a far more thoroughgoing control. It's not hard to imagine ways this technology could be used to short-circuit the power of public opinion. A simple example is the video cameras that could in the future be posted on every corner. Another is the possibilities that electronic transactions could give the state to monitor every aspect of a citizen's consumption. So it's never a one-sided development. The same technology that leads to a draining of state power *vis-à-vis* the economy can lead to an increase of that power *vis-à-vis* the people. Out of such means, a new authoritarianism could be forged that was adapted to the needs of the world economy, one that was simultaneously postmodern and authoritarian. Globalization's winners would get the fruits of neoliberalism, and globalization's losers would get the back of the hand. A new wall of anti-immigrant sentiment wouldn't keep them out, but would keep them down, would keep them from having a voice in the state. This seems to be more or less the vision of Haider: an unholy marriage of yuppie and law and order. Of which Blairism, to be honest, sometimes sounds like the up-market version.

These new means of control you mention can already be used by corporations without the aid of the state. When it is finally possible to synthesize all the data it is now possible to gather, who knows how far into a person they will be able to peer? They may know things about us we don't know ourselves, like that in three weeks we'll buy three pairs of green socks and before Easter a blue blazer.

That may be true. But I want to return to an earlier point, the difference between historical possibility and historical reality, and the fact that you can have the reality, even when it doesn't make sense. Auguste Comte and Marx and Engels, after thinking it over, all came to the same conclusion about imperialism, that colonies just didn't pay. They cost more to maintain than they were worth. Yet, just as Marx and Engels were coming to that conclusion, the age of imperialism began to enter its highest stage. A hundred, a hundred and fifty years later, historians go through all the empirical evidence and say, "Hey, these guys were right!" But just being right is not enough to stop it from happening. Even today, we as societies haven't been able to realize the insight that Engels had way back then, that the military is a very unproductive way of increasing wealth and that it swallows vast quantities of it. Engels said the maintenance of standing armies undercut and contradicted the objective interests of capitalism. A century later we've had two world wars and countless terrible smaller ones. We have to keep this sort of thing in mind when weighing the possibility of a new authoritarianism. It might not be able to solve the puzzles of the second modernity. It might just force them.

Conversation 2

Individualization

JOHANNES WILLMS *The second modernity is dissolving everything that is near and dear to sociologists, like class and caste and gender roles. But what kind of social structure will take their place? Will it be an individualized society? Is such a thing even conceivable?*

ULRICH BECK That is one of the biggest questions we have to wrestle with today, not only sociologically, but also politically.

The theory of individualization has been part of my agenda for at least 15 years now. There has been a very heated debate about it during that period in the German-speaking world, but there has also been a lot of misunderstanding. Individualization does not mean individualism in the sense of a celebratory ideology. It does not mean individuation in the sense used by developmental psychologists to describe the process of becoming an autonomous individual. And it can't be equated with the market egoism of Thatcherism or Reaganism. That's a complete misunderstanding. It is also not what Jürgen Habermas describes as emancipation.

Individualization is a concept which describes a structural transformation of society's institutions. It describes a change in the relation of the individual to society. You could write a history of sociology describing how Durkheim, Weber, Simmel, Marx, Foucault, Elias, Luhmann, Giddens, and Bauman each used and interpreted the concept of individualization differently. Markus Schroer, a young German sociologist, has recently done just that.

Individualization is also not simply a phenomenon of the second half of the twentieth century. Earlier historical phases of individualization occurred in the Renaissance; in the courtly culture of the Middle Ages; in the inward asceticism of Protestantism; in the emancipation of peasants from feudal bondage; and in the loosening of intergenerational family ties at the end of the nineteenth century and beginning of the twentieth.

But then what is specific about individualization in the second modernity?

That's exactly the main question. Or, as Scott Lash puts it, what can individualization and individualism mean in an age of flows?

First of all, what individualization means in this constellation is *disembedding without re-embedding*. In the second modernity, the individual becomes, for the first time in history, the basic unit of social reproduction.

Durkheim, by contrast, was concerned with *anomic* individualism. His was the normative idea of re-embedding individuals after they had been set free by the dissolution of feudal structures. He argued that individualism could be routinized in market structures and nation-states just as the religious world view had once been routinized in feudal structures. He was right about that. My point is that once we enter the second modernity, individualism is no longer routinized but rather radicalized.

What does that mean?

In disembedded individualization, individual action becomes qualitatively more important. It is one of those moments in history where difference in degree becomes difference in kind.

Biographies cease to be pre-given by society. Instead, the construction of a narrative that makes sense of the individual life becomes a task performed by the individual. Disembedded individualization also ceases to be a subjective content to which an objective social structure, like that of system or class strata, can be opposed. Social structure can no longer be conceived of as being in principle unaffected by individual thought and action. Disembedded individualization *is* the social structure of the second modernity.

[handwritten margin note: How to make your life]

Individualization is institutionalized in modern society. Modern law, to take a central example, is the first form of law to address itself exclusively to individuals rather than to collectivities. Rights become individual rights, rather than the rights of a class or status group. Modern legitimacy is also based on this new principle, that no group should be legally privileged over any other. Political and social rights follow the same pattern as civil rights. And the market, the other central institution of modern society, is also a structure of individuation.

Where the second modernity really differs from the first modernity is in its subsidiary institutions: in the educational system, in the labor market, in the career patterns that arise from their interaction, and in the family structure that has to bridge them all. In the first modernity, there was much less variation in reality than there was theoretically room for. Theoretically a woman could have gone to college and become a doctor and then married another doctor. There were no laws forbidding it. But in reality there were strong informal barriers that kept most women from doing it. They were constrained by family and gender roles the boundaries of which were very effectively, if informally, policed.

What changes with the second modernity is the dissolving of these rigid roles and, with them, the relatively small set of pre-given biographical patterns that were socially constructed to intermesh. It was not only gender roles that regulated the first modernity, but class and caste roles as well. In each case, the model was that you conformed to a pre-given role and sought your success and happiness within it. You could expect bitter opposition if you transgressed it, and so most people didn't.

Roles thus provided something that wasn't a superstructure or a substructure so much as an intermediate structure, a structure that meshed the two. Roles provided the clear social outline of individual lives. And, as I said, they came in role-*sets* that had evolved to fit together. You couldn't change one without wrecking the whole set and thus endangering the smooth functioning of society. That is why traditional roles were defended so fervently for so long.

All that changes in the second modernity. In a word, roles dissolve. Gender, racial, and class distinctions become fluid and flexible. The norms of democracy and justice are extended to spheres of social life where they didn't previously apply, like the realm of intimacy. As a result, pre-given biographies get torn up. Each person now has to construct her own biography from a much wider selection of elements. The small set of pre-given life trajectories is replaced by a much wider set of unknown ones. And the pre-given intermeshing of role-sets is replaced by a much more fluid situation wherein nothing is pre-given and everything has to be negotiated.

This is what it means to say that individualization is the social structure of the second modernity. It means the structure of roles has been replaced by something much more fluid. Of course, fluids can have a structure, like the Gulf Stream or El Niño. It's just that it's a different kind of structure, a fluid structure. This is where we have to look for an answer to Scott Lash's question, "What can individualization mean in an era of flows?" We have to investigate how a fluid structure performs the function once assigned to the rigid gear set of roles. We have to investigate the nature of fluid structure itself. We have to examine how fluid life patterns interact with the nature of identity and consciousness.

Under these conditions, individual agency now assumes a central place, one that was only talked about before. Individual action can no longer be treated as the resultant of group pressures. It can no longer be treated as the residue of social attributes. When individualism is disembedded, concepts like "self responsibility" and "individual initiative" cease to be elements of the "superstructure," that is to say ideology, which can be clearly distinguished from the "substructure," that is, the "actual," "objective" situation. When individualism becomes disembedded *and* institutionalized, it becomes a kind of "supersubstructure." It's an inherently paradoxical social structure. In order to analyze it, sociology will have to change its approach from the logic of self-reproducing structures to the logic of "flows" (Appadurai) and "networks" (Castells).

Let me see if I understand this correctly. Up until now, sociology has deduced the individual from his social conditions. You turn that around and ask: "How can a legitimate collective identity be produced under the new historical conditions of radicalized individualization?"

That's right. But this has wide-ranging consequences. The sociologists of the first modernity gave roles a key place in society's self-reproduction, much larger than is usually acknowledged. Roles were what connected individuals to the larger social structures of classes and systems. They mediated between the micro and macro levels of society. All of that now has to be rethought. Instead of role-sets that had evolved to fit together, we now have the institutionalization of individual options, the necessity of choosing among them, and the indeterminateness of the final outcome. The pre-given compatibility of role-sets has been replaced by one that has to be individually produced through negotiation with no guarantees that any given set of choices actually *is* compatible. They might not be.

But isn't this just the old program of sociology from Durkheim to Foucault? Those two thinkers differ on many points, but both of them seem to converge in unveiling individualism as a discourse of power and control, as a paradoxical collective norm. Almost all of sociology seems to follow them in maintaining this to be one of the central features of modernity. Isn't this just one more version of that idea?

There's a big difference. The various theories you mention are alike in having a more or less *linear* conception of the control function of individualization. This obscures both the reflexivity and the potential subversiveness that distinguish the radicalized individualization of the second modernity. Markus Schroer does a good job of explaining this difference in his sociological history of individualization.

Radicalized individualization has a horizon of *experimental* normativity. This is similar in some ways to the ideal speech situation that was developed by Jürgen Habermas in his discourse ethics. One could perhaps speak of an "ideal intimacy situation," that is, an ideal-typical situation that is regulative even though it is counterfactual. In both cases, we are dealing with something that embodies the norms that people strive to realize.

What people are trying to realize in the small scale of their self-chosen [*eigene*] lives is a cherished and internalized ideal that remains denied on the larger scale of society. They are trying to realize a more perfect democracy in miniature. They are willing to make the greatest possible efforts in order to redeem the key normative expectations of democracy – equality, justice, fairness, and the right of each individual to develop her individuality – and to accept and deal with all the consequences that necessarily flow from such efforts.

Radicalized individualization is often misunderstood as autarkic individualization. That's simply wrong. Individualism cannot be conceived of as isolation, whether of a person alone or as some kind of autistic mass individualism. Individualization is always individualization with (and against) others. In fact, all too often the individualization of the one is the boundary of the individualization of the other. Thus the idea of individualizing by oneself is a contradiction in terms. Individualization is a social concept or it is nothing. The idea of an autarkic I is pure ideology. Individualization is intrinsically defined by the normative claims of co-individualization.

Does individualization mean that everyone will become a nonconformist?

No. The "society of individuals" is often misunderstood this way. Because the norm is that one must individualize, some people think the result has to be mass nonconformity. But this misinterprets individualization as being yet another pre-given pattern that has to be followed rather than a process of choice and the indeterminate attempt to harmonize those choices. True nonconformism includes the possibility of living traditionally or conventionally. Women can decide to become housewives and mothers in the classical sense, but it's the fact that they decide, and that they are really free to decide otherwise, that makes of it a self-chosen life. Having other options changes the meaning of what is chosen simply by making it something chosen, even if superficially it looks the same.

When we do empirical research on individualization, we constantly have to keep this in mind. Institutionalized disembedded individualism doesn't mean everyone is becoming more individual in the sense that they are each becoming more of an "authentic I." The opposite might be just as probable. We might end up observing the retreat of the self into blind obedience. The desire for relief from the pressure to individuate can lead to all kinds of fundamentalism. Unfreedom becomes more appealing the more unbearable becomes the pressure to choose between mutually exclusive alternatives. Eileen Barker argues this point quite persuasively in her essay, "The Freedom of the Cage."

But, on the other hand, the lifeworlds of institutionalized individualism cannot be reduced to forms of pseudo-individualism. Individualization cannot be equated with the mere management of self-image anymore than it can be equated with mass self-authenticity. The fact that each person has had options, and has necessarily turned more of them down in order to arrive where she ends up, makes it more and more justified for each of them to be considered the author of her own [*eigene*] life. However, it doesn't mean people have to be good authors. Individualization opens the space for nonconformity and the subversion of social conventions. But it gives no answer to the question of authenticity. In itself, it provides the ground for neither cultural pessimism nor cultural optimism.

From a sociological perspective, the concept of the self-chosen life includes equally the original, the re-enacted original, and the standardized life freely chosen. Each is a self-chosen life not on the basis of its subjective or aesthetic content, but because individuals have been institutionally forced to construct their lives to a qualitatively new degree, resulting in a more indeterminate coexistence. The results are sociologically significant because such life construction is now a key part of social construction, of social structuration.

Nietzsche, one of the prophets of authenticity, himself cruelly mocked the attempt to derive authenticity from social structure. When he said: "Are you authentic? Or just an actor? A representative? Or the represented? In the end, you are a copy of an actor," he wasn't just insulting dandies. He was deriding exactly this attempt to derive the individual from the social. The whole point of authenticity is that it isn't founded in anything outside the individual. It's a perspective of the self on the self.

How do individualization and globalization interact?

They both increase the number of cultural opposites we have to be able to experience simultaneously while still being able to think and live. Everyone, in quite everyday ways, is transported into a polyvalent action situation, in which she or he is forced to "translate" across different horizons of meaning. The result is both that self-chosen lives have built-in contradictions and that they give rise to political discussion, because the pressure of having to choose and negotiate between irreducibly different cultures, certainties, and styles of life has public consequences.

This is what really erodes the role model of social life. The role model was lived as a copy of blueprints stipulated by tradition. Individualization replaces this with a *dialogic existence*, a dialogical imagination, in which the opposites of the world must be borne in our own lives, and must be bridged there. Everyone is now living in different cultures simultaneously. Each of us somehow has to harmonize their discordances simply in order to make life livable. This is what is meant by "lived contradictions." Resolutions can only be achieved through a continuous process of translation.

In short, when individualization and globalization are combined, they radically open up the nature of the social. The resultant complexity far exceeds the capacity of the nation-state to regulate or represent it.

The myth of national homogeneity continues to disguise this increase in social creativity. The ideas of integration and assimilation are still dominant. The old terms of the problem are still insisted on. Foreigners are still singled out, and the discussion is still broken off before new terms can be introduced.

Thus far in history, solidarity among equals has only meant *national* equals. The tacitly acknowledged precondition of national solidarity has always been the exclusion of foreigners.

Let's go back to the example of the family. How do private life and living together change under the conditions of disembedded individualization?

The traditional family has fallen under the normative horizon of reciprocal individualization. The result has been an ongoing struggle over the definition of family and gender roles, and thus the definition of sexuality, marriage, parenthood, cohabitation, the household, and the division of labor.

In some respects this transformation is the most difficult and irritating of all. We can try and shield ourselves against huge changes happening in the world outside. But the porcupine defense won't work when changes are taking place at the center

of our own [*eigene*] lives. Our resistance to such changes is
proportionately bigger. The debate over the family has always
been heated. Three decades ago, this debate was being held over
the equality of the sexes. But the term "debate" obscures the
extent to which it has been carried on more like a war. Strong
cultural enmities are forever flaring out of it. It's more like a
clash over fundamentalist dogma than a debate. And it's not
much ado about nothing. There *has* been a decisive sea change.
The model of the normal family has opened up towards multiplicity. Even homosexual unions are gaining acceptance as
families.

But only against enormous resistance.

Exactly. The change has continued despite the resistance. The
result is that we now have a large set of variant family forms
existing side by side. If there is anything to which the slogan
"let a thousand flowers bloom" applies, it is to the forms of what
Elisabeth Beck-Gernsheim has called the "post-familial family."
Individualization has changed private life (that is, living
together, in the broadest sense of the term) into an open-ended
experimental situation, partly voluntarily, and partly against our
will.

The international data we are receiving about variant forms
of the family – about divorce, transnationality, late marriage,
living alone and step-siblingship – are all preliminary results in
this compulsory experiment. It is as if someone set out to discover what would happen to society if certain social relationships could no longer be thought of as determined by nature or
tradition, and had to be entirely reconstructed within the horizons of reciprocity and equality, with all parties being mutually
determined by the results. What would happen to children if,
from a young age, they were no longer treated as parental property, or a gift from God, or a national duty, or the object of
socialization, but rather as individuals with the right to follow
out their own self-chosen lives? And what will happen if this
attempt to live everyday life under the aegis of partnership –
what Anthony Giddens called "emotional democracy" – is confronted with the harsh new demands of a "flexible" labor
market? When the parents, and specifically the women, are
sucked into precarious work situations, and "flexible" time

schedules that serve business's needs rather than theirs? And when radical inequality re-emerges as a result? What happens in a society where, on the one hand, fealty is forever being sworn to *family values*, and to motherhood and fatherhood and parenthood, while on the other it is preached with equally doctrinaire zeal that everyone must always place him- or herself at the absolute disposal of a labor market that offers fewer and fewer zones of protection and long-term security? What does this all mean for couples who in their everyday lives must also bridge differences arising from their different ethnic and national origins?

We have as yet no idea what the solutions to these problems will be. All we know for sure is that people are being compelled to try out millions of them. Their side effects are dissolving old institutions and coalescing into new ones. However, which new ones they are coalescing into we're not yet sure.

This all sounds very strenuous.

Yes. But nobody wants to turn back. When it comes to crisis, we each want the other person to give in so that we can follow our own dream a little farther.

There are many ways in which individualization is a structural process. One is that it involves the individualization of risks. Individuals are forced to bear more and more of the consequences of decisions they've been forced to make, and more of those consequences are unforeseeable. But there is a second way in which risks are being "individualized." Numerous social problems which are being caused by the mismatch of newly developing institutions are being off-loaded to individuals for them to resolve as best they can through the redesign of their joint private life. So if, for example, there aren't enough kindergarten places at the local school, the family is now expected to fix this by rearranging everyone else's day. If society hasn't made sufficient provision for the elderly, the family has to bear the burden. This was true in first modern society too. But it didn't affect everyone's career plans then, because there only was one career and it lasted a lifetime. In the second modernity, every shortfall of social institutions causes not only a strain on, but also a *reorganization of*, the family. This is not society's intention, but it is the result.

It seems to me a decisive factor here was the broad set of changes in education that took place in the 1960s. Without widely distributed education, the labor market could never have been made flexible. The more people get degrees, the greater the pressure to individualize in the sense you've been describing it. Would you agree with that?

Absolutely. I think one of the biggest revolutions that happened in the 1960s and 1970s was the expansion of education. One of its most important dimensions was its effect on the equality of men and women. When higher education became a mass phenomenon, it inscribed deep changes in society especially because of its effects on women. The internalization of educational ambitions is bound up with the internalization of rights and claims. When that happens to a semi-caste, which is what women were, it frees them from their caste destiny, and creates for them the risks and opportunities of leading a self-chosen life. This in turn creates turbulence in marriage and family life. Biographies not only need to be self-constructed rather than selected, they need to be coherent in two different spheres, both at home and in one's career. And now there are two of them coexisting in the same space and time.

In one of his last great writings in the 1970s, the American sociologist Talcott Parsons considered the consequences of educational reform. He put forth an idea of institutionalized individualism that parallels my own, and he traced several of its essential causes back to the educational process.

Parsons clearly distinguished institutionalized individualism from the egoism of the market. He said that what was happening here was not a generalization of *homo oeconomicus*. It was not an extension of the rational choice by means of which persons pursue economic ends. Rather it was an individualism filled with paradoxes, the first of which was that the people who were now freed to pursue self-chosen lives were at the same time overcome with the deepest kind of yearning for emotional relationships. They wanted not just any emotional relationship, but a distinctive kind of love in which you could lose your self in the other – and find yourself in the other. They wanted an emotional interaction in which the bounds of the self could be transcended, and they wanted to base their marriage and their private life on it. Parsons said this notion of love could also express itself through, for example, the love of nature; a person could find herself in the experience of nature. In fact any abiding passion in which the I was transcended could serve this function. But he thought it was an essential element of this new individualism that it strove for this kind of love.

Naturally when Parsons wrote this, he was chiefly thinking of the hippie movement of the early 1970s, the era of "make love not war." But he also thought – and this is the last implication I'll draw from his work – that along with all the other elements of a new culture, the individualization of everyday life would also produce a new religiosity. It would not necessarily take institutionalized religions as a model. It might be an atheistic, a secular, or a new-age religiosity, just so long as it was one which sought the abandonment of self.

This striving for the experience of the abandonment of self is radically opposed to the rationality of *homo oeconomicus*. It also translates into a constitutive paradox at the very heart of the biographical project. The main activity of the self-chosen life is the search for one's true self. The proof that one has found it is the emotional feeling in which we experience the transcending of our self in another. So the search for self, for individuation and self-fulfillment, has to pass through others, and for others to find their true selves, they have to pass through us.

That's a beautiful paradox. It's a very hopeful way of looking at things. But aren't we a few years older now, and richer in experience? Isn't this exactly the moment when we can see clearly that homo oeconomicus *has in fact triumphed over the kind of individualization that Talcott Parsons envisioned? You only have to watch TV. There are now ads for firms that are preparing to come on the stock market. That is, the ads aren't for what the firms make; rather they are marketing the firms themselves in the form of shares. This is a quantum leap in marketization that would have been unthinkable even a year ago.*

It is true that in parts of society individualism has been assimilated to the neoliberal project. You see it in the concept of the self entrepreneur, which merges both concepts together. Here the self-chosen life is conceived of as the business plan of a one-person corporation. Each person is exhorted to treat his self as a capitalist would his company, and to self-consciously reorga-

nize all of its features into preemptive conformity with market
conditions. It's a very peculiar synthesis. There is a certain
advantage to the previous set-up of being oppressed by someone
else, because then at least you can set up a political defense
against it. Now it seems at the next level of capitalism the
corporation is off-loading the responsibility for keeping up
the pressure onto the individual. It becomes self-exploitation
and self-oppression, and everyone is supposed to give three
cheers, because a new kind of autonomous person is being born.

This already forms a recognizable trend. On top of that, this
form of individualism is highly functional for our present social
institutions. It allows all kinds of institutional problems, not only
from the sphere of work, but also from the larger society, from
deficiencies in the welfare state to the wrecking of the environment, to be off-loaded onto the sorcerer's apprentice of the
self entrepreneur. The individual becomes the waste basket of
society's unsolved problems, and then is supposed to transform
this garbage can he's been made into into some kind of creative
project.

Now, when something is this functional for society's institutions, sociologists need only activate their normal cynicism to
recognize the huge potential for growth. But I think it is very
important to distinguish the ideal type of the self entrepreneur
from the form of individualism I am envisioning, which also has
a reality.

Self entrepreneurs, as Richard Sennet has shown, act in the
illusion of their boundless autonomy. They live in the idea
that each is a little Hercules, a mini-global player who exists

in a societal vacuum. Each really believes he is a monad; each
lives in an illusion of total independence. For this reason
each also lives in a state of false consciousness in the strong
sense of the term, because the social form of the self entrepreneur is only possible as the highly artificial product of
a very complex social formation. It presumes a huge network
of very specific dependencies that extend all the way from
one's locality and nation-state up through a transformed world
system. Each of these self entrepreneurs sees himself leading
an insular existence, as being a Robinson Crusoe of global
society. But in fact it would be closer to the truth to see them
as completely exposed in a jungle of global markets on which
they are completely dependent. A consciousness this illusory is

doomed to constantly run aground on its own contradictions because it doesn't recognize the social conditions of its
existence.

In contrast, the ideal type of individualization I focus on
is conscious of the social conditions of its existence. It might
be more prevalent in milieux surrounded by well-functioning
welfare states, as in continental Europe. Here alternative
lifestyles are usually bound up with alternative communities
and often with alternative politics. The task and adventure
of developing one's individuality is clearly perceived as going
hand in hand with the duty and necessity of reinventing social
arrangements. Although much of its descriptive vocabulary may
be pre-theoretical, this feeling that individuals are determined
by society, and that if they are to make themselves anew, they
must change many of their everyday arrangements, is regarded
in such milieux as a commonsensical truth. A sensitivity to individual nuance therefore goes hand in hand with a sensitivity to
social connections.

These two types of individualization can be clearly distinguished as ideal types. In reality, there is a great deal of overlap
and combination. We know, based on a wealth of studies, that
those people who have made living a self-chosen life into a life
project defend this project with all their strength against
external encroachments. But it is impossible to organize any
"self-chosen" life except through networks with others. Thus,
such people are forced to become tinkerer-inventors not only
of their own lives, but also of networks. No matter what
their ideology, they are almost forced into becoming an alternative kind of entrepreneur, a social entrepreneur, because they
can only construct their self-chosen lives by entering into a continuous process of harmonizing their projects with those of
others.

Leading a self-chosen life therefore means leading a social
life, and in much more conscious way than previously. Earlier,
one could get by simply by living up to one's standardized
duties. But that becomes impossible when two or more people
are trying to harmonize life patterns that they are both constantly in the process of creating and changing. In that situation,
duties must be worked out consciously and reworked continuously according to the sense of justice of all concerned. Reciprocity must be continuously reproduced.

I believe that if you take a good look inside present-day families and relationships, and into the turbulence that is working itself out there, you can readily see just how large the sea change was that began in the 1960s but which really started to work itself out in the 1970s and the 1980s. We can see by observation just how stressful it is, and what enormous efforts people are making to compensate for the contradictoriness that emerges in everyday life when pre-given roles cease to be legitimate. But we can also see how many innovations are being produced to deal with these problems and make life easier.

It is important that we be precise in grasping this point about the social orientation of individualization so that there aren't any idealistic misunderstandings. It is not a matter of altruism so much as the social becoming a desired side effect of interconnected individual projects.

But aren't you talking about an earlier idyll rather than the present reality? Wasn't the experimental phase of self-discovery of the 1970s and early 1980s completely swamped by the neoliberal upheaval of the late 1980s and 1990s, when creativity was made subservient to career, and work swallowed every moment of private life?

No. It's never just one form. Not even in the utopia of neoliberalism, the United States.

Robert Wuthnow, the American sociologist of religion, conducted a very interesting set of investigations which, while admittedly bound up with American peculiarities, can also be extrapolated to Europe. One thing that makes America so interesting is that alongside extreme individualism it also has a dense network of everyday social activities such as we don't find in Europe. These "community activities," centered on church, school, and various associations, have been an identifying mark of American democracy ever since de Tocqueville wrote about them so enthusiastically in *Democracy in America*. Wuthnow examined these activities more closely and came to an interesting conclusion. Those people who were the strongest exponents of egoistic values, who most came out in favor of the importance of career and self-realization, were almost always also people who not only valued communal activities highly, but who spent a great deal of their free time taking care of others.

This seeming contradiction, that people can value egoism so highly while at the same time showing a great willingness to care for others, is an interesting phenomenon. If we wanted to typologize it, we might call it something like altruistic individualism or cooperative egoism. But for me, this is simply the limit case of a general rule: that the question of what kind of social morality is being created by individualization has to be explained from the perspective of the individual project.

Wuthnow asked one woman why she devoted so much time to teaching illiterates to read, and she stated this relation with unusual clarity: "I do it out of pure egoism, because being with these people is extremely important for me. I learn things about myself that I experience in no other social context and in no other social relationships." But while her clarity of expression is rare, her behavior and ideas are common. There is a great deal of literature and analysis that confirms Wuthnow's argument that social morality can arise as the direct function of the individual, egoistic project.

I think this point is extremely difficult for most of our social welfare institutions to accept or even comprehend. There are many people who are unwilling to be soldiers in the hierarchically organized tasks of social welfare, not because they object to the morals, but because they object to the hierarchy. What we need is a form of social organization that will allow the "victims" of social work to be recognized as subjects, to be taken seriously. This system also has to recognize that most people who want to engage in these activities don't want to do so as the agents of a welfare army, but rather as a form of personal exchange that gives them self-fulfillment in return. Our goal should be to be to come up with an alternative form of social organization that both encourages this behavior and makes it into an enduring part of the social fabric by facilitating people's ability to weave it into their self-chosen lives.

When people in Europe ask how political parties, or unions, or churches, or the great welfare institutions, can come to terms with this new individualism, they usually foreclose any answer by assuming individualism means a new form of radical selfishness and a farewell to every kind of social morality. This is not only false, it erects a self-defeating opposition. Radical individualism does not mean a society of radically egoistic monads. If one were forced to simplify and come down on one side or the other, it would be truer to say that this is a generation and a culture that is determined to risk the experiment of finding out how individualism and social morality can be harmonized in a radically new way – how free will and individuality can be reconciled with being there for others.

For such a culture to grow and take root, we must first supply the preconditions. This presumes first of all that we recognize it for what it is, in all its complexity. It is a historical and political mistake to keep on forcing it into old stereotypes which make it look like nothing more than a farewell to old institutions, as nothing more than the culmination of egoism.

Even if we grant this point, isn't it still possible to argue that radical individualization will introduce a new kind of stratification? That it will divide society into those who, on the basis of their education, their job choices, and their mobility, are capable of fully undertaking these experiments in individualization, and who become deeply invested in them; and those who, because of their lack of education, lack of job choices, and lack of mobility – and the lack of social imagination that often flows from such a constrained social reality – are therefore less capable of, less inclined towards, and less well-disposed towards this sort of individualization? Is it possible to see things like this?

Partly. There is certainly the material for a new division along such lines. But we have to think through more precisely what the conditions are that put people in a situation where they are able to respond creatively to these new possibilities.

The more immediate cause for division is internal to individualization, namely that it's so extremely nerve-wracking. This goes for both the neoliberal version and the social-experimental kind. Everyone who isn't pursuing individualistic goals of her own, but instead experiencing them from the outside, as the victim of someone else's plans and whims, reacts against the process with aggression. Individualism produces its own enemies precisely to the extent it is successful.

Each of us claims for herself the right to keep reorganizing the world so we can follow to the fullest our interlinked set of desires. We call that self-realization, and its opposite self-stifling. But when an intimate other claims the same right, and it comes into conflict with ours, it strikes us as an ego trip. This is how people become the victims of individuation. The immediate crisis that turns a person's life upside down is something like divorce. But behind it is usually a history of clashes and being balked, like one person having to put their own desires on hold in order to adjust to the needs of someone else's career. This is something women once did for men and accepted as fate, but now it's generalized and never accepted entirely by anybody. We are all pursuing the same goal of personal realization, and these projects can't but come into constant conflict with each other over the limited resources of shared time and space. That's what we all feel: that we are under constant time pressure and we don't have enough space. And that's what we fight about, the organization of time and space.

Many people think that the central indicator of individualization is the number of people who are single. But the number of singles is a superficial figure behind which hides a complex reality. In most big cities, the number of single-person households hovers around 50 percent. However, it's important to note that divorced people are just one category of singles and make up a relatively low proportion of the whole. There are many kinds of pair-relationships which take a physically divided form for various reasons and so get counted as two single-person households; for example because the man has his primary residence in another town during the work week. There are also a lot of widows in the world, who we don't normally think of when we think of "single" people. We men seem to labor under a clear structural disadvantage; we die sooner. But the point I'm getting at is that even the simplest sign of individualization actually represents a very heterogeneous reality. It is important to look beneath these signs to see how individualization is actually changing the social architecture of society.

Speaking of changing architecture, the history of architecture is a veritable fossil record of the history of individualization. The project of having your own life presupposes having your own room. That seems like a commonplace, but historically it represented a radical change in our living arrangements. In the early years of the modern era, workers' homes basically only had one room in which family life played itself out, the kitchen, and another one where everyone slept, parents as well as children. Maybe the family of a well-off worker would have two bedrooms. But in today's Germany it's considered an index of poverty if everyone in a household doesn't have her own room. Over time, this norm that everyone should have her own room has found concrete expression in the architecture of apartments and buildings and neighborhoods. The process of subdivision is still ongoing in the middle classes, where there is growing trend for both members of a couple to get their own bedroom because everyone should have a room they can mess up and organize as they see fit.

A room of one's own is clearly a symbolic as well as a spatial category. To have a room of your own means you can lock other people out. You can become a self for itself. You can read pornography, or write revolutionary tracts, or do whatever you want. Virginia Woolf wrote a wonderful book by that title, *A Room of One's Own*. She starts out by saying, "You asked me to speak about what a woman needs to become a writer, and my answer is: a room of one's own." A room of one's own, as Woolf makes clear, is room to develop one's own perspective.

Historically, the struggle of people to have their own time might accelerate after they've secured their own rooms. By the way, there's evidence of this going on in almost every social milieu we've ever observed, including many not usually associated with radical individualization, like farmers' households. People there are also struggling for their own time and space.

So far we've been discussing the effects individualization has had in the microcosm of the family. Let's step back and look at society as a whole. What is the relation between individualization and the social safety net that is supposed to catch us when we're old, sick, unemployed, etc.?

The interaction between disembedded individualization and "social assistance" in the broadest sense is one of the most important dynamics in the second modernity. How we manage it may well determine the result of this social experiment.

In order to analyze this, we need to introduce a new distinction. We have already contrasted the phenotype of neoliberal individualism, the self entrepreneur, with the experimental form of individualism. The latter form involves a pressure to harmonize your life choices with those of others, and for that reason necessarily opens out into an experimental culture. It creates new social forms. We must now make a further distinction between an individualization that takes place on the basis of relative social security, such as we experienced in the 1960s and 1970s in Germany, and an individualization that takes place when the collective system for providing such security is being dismantled. The first I would call individualization in the full sense of the term. The second should really be called *atomization.*

Individualization in the experimental sense can only really take place under certain conditions. We're not certain yet what all of those conditions are, but so far we can say that people require a certain foundation of security – and one they can take for granted will be there in the long term – in order to be able to bring these sorts of experiment to fruition. For this form of life to be possible, certain kinds of problem have to have stopped intruding on everyday life. This is why we should consider very carefully the repercussions of remaking, or unmaking, the system of social security.

Let's examine one of the classical theories for the rise of fascism in Germany. Hannah Arendt explained it using the concept of "individualization," but what she actually meant was "atomization." She was speaking about people who had been uprooted, who had been not only freed from tradition but also cut off from it, and who hadn't managed to achieve a new basis in private property. People, in short, who had lost the ground beneath their feet. Ungrounded in either a middle- or working-class existence, they were now delivered over defenseless to a massively effective propaganda machine. What made it possible for these malign societal definitions to remold them so completely? Arendt argues it was because they had already been robbed of the fundamental prerequisites of a self-organized, self-conscious, and therefore political existence.

Today this description holds true for broad regions of the world, where a form of modernization that is almost entirely driven by the needs of the world market is killing the social preconditions of freedom. One of the most important questions today is how far the systems of social security and the traditions of family-based mutual assistance can be weakened without atomizing people. What will the consequences be of a worldwide "tabula rasa" modernization, which so shakes the foundations of people's security that they become ready for any sort of indoctrination? It's quite thinkable that they'll lash out at others in order to give some meaning to their own lives. Or they might become rubber stamps for other people's ideologies and the tools of their mad delusions.

Atomization is now going on even in the centers of rich western societies themselves. Many middle-class people are so insecure in the basic conditions of their existence that they too have begun to experience this creeping fear of losing the ground beneath their feet. This existential anxiety has been growing behind the façades of prosperity and security. This could be a fatal development precisely because it erodes the prerequisites of experimental individualism, which is now the prerequisite of effective political freedom.

What do we need to do to foster the conditions that make experimental individualism possible? To start with, we have to realize that all of our current systems of social security are coupled to paid labor. The distribution of income is the precondition that determines who enjoys security. We've widened the radius of social security over the years to include, for example, housewives who aren't in the paid labor force. But so long as the basic logic is left unchanged, that everyone should get back what they put in, and should earn their rightful share in the market, such inclusions simply lead to fiscal overburdening and the threat of system breakdown.

The generalization of the individualization process confronts us with the problem of generalizing basic security so that more and more people have access to the prerequisites of a healthy individualization. The problem is exacerbated by the fact that even paid labor is now bringing with it ever less security because it is organized ever more flexibly on a short-term contract basis. What we have to figure out is how people can be compensated for the extreme insecurity of their private lives (in relations between the sexes, in the changing demands of the labor market, etc.) by being provided with medium- or long-term basic security as a backdrop.

A good way to illustrate this problem is to examine the measures that were undertaken in Great Britain to reintegrate people into the labor market and why they failed. The plan was simple: take people living on the dole and offer them jobs. But the jobs offered were ones which only offered short-term employment. They were "highly flexible" jobs, in which one could make a short-term economic gain at the price of possibly being let go at any instant. The fact that these "opportunities" were not widely taken up outraged many economists. They accused the unemployed of being lazy, and said they only wanted to make themselves comfy in the niches of the welfare state. But what these economists overlooked in their critique was the fact that the behavior of the unemployed actually embodied a very rational economic calculation. The odds were that a person could expect to be forced out of one of these short-term jobs in a short period of time. Then he or she would be back at the unemployment and welfare offices. The welfare office is the real enemy of the poor. It's the main obstacle they have to overcome before they can get on with their lives. Once they get past it, social assistance offers them a basic security on which they can build through legal or illegal activities. So the problem with these jobs was that, while they were economically more attractive in the short term, they took away this basic security and put the poor back to square one in trying to get it back. So the poor were making an economically rational calculation and finding it unacceptable. They judged that as little security as they had, it was worth more to them than short-term gain.

It's considerations like this that make it clear why a de-traditionalized and individualized culture requires basic security. We have to ask seriously why we can't have a decommodified system of basic security, one that is independent from paid labor. It would have to provide more than is currently offered by social assistance, of course. But the goal would be essentially the same, to provide a dependable basis upon which a multitude of various activities could be built, including super-flexible temporary jobs, but also work in the home as parents, as citizens, etc. (See pp. 160–2 and pp. 166–7).

In other words, a basic security system that would put the kinds of work you were discussing in your American example, which are now called charity work, on an equal footing with paid labor.

Right.

So you'd let the lame care for the blind?

It's more probable that what this system would allow would be for the blind to care for the blind and the lame to care for the lame. It would foster such self-organization as there already is and allow it to develop to the next level. It's amazing what this does for people's hopes and for their power to aid themselves. You can see it today in South America among even the poorest of the poor. Even in favelas, if the proper framework is set up, people start organizing, and they start to pull themselves out of hopelessness.

But doesn't this also show (I have to slip a critical question in here sometimes) that the magic of individualization really only functions, and really only can function, when people do it voluntarily? If the iron cage of social roles (or class context, or what have you) is broken down by external forces, and people are not yet psychologically ready, this is a real problem. Forcing people to individuate is no more promising than forcing people to be free.

That's an important point. If we look at how people are reacting to globalization in parts of Asia, or in the Arab countries, or in South America, they are almost universally seeing themselves as victims of it. Even among the elites who are profiting from it, we find enormous emotional resistance and anger. Part of this is injured national pride, of course. Only in America do national interests and globalization converge so closely as to be invisible; only there can imperial interests appear identical with the national interest. On the receiving end, the imperialist aspect stands out a lot more clearly. But even granting that, I still think the main source of the really virulent resistance to globalization is less injured national pride than the injuries of individualization.

There is a deep connection between globalization and individualization. Globalization increases the lived contradictions that people are forced to bridge in their everyday lives. That creates more space and more necessity for individuation. In Europe or America we have such a ready context to apply to these developments that we actually miss the part that is qualitatively new. If we speculate about how the internet might give rise to an "anarchy of individualism" it's an image that probably holds more attraction for us than fear. But in Asia, in the Arab countries, or in traditional parts of South America, the same phenomena are experienced as an enormous aggression against the traditional order of society.

It's important to look at this self-critically. It is not only in the so-called periphery that people complain about the corrosive effects of individualization. Even in Germany over the last few years there has been a heated debate about the legacy of the 1960s and 1970s and 1980s. Now here are people who have clearly enjoyed the fruits of individualization. But the more the process is generalized, the more each of us runs into its nerve-wracking nether side. Each of us becomes more of a victim of individualization to the extent that all of us are individualizing. Every act of individualization has the potential to make others the victims of its consequences. Eventually the public debate heats up, and people begin to say, "Are there no limits to individualization? Have we not reached a stage where we have to say Stop! No further!"

It is important to note, however, that this desire for limits is directly caused by the increase in individualization. If we ever agree to set limits, it will mean the boundaries of individualization were produced by individualization itself.

If I understand correctly, there are two superimposed discussions going on here. One is about experimental individualization, and how it is fundamentally premised upon an expanded and decommodified welfare state. The second is a critique of the conservative argument that the present-day welfare state is being chronically abused by lazy scroungers. I think we could contribute something by clarifying this second argument, because this conservative outcry, that smart guys have made the social safety net into their own private hammock, is growing louder every day in Europe. Conservative critics give examples of people who are unemployed and still go to Italy three times a year. They say this is outrageous, these people should be forced to work, and all their payments should immediately be cut off so they can't ever do anything like this again.

From my perspective, one could argue almost exactly the opposite. I think I would like to claim these people as the pioneers of a new form of existence. They exemplify a fundamental truth, which is that many of our non-paying activities are just as important to us as our jobs, often more important. The reason they make this point starkly is because they are living in economic extremity. The *only* advantage they have over people in the labor market is that circumstance has granted them some flexibility to structure their lives differently. It's therefore interesting to see what they choose to do, and what to sacrifice.

Their case also underlines that the precondition for allowing individualization to develop to the next stage is the provision of basic security – not total security, but *basic* security, something that would allow individuals to decide themselves how much more time they wanted to spend improving their material existence, and at what point they would prefer instead to stay at a lower level of material existence but branch out into other activities useful both for society and for themselves, contributing to both social cohesion and personal development.

What these people also make clear is that in a society where paid labor has absolute primacy, this form of development has been criminalized. The only allowable option is to undertake these other activities after you have devoted most of your time to paid labor. If there are social deficits, they have to be provided through other people's paid labor, whether those people are employed through the market or by the government.

By contrast, I think the real solution to both the personal and social problems of individualization is many-sided development. And the key to that is breaking the monopoly of paid labor. By monopoly, I mean the centrality of paid labor in bestowing meaning upon activities, such that they can't really be taken seriously unless they're paid for. Paid labor is not only the foundation of our material security. It's also the basis of our identities and the precondition for our participation in democracy.

This is no longer consonant with how we think, or with how we strive to structure our lives. Throughout society, we are struggling to integrate a broader range of activities, to give more importance to non-market activities, to achieve a balance in multi-sided lives. Those welfare state "spongers" who are so demonized are simply achieving at a very low level what the rest of us are inchoately striving for: to develop a many-sided form of existence, where many kinds of work are equally important in building up a single existence, a life one can truly call one's own.

But aren't there also many people who have fixed up the "iron cage" of social roles quite nicely and don't want to leave? Whose individual decision is to wallpaper it over and redecorate, but who really want to stay there because they are afraid of freedom? What can be done for them? Isn't that also an individualized decision, when I say I want to stay here? If the cage is then ripped open and I am thrown into freedom, I'm forced to confront problems I find insoluble.

Yes, that's a possibility. The attempt to try and reweld the cage as it's being broken down by both external and internal forces, that may be a considerable temptation for a large group of people. It could be that for some people individualization represents a demand that exceeds their resources. As we said before, as individualization grows, so do the temptations of fundamentalism.

Does the culture of the individual have a concept of an enemy, of a culture it opposes itself to?

It has several, actually. One is the counter-ideal that a collectivity should be based on a closed, ethnically defined culture of origins. Another is the new ideology of communitarianism, which often seems to preach community as if it were an antidote to individualism. However, the most interesting opposition may be the opposition of this culture of freedom to the culture of aggressive capitalism that is now widely known as neoliberalism. It may be in the future that people will think of this as the most important opposition: freedom vs. neoliberalism.

That would almost turn on its head the current understanding, where neoliberalism is identified by everyone, even its opponents, with the policy of increasing freedom, even at the expense of other civic virtues.

That's right. But if neoliberalism continues to strip away the social foundations that are necessary for a cohesive society to emerge out of self-determining, self-developing individuals, it will emerge ever more clearly that the two are in fact deeply opposed. True freedom is the individual freedom to develop freely.

What are the political implications of the disembedded individualism that you've been describing?

Politics in its parliamentary form presupposes aggregated interests. Aggregated interests presuppose the relatively stable and easy to survey social structure of collectivities. And collective society is exactly what is being dissolved by disembedded individualization. The question then becomes, "If individualization and atomization are removing the social structural preconditions for the old kind of state-centered politics, what kind of politics will take its place? How can disembedded individualization be made into a basis for collectively binding decisions?"

One possibility is that a form of politics is coming into being based on human rights. Can human rights become the building block of a cosmopolitan society? If human rights come to be understood as the necessary basis of every individual's autonomous life, will people someday feel they are defending the foundations of their own identities when they defend the importance of human rights for foreigners? Although it is not often noticed, I think the age of the self-chosen life has already introduced a fundamental change into our concept of democracy. The cultural and political diversity that is essential to this kind of life has been slowly elevated to a central political principle. It sometimes seems as if it were even more highly valued than the representative principle with which it now shares pride of place.

The real question is whether cosmopolitan individualism can effectively oppose the two main political currents that currently dominate the world. On the one flank is capitalism gone wild; and on the other flank are counter-individualistic forms of communitarianism that want to go back to authoritative, even authoritarian, collective values. The values and preconditions of the self-chosen life are something both sides are aiming at undermining.

Under the conditions of disembedded individualization, society can no longer be integrated by means of pre-given norms and values and hierarchies. Now, rather than integration being the basis of freedom, freedom has to become the basis of integration.

We have to inquire in more detail into the nature of freedom, into the interaction of its social, legal, political, and economic

aspects. And we have to keep foremost in mind that it's forever-
more impossible for there to be one set of normative patterns
that we can all just copy and which will then hold society
together. There are no longer any legitimate essentialist definitions. Not of men, not of women, not of wives. Not of
Christians or Jews or blacks or Muslims or Germans or Chinese.
Our culture has been irreversibly transformed into what Alain
Touraine called "an experiment whose ultimate goal is to figure
out how we can live together as equals and yet be different."

*It's interesting that on your interpretation, the two things the self-
chosen life isn't threatened by are the spectres that usually play
the central roles in this debate: the destruction of all values and
the addiction to the self. You seem to be saying that the real danger
is that the self-chosen life won't go far enough – that it won't
succeed in translating its creative impulse, its experimental normativity, into a societal program.*

That's right. Although I do admit the possibility that the search
for the foundations of the self-chosen life could lose its way
in psychological and new-age byways and become an infinite
regress into the private. But yes, I consider that a much lesser
danger than the others we've discussed.

For me, the central point to keep clear on is that in the age
of the self-chosen life, individuals can no longer be integrated
by *control* norms and their pre-given either/ors. Priority instead
has to be given to *constitutive* norms, which encourage and
provide security, which make the experiments of the self-chosen
life possible, and which keep individualization from careening
off into atomization.

In some ways, the question is the same one that de
Tocqueville found insoluble two centuries ago. How can a
socially and politically creative individualism be grounded *in
itself?* Is there anything inherent to the individualization process
that keeps alive the consciousness that the foundations of the
self-chosen life can only be secured and defended through
public and political exchanges with others? Or does the old rule
still hold in transformed form, that for there to be political
action there must be gods? That is, compulsive collective beliefs.

All these questions have to be placed in a wider and still
emergent social context. We have to examine the role transna-

tionalization plays, both in the way it changes people's experience of the world and in the way it changes their capacity for action. Remember, this is true not only of the people at the top, the so-called global players, but just as much (if not more so) among the migrants and illegals at society's edges and bottom. They are the ones who really have to juggle different cultures and systems of law. Similarly we have to ask how it can be made possible for men and women, blacks and whites, Israelis and Arabs, Christians and Muslims to share non-essentialist definitions of the human condition.

That last question hints at the ambiguous legacy of religion. We can learn a lot from studying the history of religion. Historically, religion mostly vilified individualism. But it also produced a universalist framework that was integrated into the self-image of humanity. It is this legacy of the world religions that has made it possible for strangers living across ethnic and national boundaries to recognize each other as "brothers" and "sisters." Religion made an essential contribution to the possibility of establishing a cosmopolitan basis for political action.

However, religion is not just a historical ancestor. It's a present-day reality, and it too is being transformed in all sorts of ways by the second modernity. Sometimes, in the trendy zone between individualization and new-age thought, it almost seems like there is a constant sum of religious energy that is simply expressed in different forms. Could that be true? Could it be because a transcendental framework really is indispensable, even in the era of the self-chosen life? If that turns out to be true, then the age of individualization might turn out to be the age of tinkered-together religions, in the broad Parsonian sense of religiosity.

On the other hand, if it's not true, it opens up the possibility of a historically unique future. In place of a world of heretics and atheists and nihilists, we may someday see one dominated by the religiously indifferent. Perhaps not only the belief in God, but even the belief in substitute (for example, national) gods will finally be dislodged. Perhaps we'll learn through experience that a transcendental framework in fact isn't necessary to lead a self-chosen life.

These, however, are questions that can only be answered historically – by the history of the future.

They are intriguing questions. I think the question must still be answered first, however, of how this wonderfully free and individualized society, saturated as it is with the politics of the everyday, will ever manage to erect itself against the foreseeable resistance of the many, who out of weakness, or a poverty of imagination, or the comfortableness of their particular cages, cling to their bondage. Isn't there the danger that these people who don't want to leave their iron cages will run en masse after any pied piper who tells them, in essence: "I'll make it so you can avoid all that. I'll protect you from all the evil riders of the Apocalypse, from multiculturalism and globalization and having immigrants up to your eyeballs. I'll guarantee that the old familiar bars and fences will hold up. All you have to do is vote for me."

That's certainly one possible reaction formation. It's one of the political scenarios individualized society could produce.

Perhaps then we should give some time to sketching out the various scenarios of what the political consequences of individualization might be. Where do you think we should we start?

The decisive question will be whether the culture of political freedom we've been discussing can win a public voice and find appropriate organizational forms. That would mean empowering civil society to open an institutional space between state and market for the creativity and self-responsibility of individuals. But there are at least three counter-tendencies that we have to watch out for which could end up prevailing.

One is a kind of *postmodern nationalism.* This accepts that the essentialist definition of ethnicity and nation can no longer be defended. But it then manages to breathe new life into the old demons by creating a new basis for ethnic identity that is compatible with the new conditions laid down by disembedded individualization.

You can see this in incipient form in various varieties of identity politics. In the USA, for example, some members of minority groups have used postmodern means to re-mark the boundaries between themselves and the rest of society. They accept the postmodern argument that everything is relative. But they then use that as a starting point to refortify the old essentialist battle lines on a new basis. Their fundamental proposition is that the truth of a minority group can only be known (because it can only be experienced) by its members.

The result is a paradoxical mixture of relativism and fundamentalism. Its proponents seek to draw a line separating this identity from all others while at the same time evading the discourse of justification. Over time this model is being extended to cover not only minorities but all possible identities. This means there is now an acceptable language for any identity, including ethno-nationalist identities, to assert the uniqueness and endangeredness of their culture. They can base their claims on a new higher ground that is harder to assail. The marriage of relativism and fundamentalism may be paradoxical, but once formed, it is hard to break.

The second counter-development is something we've already discussed, namely *globalism*. This is the dominant political form assumed by global capitalism. It takes as its main opponent exactly the political alliance that once defined the first modernity: the alliance between nation-state, market, and democracy. It not only opposes the extension of this alliance into global society, it seeks to break it down in its original strongholds. Globalists claim that politics can and should be vastly minimized if not done without altogether. They claim the state is no longer needed because most of its functions can be assumed by the market. When it comes to the culture of freedom, they go both ways. They minimize the importance of political freedom and maximize the importance of consumer freedom. They let the difference get obscured in the spectacle of having ten kinds of yogurt to choose from.

Globalism claims to enthrone a seemingly unpolitical form of market rationality. But it misunderstands the extent to which democratic culture was one of the preconditions of market extension. If it systematically dismantles that culture, it will become *forced* to accept un- and anti-democratic forms of re-ethnicization or re-nationalization as the only ways of pushing through the expansion of the market against resistance. But if it comes to that, I think globalists will be perfectly willing to work out an arrangement with the ethnically defined Haider capitalisms of this world.

Finally, a third scenario could be what I've called *democratic authoritarianism*. We've already discussed the increased possibilities for domestic surveillance and control that the new information technology places in the hands of government. The advance of technology will only extend this capacity in the years to come. Technology also increases the opportunity for a new kind of caesarism ruling through more effective use of the mass media. In combination, they hold forth the possibility of combining democratic forms and authoritarian substance.

I think there are several reasons why this marriage of opposites will become an increasing temptation in coming years for ambitious nation-state politicians. One is the "logjam of reform" that presently haunts German public discourse. There is a great deal of truth in that description. The argument is that society stands before enormous political changes, which everyone knows have to be pushed through, but they are stalled by the democratic means of implementing them. In other words, reforms that are recognized as necessary are getting scuttled, contrary to our collective interests, by our individualistic culture and pluralist constitution. The more this argument gains assent, the more the tacit consensus might grow that democracy needs to be circumvented, that we need a technocratic solution, or a grand coalition, or some other means of limiting people's input and weakening the pluralist power structure.

The fact that governments are losing their influence over the economy and the labor market also feeds into this temptation. This loss of influence weakens the core of their legitimacy. They need different means of looking strong and capable of action, and one way is to take up the mantle of reform. It bestows on its proponents the air of decisive action and a reputation for order. But let's be honest. The "reform" movement is largely an anti-democratic movement.

So we can find the palpable stirrings of each of these three bad scenarios: anti-cosmopolitanism, anti-democratization and de-democratization. And if the landscape of European parties is broken up through social stress, these tendencies could gather momentum. We have already seen how new extreme-right populist parties and anti-immigrant movements have come into being in recent years in countries where conservative parties have been marginalized. It happened in Austria, France, and Denmark, and it could possibly happen in Germany.

This reminds me of Weimar and the aftermath of World War I in Europe, except this time in global terms. Party politics is just not equipped to cope with things like this.

Especially not when they have a transnational dimension. Brecht's line that "those in darkness go unseen" is especially true of the world's majority today. They are painfully poor, their voices are unheard, and they have no votes. What little social justice they see is mostly in the form of alms, when funds are sent to help cope with some natural or social disaster. To babble about "equality of opportunity" in such a world as if this were the same as social justice, and to sweep aside the fact that it pretty much ensures inequality of results; to regard this as if it were simply an unfortunate fact of life we have to be realistic about; and then to try to sell this as "modernization," as a cure-all for all the world's problems – this makes Orwell's Newspeak look good. The fact that those in darkness are mostly dark-skinned should disturb us even more.

Political and methodological nationalism has always conceived of social justice as something that only happens among national equals. It's time to question this way of thinking. It seems clear on a philosophical level that real justice can't mean "justice for everyone except 'foreigners.'" But justice that included rather than excluded "foreigners" would have to be transnational justice. What could that possibly mean? What would it mean to have transnational justice just within Europe? And how can any concept of real justice be reconciled with the existence of massive global poverty? Our dominant ideas of social justice, such as those embodied in the philosophy of John Rawls, look completely feeble when placed in the context of global injustice. Global injustice is all over the newspapers, but it hasn't penetrated our philosophical consciousness yet. It hasn't penetrated our basic categories of thought.

The interesting thing about an individualistic culture is that it could conceivably embrace a concept like cosmopolitan justice in the same paradoxical way that it is able to embrace the politics of ecology. In many ways, ecology embodies a conservative perspective. It takes the values of locality, the idea of communal responsibility, and blows it up to the level of civil society. In effect, it treats civil society as a great community, one which should have control over its environment. It treats society as something that can be treated for these purposes as a single community, despite the fact that it consists of very different subgroups and classes.

Democracy has always been in part about representing and enacting a national communal experience. The various demands for participation that changed the political landscape in the 1960s and 1970s were in part an attempt of previously excluded groups to claim their rightful place in this national community and to co-determine its outcomes. But paradoxically, local elections, which represent the most communitarian experience of democracy, always get the lowest turnout. That puts into question just how much weight this current can bear in real life. Yet conservatism, in the root sense of "conserving," clearly has a role to play in the second modernity. There are many values that we very much want to preserve and reshape. There is a kind of forward-looking conservatism in the culture of freedom that sets itself against the over-aggressiveness of the market, and which wants to preserve things like self-reliance and the power to determine one's fate. There is also the question of whether "progress" has the same meaning in the context of the second modernity. I mean, think about the revolution in genetic engineering, which is on the verge of becoming human engineering, without there ever having been a vote taken. How exactly should we categorize a resistance to letting gene technology rewrite our most basic human taboos without having any democratic input? Is asserting society's right to decide such questions progressive or conservative?

In the end, we are still left with a fundamental problem for which no one has a pat solution. Individualistic culture erodes the soil in which political parties and other large-scale organizations have to be rooted in order to work. It robs them of their social structural prerequisites.

That's right. But in fact the problem is even bigger because the political system is being subjected to ever larger tasks and expectations. The welfare state does have to be reformed, whether it's by the neoliberal reform plans that the political system finds it so hard to carry through, or by a completely alternative reform plan that relativizes the importance of paid labor. Similarly the political system has to find some way to manage

the opening out of the nation-state into a transnational dimension. It has to come up with a workable model of cosmopolitan democracy and a path to get there.

*Then there are also the new demands on its steering capacity posed
by the transition to risk society . . .*

. . . which is really another variant of the same system overload.
Risk society presents unprecedented problems which demand
unprecedented political solutions. So coping with them successfully seems like it will require a huge empowerment of politics at the same time as the current foundations of politics are
being stripped away.

There is a school of thought in political science that thinks
the solution to all these problems is to build up the intervening levels of political will formation. They say what we need is
to organize lots of new little groups and subgroups, and hold
forums and round tables and side tables, and basically work at
networking all these intermediate groups together until we
weave a grand new "network of networks." The only problem is
that this plan doesn't address the basic problem, which is how
to produce collectively binding decisions. It would actually
make that aspect of the problem worse by increasing the
pluralization of decision-making forums. The real problem is
how to incorporate many, many preferences into a single, joint
and binding decision. How to make their members feel both
represented and obligated at the national and transnational
level.

The political problem with pluralization and individualization is that they diminish what have up until now been the
necessary prerequisites for reaching collectively binding decisions. The possibility of pushing through real political decisions
at *any* level of society is getting increasingly difficult. This isn't
fixed through network democratization. Instead it's multiplied.

I think this is the nub of what you have repeatedly called "the
end of politics." It appears as an "end" from the perspective of
established political dynamics. But there are important aspects
that perspective doesn't capture which suggest an alternative
perspective.

There is a lot of support expressed out there for new kinds
of politics on a larger scale, as with the politics of global

warming or human rights. And these new political developments are not opposed to, but rather based on, this multiplication of political forums that reaches all the way into the
bedroom and the kitchen. The same *subpoliticization of society*
that disempowers parliamentary politics provides a nurturing
soil for these new kinds of politics.

There is now a continuum of negotiation that extends from
how we make love and how we set the table to the reorganization of the world economy and how we can best help sweat-
shop workers. New centers of action are developing all over.
This subpoliticization of society is a form of politicization. It is
not immediately apparent how this subpoliticization can re-
empower state political institutions or party politics, or how it
can be harnessed into new forms of democratic political organization with the power to shape society. But that is how the
question ought to be posed, in my opinion. That is where we
need to begin.

*Is subpoliticization the political expression of individualized
society?*

That's the view I've been developing, and I think it provides
answers to several key questions. Subpoliticization results
from the democratization of democracy, also known as cultural
democratization. This is something that was never foreseen in
democracy's original blueprints. It probably wouldn't have been
desired if it had been foreseen, but it flowed naturally enough
from its further development. It is a perfect example of modernity modernizing its own foundations and producing a qualitatively new dynamic.

Cultural democratization is an unintended side effect that is
produced when civil, political, and social rights are internalized.
With this step, democracy enters the family. Divorce makes
marriage into something we can vote to dissolve, like a parlia-
ment. When the "natural" intermeshing of gender roles and the
division of household labor breaks apart, the question of who
does what becomes something that is not only negotiable but
in need of justification. With this, the family takes on qualities
that are the hallmark of the public sphere and it becomes difficult to divide them. Public debates people see on TV remain
in their heads when they enter their bedroom, and affect what

goes on there. And vice versa, the changing mores of private interaction are carried into public forums.

The redefinition of gender roles is an excellent example of how subpoliticization can result from the boundary between public and private becoming blurry and permeable. Another is provided by the politics of risk society. The discovery that some risks are literally incalculable is a truth that has gathered momentum outside society's established institutions and forced itself upon them against their strenuous opposition. Ironically, it is precisely in overcoming institutional resistance that subpolitical processes build up their power. Similarly, when corporations find themselves forced for the first time to take ecological standards seriously because otherwise their stock price will drop or their sales will plummet, they are facing powers of resistance that are based in subpoliticization. The recent flap about genetically modified food is another good example of how this works. It even had reverberations in the United States, which had previously been thought to be beyond the reach of such movements.

Parallel to the subpoliticization of society is the pluralization of political space. The main divides of our time, between New Labour and Old Labour, between new social democracy and old social democracy, are really countervailing movements that are taking place *inside* the old party-political facades and institutions. This is also why we can't be immediately sure anymore which banners and which political labels should count as "progressive." It's become almost impossible to answer the simple question of what each of the parties stands for anymore. It's even harder to draw clear lines that capture the change and division beneath their façades.

Subpoliticization takes the same pluralization of political space that weakens the old party parliamentary system and creates new arenas for staging battles. Both the pluralization of political space and the subpoliticization of society involve tearing down the borders that separate the arena of specialized politics from a depoliticized society. This is why our definition of politics has to change. It was this social structure that made the central meaning of "politics" into "politics as an activity separate from all other activities." It was this relation that defined the first modernity.

All of this serves to make the central question clearer: in the face of such political pluralization, how are democratically legitimate and collectively binding decisions possible? The answer has to be found in the structures of subpoliticization. That is where we need to start. We need to examine this phenomenon much more closely.

You seem to have just described a reality that can't be summed up. Everything seems possible, everything is political, everything is dissolving and re-forming, but no one knows where any of it is headed. Is it possible to sketch it provisionally with our old, outmoded concepts?

The main theoretical rival to the idea of the individualized society is the idea that we are entering a new class society. Proponents of this view agree that there was an expansion of social freedoms in the 1960s and 1970s, but argue that since then it has been more than swamped by the counter-tendencies we have already mentioned, like chronic high unemployment, and an ever growing number of people falling out the system altogether. They believe that increasing class polarization is overwhelmingly the wave of the future.

This process of people falling out of civil society altogether has been widely discussed in Europe under the title of social exclusion, and it can be observed even in countries which have maintained seemingly full employment, like the USA. On this view, poverty, rather than being eliminated, is instead being radicalized. The dark side of millennial neoliberalism is that the gap between rich countries and poor countries has increased. Proponents of the "return of class" view read this as a sharpening of class lines, and see the ultimate outcome being a new class system on a world scale, simpler and starker than ever before. They see transnational proletarianization leading to a transnational two-class system, just as Marx originally predicted long ago.

Now if this were true, it wouldn't be the first time in history that one class system declined only to have a new one come in through the back door to take its place. And there are interesting warrants for this argument in a deep reading of Marx himself. One of Marx's central points is that everything is historically finite. It's possible to start from that premise and arrive at the conclusion that the nation-state form of capitalism was only a historical episode; that its last and highest development was the welfare state; and that it was only in this form that capitalism was successful in developing a class compromise and staving off proletarianization. Furthermore, one could argue that this compromise only succeeded because capitalism, like modernization, hadn't been completely carried through.

If you start from those premises, it doesn't seem far to argue that this historically short transition phase, where individual national capitalisms were surrounded by borders and buffers, is now coming to an end. And that from this point on, society will be thoroughly capitalized from top to bottom. The welfare state will be dismantled, of which there are already signs everywhere. And then, so goes this argument, individualization will necessarily turn back into proletarianization, because the only dam that was holding it back will be taken away. The middle class, whose rise and continued existence has refuted the two-class model in both practice and theory, will be fated to diminish and disappear, since the welfare state class compromise was what allowed it to come into existence in the first place. So proletarianization really will be our collective destiny, just as Marx originally predicted, after an unforeseen long delay.

It's a powerful argument. Looking at it, one can almost believe that Marx's ideas really were meant to apply to the third millennium. Maybe the twentieth century really was just a brief intermezzo of stability between the chaos of the industrial revolution and the supersession of the nation-state. Maybe now we really will see the social reality that corresponds to his theory.

It's easy to see why classical marxists feel like they smell a new dawn. They feel like they can dust off the old speeches and give them again. They have a serious counter-perspective against which the scenario we've been laying out has to be rethought and re-justified.

To start with, I think it's absolutely correct to highlight the new radicalization of inequality. We should lose our shyness about taking such worst-case scenarios seriously and developing proposals early on to deal with them. It is a real possibility, something that could grow out of current developments, and something that has to be accounted for in any serious interpretation. But I think those who want to found a renaissance of class theory on this radicalization of inequality are not thinking radically enough.

The main result of disembedded individualization is to blur the distinction between substructure and superstructure, between consciousness and class. In this context, individualization can no longer be understood as a merely subjective phenomenon whose deeper reality is revealed by objective class analysis. Individualization no longer only affects the superstructure of ideology and false consciousness, but also the economic substructure of "real classes." For the first time in history, the individual rather than the class is becoming the basic unit of social reproduction.

What are the implications for a sociology of class?

Instead of individualism being placed in context and relativized by class analysis, in order to understand class we now need to place it in the new context of individualization.

This is true of every social collectivity. They all have to be reinterpreted in the context of disembedded individualization. They are all being transformed. Individualization is the social structure of the second modernity. The classical conception that regards sociology as the institutionalized rejection of individualism is no longer tenable.

However, we also have to realize that this sort of institutionalized individualism represents a radical departure from Talcott Parsons's idea of a linear, self-reproducing system. What makes an "individualizing structure" so paradoxical at first sight is precisely that it is a non-linear, open-ended, ambivalent, and continuous process.

Another point that is important for class analysis is that this sort of individualization necessarily entails a decline in overarching social narratives, paradoxically by multiplying them so that no single one can achieve an undisputed hegemony.

Besides its consequences for social theory, what does individualization mean for society?

One of the central risks of global risk society is the possibility of a mismatch between disembedded individuals and global problems. The individualized society encourages and makes it increasingly possible for us to seek biographical solutions to systemic contradictions. But it is precisely this process that sharpens and radicalizes social inequality.

We should proceed on the assumption that, under the conditions of individualization and globalization, pre-given social collectivities will be disintegrated by individualization, and with them will go class consciousness and its political dynamics. At first sight, this might look like a bleak take on things and one that portends an even bleaker future. It might turn out that way, but it might not. Not only because no outcome is predetermined, but also because individualization is a much broader phenomenon than it is usually given credit for.

It is a misunderstanding to think of individualization as something that happens solely to people who are well off economically. There is also an individualization of poverty. In many ways the individualization of poverty is actually easier to measure. Stephan Leibfried and Lutz Leisering's study, *Time and Poverty*, is one of many which have shown how poverty loses its collective meaning and takes on a new shape under conditions of individualization.

Poverty in rich countries is gradually becoming more of a phase in the average working life that most people pass through rather than a lifetime situation. This means the experience of poverty is now more widely generalized. The majority of people in rich countries are now poor in income terms at some point in their life. But for most people this is only a temporary experience. The permanent poor are those who get stuck in the valley of poverty while everyone else is passing through. Those few end up as the professional poor. They develop negative careers which take them further and further away from the normal labor market and everything that goes with it. So this is not a class destiny; it is a starkly individual destiny. To update the image from Schumpeter, we might say the bus of the poor no longer takes everyone to a collective fate. There is instead a permanent getting on and off. The few who are left on the bus conceive themselves as individual failures precisely because their fate is no longer experienceable as a collective one. That's why it's no longer possible to organize them as if it were.

But we are still speaking of life on the rich continent of Europe. On a world scale, things look different. As you said yourself earlier, in the exploding megalopolises of the first and third worlds, the center and the periphery now run up against each other rather than being separated by oceans. As a consequence, the super-rich are retreating into new walled communities reminiscent of the middle ages. They fly to their business meetings by helicopter and drive bullet-proof limousines through the streets of the wretched. The rich fear the poor as enemies even as they remain dependent on them as cooks and security personnel. At first sight, this looks like the twilight of common humanity. Calling it a new class society might be almost too idyllic a description.

This is what the archbishop of São Paulo was saying when he described his city as a Switzerland surrounded by three Biafras. But again, we have to realize that individualization and class analysis are not on a continuum, with the former always describing something more pleasant and the latter always describing something worse. Class analysis misses what is new about this ghastly reality, which is a large part of what makes it so ghastly. It's true that in part it's a return to something we know from the past, what Otto Karl Werckmeister described so well in his work on medieval art history as "the return of the citadels." Supermodern castles, full of security and pomp, are being erected right next to scenes from *Apocalypse Now*. But Zygmunt Bauman put his finger on what distinguishes the current monstrous, urban poverty from that of the past: these people are simply no longer needed. Marx's discussion of the difference between the proletariat and the lumpen proletariat still presupposed actual or at least potential exploitation in the labor process. Here, where civilization topples over into its opposite, into populated garbage heaps, even "exploitation" is a euphemism. Bauman talks about the "globalized rich" and the "localized poor" as two groups who are no longer connected by any common social bond. That might be going too far. But it is true that at the same time as globalization is abolishing distance and borders, it is opening up new unbridgeable gulfs, and the abolition of distance only makes them worse. The globalization of poverty and wealth puts the glitz world of the super-rich and the de-civilized world of the propertyless right next to each other. The rich may only depend on the poor for a limited range of services. But the poor haunt their days and probably their dreams. The rich fear the poor.

So don't we have to look at this and say a new revolutionary subject is growing up here out of pure despair?

No, because the frame of reference is completely different. Our model of class struggle and class society presumes the nation-state. The old marxist argument that the worker knows no nation has today been turned on its head. It is capital's activists, those who have made globalization their profession, who don't have any fatherland, while the workers and their unions call on "their" governments for aid, and ask "their" states to protect them against the injustice of globalization. The globalizers are already acting in a transnational framework, one in which the question of which workers and which poor they should most be held responsible for is already getting difficult to answer.

The deterritorialized "class struggle" has become a power game in which at least two different frames of reference are being used simultaneously. On the one side is denationalized capital, and facing them is a labor movement that is still place-dependent, and which still thinks and strikes within the categories of national solidarity. Sooner or later the question of which frame of reference distributional struggles ought to be organized in will itself become the object of a deterritorialized struggle. Should it be a national framework, or a transnational one? And if the latter, which one?

The problem with class concepts is that they deeply, intrinsically depend on the ontology of the nation-state. If we use them in an unreflecting way, as if it was obvious what they meant in an age of globalization and radicalized inequality, we are ignoring at our cost the collapse of that ontology.

Class concepts presume a common framework that includes both sides. What distinguishes the present period is that people's lives are organized in more than one framework simultaneously – not one true and one false, but more than one real framework of existence. It is not only the global elites who live this new transnationality. It is also true for poor and exploited migrants. They are treated in western countries as "others," and as the "excluded." But at the same time as they exist as Filipinos in the USA or Chinese in Indonesia or Turks in Germany, they are also contributing to their households "at home," where they are engaged in communal projects or are protesting against corrupt regimes. So they too are living the transnational life of a double frame of reference. While they might appear to be settled at the edge of their so-called "guest" countries, where they are discriminated against on account of their origin or skin color, "at home" they count as people who are rising into the middle class, and they are honored and respected as such, if also sometimes mocked and laughed at for their bi-nationality. In short, they live here *and* there at one and the same time. They are positioned simultaneously in two different frameworks of social inequality, two different frameworks that are both being enlarged and brought into a new relation with each other through their mediation. This ambivalent and transnational placement completely stamps their lives and their identities.

The categories of class are simply not differentiated enough to capture such interlocked relationships of border-spanning, multi-perspectival inequality. Pierre Bourdieu is a good example of how you can expand the idea of class and still end up unreflectively trapped in the categories of the nation-state. He starts from the premise that economic capital can be translated into cultural capital (like educational credentials) and social capital (like professional connections). But this system of exchange functions only in a national framework, not in a transnational one, and especially not for those who live on the edge of society. Attempts to make such Bourdieuian exchanges run up against national blockades and ethnic discrimination. Class concepts, no matter how subtle, simply can't capture the existing complexity of radically unequal living situations, either within nation-state societies or between them. What they do instead is deceive us with a false simplicity. To many they may seem worth striving towards for exactly that reason, for ideological purposes.

Does this rule out poor people's movements?

No. In order not to be misunderstood, let me say clearly that the current situation is extremely full of conflicts. It's just that the pattern of classes and class struggle is not the key to understanding them.

I am not ruling out Marx's prognosis, that when the poor reach a certain point of despair, they are capable of transcending their "false" images of individual and transnational isolation. But in all probability the new movements will not follow the classical forms. I can imagine, for example, a new global social

movement to abolish poverty that would be made possible by
the new global media, that would "discover" world poverty as a
scandal, and organize against it, and create events to call attention to it. But such consciousness and solidarity would not be
at all like what marxism conceives class consciousness to be.

I think if such a movement does arise, its more likely shape
will be a transnational antipoverty movement on the model of
the environmental movement, something like the Greenpeace
of poverty. We could end up with an anti-globalization movement against worldwide poverty, one that arose in reaction to
the radicalization of inequality, and that succeeded in awaken-
ing the world's conscience. But such a worldwide movement
would have a consciousness mediated through the mass media.
Its central connecting links would arise out of concerns *for* the
poor, not *of* the poor. We cannot infer the actual presence of
classes from this sort of consciousness the way we can from classical class consciousness. In this hypothetical case, most of the
worldwide consciousness in question would be virtual consciousness, produced through events that were created for the
media.

This brings us back to the discussion of individualization. It
is very important to recognize that individualization and exclusion are not opposites. Rather they are two axes of an analysis
which together give us a fuller picture. In the same vein, individualization is not solely the individualization of riches. It is
also the individualization of poverty.

Another aspect of class analysis that is placed in question by
individualization is the issue of the kind of political project it
points to. Marxists use class analysis in part as a means of finess-
ing their way around the central problem facing us, the question of what we can find that can successfully serve as the basis
of long-term, progressive solidarity.

Class analysis has always been in part an attempt to conjure
up class solidarity, to postulate the collective subject as a historical subject, and then to build a political program around it.
But as a utopia, and as a political program, class leads to a
picture of society that is exactly the opposite of individualized
society, and to politics that are exactly the opposite of political
individualism. If you ask what are the new ideas and political
strategies that class analysis can generate for the present situation, all you get is antiquated answers or total hopelessness.

Those who say they are going to bring the solidarity of the workers and the solidarity of class back to life simply can't be believed, because the disintegration of this solidarity, and the disintegration of this collectivity, has been one of the central historical experiences of recent times.

In a certain sense, this same story was told by the collapse of the Eastern bloc, and socialists would do well to take notice of it. It was a system that repressed the individual, and in the end, it was collectivities *of individuals* that contributed most to its overthrow, not people organized as classes. The main forces that did in the Eastern bloc were social movements based on rights, on civil rights and human rights.

There isn't any basis at all for thinking that the historical subject of the working class will provide the solidarity for future progress. And the attempt to sneak that idea in by sleight of hand while talking about class society and class analysis is intellectually dishonest.

It's also politically doomed. This is why what we are usually facing is a politically castrated marxism that stands a lot closer to neoliberalism than it wants to admit. The only real difference between their analyses nowadays is the positive or negative emotional tone they place on the same developments. The marxist line nowadays consists largely of outlining the worldwide consequences of the overpowering spread of the market without having a political answer for it. When a political answer is proffered, it's obsolete.

So in the end the attempt to found a renaissance of class theory on the experience of the radicalization of inequality, on the exclusion of large parts of the population both nationally and transnationally, is doomed to failure. In the first place, a collectivity is presumed to exist in a situation where that collectivity has already been dissolved through individualization. The only way to continue with this line of thought is to ignore the main difficulty facing politics today, which is how to construct a new collectivity out of parcelized individual existences and the self-consciousness that goes with them. Nothing is gained by pretending that problem is going to solve itself. Society can no longer look in the mirror and see classes. The mirror has been smashed and all we have left are the individualized fragments. To try and stick them back together with the glue of a wished-for class solidarity is hopeless.

The second question class analysis sidesteps is the consequences that an unleashed capitalism, one that reaches into parts of society that have up until now been run on different principles, will necessarily have for any political project. It avoids, as do the conservatives, the challenge of rethinking politics against the background of an individualized and transnational culture. Like conservatism, it refuses to grasp the opportunities presented through the recognition of human rights and greater possibilities for individual development. We said earlier that we are facing an opposition between *the further development of capitalism* or *the further development of freedom*. It's an opposition that both sides of the old debates have yet to discover.

Conversation 3

Global Risk Society

JOHANNES WILLMS   *The concept of risk society plays a central role in your sociological thought. But doesn't it describe something very old hat? Hasn't society been about the socialization of risk ever since it started? Wasn't it to defend against surrounding dangers that people formed societies in the first place?*

ULRICH BECK   That question seems almost designed to throw the originator of the concept into a huge embarrassment. But of course it's not the first time I've been asked it, and the real danger is that I might answer too glibly. It's a fundamental question, and it deserves a fundamental answer.

Certainly all societies can be seen as the solution to danger, but the concept of risk is a modern one. When danger mainly meant natural catastrophe, people felt themselves to be in the grip of gods, and nobody could conceive the concept of risk. Risks are bound up with human decisions. They are a necessary by-product of the progress of civilization, and a conceptual by-product as well. As human action passes from being under the sway of nature and tradition to being under the sway of its own decisions, alternative courses begin to be conceived in terms of risks. Risks appear where nature and tradition have become decision-dependent.

Etymologically the concept of risk can be traced back to the intercontinental shipping trade. The word "average," the central concept of statistics, derives from an Arabic word that means "losses at sea" which entered various European languages in the thirteenth century. Risk was thus understood from the very first as "venturing" and was from the beginning tied up with the concept of insurance.

When the first merchant adventurers sailed out to conquer a strange new world, the danger was extremely high that at least one of their ships would go under. To the extent – and this is the birth of the concept of risk – that this individual fate could be redefined as the probability of a negative outcome that was experienced equally by everyone in a defined group, it was possible to forge a complete solution to it. The defined group consisted of all intercontinental trading companies, and the solution was that each one would pay into a common fund out of which compensation would be drawn when a ship went down. With this step, loss was reformulated into risk, and a problem that represented a mortal danger for any individual company became easily soluble through being reorganized on a collective basis.

Risk is the inescapable flipside of opportunity. Each time you choose the one, you get the other as well. Risk is also inseparably bound up with a collective calculus in which individual, random acts are redefined into calculable social events. It usually also entails an attempt to render it controllable through insurance models and the institutionalized principles that underlie them.

It is possible to see the entire process of industrialization, that is, the development of productive forces from the eighteenth through the twentieth century, as a dialectic between the growth of risk and the development of its institutionalized solutions. This perspective brings many details to light that we might not otherwise notice. It is worth analyzing how such a system functions, how it grew up historically, and what preconditions are required for it to function smoothly. Private insurance is the simplest model of how collectivities provide for risk, and one way to frame this perspective is as the social insurance model of modernization.

Let's return to our historical periodization of how risk differs from danger. Danger is what we face in epochs when threats can't be interpreted as resulting from human action. Rather than being experienced as decision-dependent, they are interpreted as being unleashed by natural catastrophe or as punishments from the gods. They are experienced as unalterable collective destiny. Risk, by contrast, marks the beginning of a civilization that seeks to make the unforeseeable consequences of its own decisions foreseeable, and to subdue their unwanted side effects through conscious preventative action and institutional arrangements.

Let's say, for example, that an accident takes place in a factory or a mine, or someone loses his arm in a machine. What caused it? Was it the negligence of the employee, who should then bear the consequences? Was it a technical failure of a system that didn't shield the worker sufficiently? Or was it the capitalist self-interest of the entrepreneur, who purchased an insufficiently safe machine in order to save money? If you start from ground zero, these are all perfectly reasonable questions, inevitable ones even. So there is an impulse from the very beginning for a struggle of interpretation to arise. In this struggle, questions of causality are much more than findings of fact. They are instruments for distributing costs and assigning responsibility.

In the nineteenth century, competing ideologies and world views grew up precisely out of such struggles. On the one side stood liberal, market-oriented ideologies. Their proponents wanted to shift these risks onto individuals. They were adamant that hell would open up and swallow the economy if events like this were defined as a collective danger we all faced together.

Opposed to them was a cluster of interpretations whose first principles were the same as those of sociology. They sought to show that what were perceived as individual cases could in fact be empirically shown to be obeying laws when examined in the aggregate. What seemed random and unpredictable at the individual level was in fact perfectly predictable at the level of society. For sociologists and social reformers alike, this meant that the aggregate level was where we found the truth of the situation, where we found laws of society analogous to the laws of nature. If the individual case was analyzed statistically, according to the laws of probability, its general features and its social nature stood revealed.

Thus social causes were brought into view, and social arrangements were identified as the solution to social problems. The truth of accidents lay in abstracting from them to laws. As the nineteenth century turned into the twentieth, this view became dominant. Accidents were described in statistical terms as stochastic events that at the aggregate level could be considered constants, and for which legal and political institutions had to be built that would enable responsibility to be evenly distributed. The institutions that finally resulted were the accreted result of a historical process of political conflicts and negotiations.

The key thing to note is that the conceptual scheme and the institutional scheme were mutually dependent. The conceptual scheme would never have been accepted as valid unless the claims of causality were accepted. But there was more than one possible scheme of causality to choose from. The reason this one became hegemonic is because it was the necessary precondition for a system of apportioning risks that people felt to be basically just. So the system of social insurance was necessary for the conceptual scheme to be accepted, and the conceptual scheme was necessary for the social insurance scheme to be created. They were two sides of one social whole.

The assignment of causality can only settle things unequivocally if it operates as part of an encompassing and interdependent social system. In the first modernity, this system grew out of a history of political conflicts and it embodied their solution in a network of regulations. The reason this larger social system provided the indispensable preconditions for reaching unequivocal decisions is because it settled beforehand a host of subsidiary questions, such as who had valid claims and who paid whom under what conditions. This is what finally enabled the individual case to be treated as a normal event rather than as an individual moral failure.

Conversely, if these questions are *not* taken care of automatically, and they are *not* settled in advance of the causality question, then the assignment of causality settles nothing. We can easily see what happens in this converse case if we look at the contemporary debate over environmental dangers. When authorities today attempt to apply the same interpretative schema, but without its institutional underpinning – in large part because the "events" themselves don't fit the institutional definitions the whole system is premised on – it settles nothing. It fuels conflict rather than solving it.

Before this evolution took place, the state basically had three classical functions, going back at least to the absolutist era: the defense of sovereignty from without; the maintenance of civil peace within;

and the laying down of standards for economic interaction. You seem to be saying that in the nineteenth century a fourth function was added as a consequence of industrialization in the form of state insurance that provided for accidents and old age.

By the way, I think Bismarck gets more credit than he deserves for being the inventor of state insurance. For one thing, the idea was already in the air. Napoleon III actually introduced it before him; he just wasn't able to fully realize his intentions. Bismarck's intentions, on the other hand, were supremely cynical. He called in a sociologist, or a statistician, and asked him: "How long does a worker live, on average?" The answer was: "Late fifties, early sixties at the most." So Bismarck said, "Excellent. Set pension payments to begin at 65."

Let's go back to the nature of risk. You've distinguished risk from danger. But aren't there also fundamentally different kinds of risk? Say between those that obtained when merchants first outfitted ships to haul pepper, and those that began to multiply with the advent of high technology?

Let's deal with your first point first. The dialectic of risk and the logic of insurance were historically essential in establishing the nation-state's internal order. State insurance sharpened the border between the state's inside and its outside. It deepened its legitimacy. The state became the respected judge who mediated between the claims of its internal conflicting parties. By codifying and then embodying this mediation, the state tapped into a deep well of legitimation. At the same time it progressively disarmed the explosive conflict potential such risks contained.

One interesting aspect of this political functionality was how it set up a system of standard equivalents and enforced the acceptance of their exchange. Once this system was in place, if someone lost an arm, or the sight in one eye, he came to accept that he would get, for example, 15,000 marks for an arm, or a certain pension level for blindness in one eye. In enforcing standards of compensation, the state enforced standards in a deeper sense. People were forced to accept the logic by which life and health were exchanged for sums of money. There were two ways this smoothed the path for capitalism. On the one hand, it internalized the moral rightness of the exchange logic of capitalism, whose path can always use some smoothing. But the even more important result was that it depoliticized and de-moralized risk conflict.

This latter result of the dialectic of risk is really quite a spectacular accomplishment if you compare it with the state's management of the overall conflict between labor and capital, which remained very explosive for decades more to come. This large historical accomplishment is easy to miss, however, because it consists largely in the production of an absence.

In my opinion, the smooth manner in which individually unforeseeable costs (and the costs of preventing them) were distributed among the members of society was an essential precondition for society's faith in progress. This distribution was progressively negotiated and institutionalized over a long historical period, which is what gave it such solidity and legitimacy. Only against this background, when it was assumed that the side effects of modernization would always somehow be compensated for, could faith in progress become popular and widespread. Only then could it become a sort of a wind beneath the wings of economic and technological development.

Now let's turn to your question about whether there has been a qualitative change in the nature of risk. The risk society that arose during the first modernity was premised on the controllability of the side effects produced by industrialization. It was a highly refined system of institutionalized answers for anticipating and dealing with the unforeseeable. It was based on the premise that accidents in the aggregate were absolutely predictable. Thus in the first modernity, risk society means perfect control society. It not only claims that it can predict and master all possible outcomes, including the uncertainty it produces itself, but it extends its control claims into the future. In a sense, the first modernity systematically colonizes the future under the aegis of risk.

But is this claim still valid? Do we still live under the conditions of a controllable future?

No, and the best way to bring all the difficulties into focus is to once more examine closely the concept of risk. The calculus of risk presupposes the concept of the accident. Both the individual accident *and* the large statistical aggregate of which it is a part are conceived of as spatially, temporally, and socially defined events. They are clearly bounded. Accidents happen to a defined group of people in a defined area during a stipulated time period. Using this model, we can interpret and process any set of accidents, be they ship sinkings, train mishaps, mining accidents, auto accidents, or bouts of long-term illness or unemployment.

Unfortunately, this model loses its validity in a case like Chernobyl. Chernobyl is a paradigmatic counter-example that bursts though this model of clearly defined accidents in all three dimensions. The way its consequences overleapt geographical and political boundaries was of course spectacular and immediately obvious at the time. But it was just as true of temporal bounds. How does one define an affected population when some of those affected have not yet been born, even today, fifteen years after the accident? This is why the question of "How many people died from the accident at Chernobyl?" is still statistically undecidable in principle. The arguments that rage over it are like battles between phantom armies.

But if Chernobyl was a big exception to the old way of thinking about risks, it is now the rule for most of what we now perceive and define as environmental dangers. They all cross social and political and geographic boundaries. By their very nature, the various poisons that course through the air and the water and the ground cannot be spatially confined. For that reason, neither can ascriptions of ultimate responsibility, nor of their ultimate effects.

This is what fuels debates over the greenhouse effect or the ultimate dangers of genetically modified food. Events like these (and there are many which fit the bill) are all illustrations of a qualitatively different kind of risk, one that is not clearly bounded, and which therefore can't fit into the old calculus of risk, nor into the interdependent social system of which it was a part.

The main thesis of the theory of risk society is that this institutionalized program of making side effects calculable is being eroded away by the political, economic, social, and technological changes that result from the continuing radicalization of the modernization process. First modern risk society presupposes side effects that are spatially, temporally, and socially bounded. Without that precondition, it can't function.

Chernobyl happened just as I was just finishing the proofs of *Risk Society*. One thing that made it so dramatic was that German contingency plans for nuclear accidents at that time foresaw a maximum possible radius of 28.5 kilometers. The idea that an accident in another country could affect us in Germany had never come up during planning.

That was a great turning point. It was like a flash of lightning that made several things clear at once.
So first modern risk society proceeded on the premise that both risks and their consequences could be localized; that they affected defined populations in bounded areas; and that they were therefore completely manageable within an insurance logic. But the very success of this system led it to be taken for granted and ended up nurturing blind spots in our thinking. We were incapable of imagining that the modernization of modern society could produce qualitatively different kinds of risks, never mind something on the scale of Chernobyl.

That's exactly right. The epochal difference between the defined risks of the first modernity and the global risks of the second modernity is still not being taken seriously either conceptually or institutionally.

By conceptual unseriousness, I mean our continuing blithe equation of risks with probabilities. We still seem unable to accept the crucial difference between probability and radical uncertainty, and to come to terms with the fact that the latter now dominates, at least among the risks that occupy the public stage. This basic misunderstanding permeates even the mindset of the natural sciences.

By institutional unseriousness, I'm referring to everything that touches on catastrophe planning, like inspections, the provision of medical services, and all the means by which costs are reckoned into our present accounts for future planning. Every time a global risk crisis occurs, it reveals to us in a panic that for all our calculations we had absolutely no idea of what was involved or how to deal with it. This has many implications. Chernobyl is a perfect illustration. As you probably remember, we were having a wonderful spring that year, the weather was just fantastic. And then through the media spread this news that there was this deadly danger.

That you couldn't see any sign of.

Our five senses failed us and there was no sixth! I think it was this experience of cultural blindness that was the kernel of our initial shock. We were suddenly exposed to a danger that was physically imperceptible and which could only be experienced through mediation, through the media, which meant through the contradictory statements of experts. It was not so much the physical danger that outraged people as it was this tutelage, the fact that people as citizens were no longer in a position to determine what was dangerous and what was not. We felt like we were hanging from the marionette strings of these experts and institutions who continually contradicted each other. They kept saying they had everything well in hand, and it constantly turned out not to be true. To get answers to the most everyday questions, like "Can I let my kid play in the sandbox? Can I buy mushrooms? Are all the vegetables poison, or just those from specific regions?" we were dependent on the minute to minute statements of experts who were simply blinding in their contradictoriness. And underneath it all was the horrifying thought that maybe food itself might now be poison.

There is a long series of differences between the risks of the first and second modernities. To start with, first modern dangers are clearly perceptible through the senses. A mining accident is an event perceivable by everyone. It is characteristic of first modern dangers that they can be captured in images, like the image of puffing smokestacks, which were once the symbol of boom times, and which even today are still spreading a haze along the banks of the Ruhr.

In the second modernity, society becomes ever more technologically advanced, which seems at first to promise ever more perfect technical solutions. However, this higher technology generates subtler side effects that more often than not escape the immediate perception of those affected. To add to the difficulties of perception, the people most affected are often not the workers, who have some proximity to the process and thus some access to the signs of something going wrong, but people much farther afield, like consumers, or sometimes even people who have no connection to the products at all, who neither make nor use them or even live nearby.

Industrialization gives rise to job cultures. These cultures draw much of their substance from behavior that grows out of dealing with job and health risks and the consequences they have for workers and their families. When a mining accident happens, everyone involved knows exactly what it means. They know what needs to be done, and what can be expected, feared, and hoped for. It's part of their working culture, and everyone knows how to deal with it. This is the normal case in the first modernity. Those who bear the risks are those who are involved in their production. They can therefore also contribute directly to minimizing or avoiding them.

In the second modernity, by contrast, we are dealing as a rule with a radical separation between those who produce the risks and those who bear the consequences. This gap is only seemingly spanned by causal analysis, because such analyses don't actually lead anywhere most of the time in such situations. The problem is that the causality is so complex. Those who have been affected must be able to prove exactly who it is that has harmed them before they can collect compensation. They are usually facing an impossible task.

Just how complicated this task can be can be illustrated by an example from France. There was a factory there which was spewing every noxious substance you can think of out of its smokestacks. All of it fell to earth in a nearby neighborhood and ate away the houses and sickened the inhabitants. So at first sight, this seemed to fit the first modern, industrial society schemata. You could see it and you could feel it. Those affected went to court. The court held that they were definitely the victims of toxins that the factory produced. But the problem was that there were several factories in the area that produced the same toxins, and the court said that made it legally impossible to clarify the question of causality. The plaintiffs couldn't prove that it was this factory in particular which had produced the toxins which had affected them personally. So the guilty party could not be identified and the accused was acquitted.

What's important to note here is that, under the conditions of a seemingly very legitimate administration of justice, which requires only that you be able to prove a clear line of causality before you can convict a particular agent, the multiplication of possible sources of pollution makes it increasingly impossible to get a conviction or compensation precisely because it makes it increasingly impossible to draw such clear causal lines. So the more pollution is thrown into the air, the more difficult it is to show anyone is liable, and the greater the probability that collective damage will be suffered without anyone being held responsible.

So the problem is that risks are in a certain sense losing their place-ability, and with that, their accountability. Because of this, the classical way of administering justice, based on the principle that he who causes the harm is responsible for curing it, begins to lose its effectiveness. The end result is that threat becomes something that permeates society. Literally: risk is now something that can force its way into the securest home and hide in the wood preservative. Years ago there was a huge scandal over wood preservative. If you used a brand with a certain ingredient the people who lived there got cancer.

What kind of defense can there be to something like that? It poses an enormous challenge for society. One of the most important bases of the state's legitimacy is that it provides security for all its members. That's what it collects taxes for, that's why people agree to finance it. But in this case it's like an insurance company that demands ever greater premiums while at the same time constantly narrowing the protection it promises.

Another result of the divorce of risks from place is that it gives them a banal cosmopolitanism similar to the banal cosmopolitanism of cuisine we discussed earlier. (See pp. 36ff.) And once again, at first sight it may *seem* like it's giving rise to banal nationalism instead. For example, I only have to say two words, "British beef," to immediately conjure the spectre of mad cow disease in every listener's mind. But even more so than with food, closer examination will show that banal nationalism will turn out to be the exception and banal cosmopolitanism the rule. It is in fact exceedingly rare that people are able to *successfully* hoist the national flag against the cosmopolitanization of risks, and mad cow disease is precisely the exception that proves the rule. The fact, as you just pointed out, that these risks have now penetrated into the innermost sanctum of our private lives makes this kind of banal cosmopolitanism even more pervasive and volatile. Unlike with food, this is not just about tastes. It's about our will to survive.

It is important to emphasize that risk is not a thing. It's a social construct, a social definition. It is something that must be believed in to have real effects. First modern risks, risks defined as probabilities rather than as uncertainties, presuppose several key rationality claims before they can be successfully constructed. It's because those preconditions are lacking that second modern risks almost always give rise to risk conflicts.

A typical second modern risk conflict starts existence as a media tale that gravely unsettles consumers, and usually parents of small children in particular. This is the first stage of the development of risk consciousness. In the second stage it enormously increases its political force through the efforts that are necessary to overcome official resistance.

This stage of initial official resistance seems like a constant. The first thing incipient risk consciousness always seems to run into is an institutionalized rationality that systematically blocks off any acknowledgment of the risk in question. It is institutionally incapable of comprehending that a risk can be based on uncertainty rather than probability. Instead the forces of order always seem to translate "uncertainty" as "minuscule probability."

This misunderstanding is inscribed in all first modern social institutions. The legal principle we described in our French example is true for all law, including administrative and scientific law. It is a general, institutional principle: in any case where a clear chain of causality cannot be demonstrated, there is therefore no risk.

When the affected and worried people take their case to the scientists, they find themselves talking to a group whose most identity-defining belief is that the canons of causal evidence and inference must always be strictly adhered to. When these criteria can't be satisfied, scientists can be depended upon to explain away any new risk as a mere fantasy without giving it any further consideration.

So in both directions, the affected run into the solidly institutionalized walls of risk denial. We might even expand on our paradoxical formulation. The more the rules of law and the rules of science (working in conjunction) find no valid evidence that a risk has been produced for, which someone can be held individually accountable the more risks it is possible for society to produce, and the more the total potential threat increases.

But however much it is denied, this potential threat continues to be perceived by those affected. It becomes a social fact which has consequences. The next step is usually that the affected or concerned population organizes itself into a social movement which, after gathering together alternative cognitive instruments that are more or less credible (other statistics, other experts), throws itself against these walls of institutionalized denial.

This is how risk conflicts arise. On the one hand, such movements continually renew the credibility claims of the dominant institutions by demanding and requiring their seal of approval. On the other hand, they are continually calling those credibility claims into question. In the end it's never just about a factory that stands there dumb. It's about a legal system, and a political system, and a system of science which, by holding firm in their old rationality, seem, when seen from the outside, to be equal participants in a conspiracy to systematically deny the risks the total system has produced.

This seems to make mad cow disease an exception on several grounds. Not only did nationalism seem to play a big role, but the danger was played up by governments. This seems to contradict the rule that the system strives to deny any danger that it can't control.

Of course it looked at first like we could construct a clear line of causality. People said the foremost thing was that the cattle came from England, and they became mad there because the fiendish English had fed them on meat and bone meal in order to lower costs and increase production. The meat and bone meal was made, among other things, out of sheep who had scrapie, a disease which attacks the brain. The disease therefore seemed to have entered cattle through their consumption of diseased sheep's brains, and to have entered humans through their consumption of cattle. The last step in the chain was that some human consumers, under certain circumstances, contracted a variant of Creutzfeldt-Jakob disease (something which in earlier times had simply been called "softening of the brain").

Then when other countries scrambled to erect protections and regulations and import bans in order to keep out the beef and calm their populations, Great Britain not only kept on eating roast beef, but started eating it demonstratively, to show that everyone, on

*every rung of the British social ladder, from the workers to the
Queen, were taking and surviving the same risks together, all in
order to affirm what by then seemed like almost a national credo,
that "British beef is the best in the world."*
  So how is this the exception that proves the rule?

I'll come to that in a second because it's a key point. But first I
want to finish up an earlier argument. The explosiveness of risk
conflicts lies in the fact that they delegitimate the political
system. Even though its institutions continue to function and
continue to deny that there can be such a thing as an incalculable risk, such risks force their way into institutions like a virus
that weakens them from within. Everyone tries to free themselves from risk, but it continues to multiply and permeate. It's
as if we've knocked over a honeypot, and in our efforts to rub
it off, we succeed only in getting honey stuck to every part of
the social body. It's a self-negating process, in which everything
society's institutions do to free themselves only spreads the risk
and helps to dissolve their legitimacy.

  Hobbes, in his theory of the state, actually put his finger on
the explosive core of risk conflict. If you ask when even this
deeply conservative thinker thinks civil resistance is justified,
you find a formulation that strikingly if unintentionally antici-
pates environmental problems and the spectre of risk as uncertainty. To paraphrase, he says the ultimate resistance is justified
when the state can no longer guarantee its citizens pure air and
healthy food and the security that goes with them. When their
air is poisoned and their food endangers them, then citizens are
justified in rebelling against the state.

  What this makes clear is that risk is not something limited to
the environment. It doesn't only affect the environment of the
political system . . .

. . . but also the political system itself . . .

. . . and it does so because it strikes at fundamental rights, institutionalized fundamental rights, namely the right to life and
security, rights upon which both state and citizenry may even
place a higher value than on freedom. When it's a matter of life
and death or health, people stop kidding around. People feel
this as an attack on the core of their existence. *It is not the size*

of the danger that makes these risks so politically explosive. It is rather the size of the contradiction, between the security that it is the state's *raison d'être* to provide – and which we have up until now expected it to provide – and the systematic injuring of that expectation that takes place in risk conflicts. Diffused poisons are like diffuse enemies, which industry has let in through its sluice gates. And then the state, rather than declaring war on them, declares them to be harmless.

I bring up this point because it makes clear both how explosive these conflicts are, and that their epicenter is not where people think it is. It lies not in the risks themselves, but in how strongly they undermine the core of what legitimates state institutions and political action in the first modernity. This crisis of confidence then reacts back to increase risk consciousness. If a risk crisis goes far enough, we eventually reach the point where no one places any trust in the repeated announcements of the authorities that they have everything under control. At that point they start to have the opposite of their intended effect. Each announcement conjures up another image of imminent catastrophe.

That was part of why the BSE scandal went into overdrive, wasn't it? The various states were seeking to prove to their doubting citizens just how seriously they took their safety and security. They wanted to show they were taking every possible precaution to guarantee their health.

Yes, and this brings us back to the inescapability of the transnational dynamic, and how all attempts to evade it simply make matters worse. Let's reconstruct how it all began. I was actually in Great Britain the very moment it started. I was able to experience it at first hand, as it were. It began with a press conference by a government spokesman who in retrospect had clearly been given too much leeway. He said on behalf of the government that we could not rule out that there was a connection between mad cow disease and the brain disease that had recently appeared in humans. I repeat: he didn't say there was a connection. He just said it couldn't be completely ruled out. That was enough to set off the avalanche. The next day, when the same spokesman appeared, he was clearly on a much shorter leash, and the government forced him to make a retraction. But it no longer made any difference. The avalanche had already been let loose.

In the very beginning, the British looked for the cause locally. They even enacted various local bans. Gradually it became more and more clear that the causal links couldn't really be corroborated. They found themselves dealing with what I call *known* or *regressive* uncertainty, where the more facts we know, the more the uncertainty grows. In such situations, real knowledge consists of the realization that the uncertainty can't be removed and has to be dealt with accordingly. This is usually true of risk conflicts. Only in rare cases can unambiguous causal relationships be established, and even then they require more time for research than events will allow. What you get instead at the height of a risk conflict is competing theories (many of which previously existed and warned of the danger but were ignored). Then a struggle ensues over defining the risk, for example, what the chain of causality is, what the affected population is, etc.

This is usually an important turning point, because the details of this definitional struggle always have economic and political consequences. And those consequences are themselves unpredictable and full of systemic risk. So, for example, at first sight it seemed that deciding on a certain causal chain would make the entire British beef industry collapse, and this would mean an enormous windfall for the French and German beef industries. But that expectation and the strategy based on it couldn't have been more misguided. Instead what happened is that consumers in France and Germany immediately renounced almost all meat consumption regardless of origin.

This was an excellent example of the paradoxical honey-scraping effect, where the more you try to get the risk off of you, the more you get all over you. People tried to use the definition of risk to push through protectionist interests. It seemed obvious that if you could brand your national competitor's products as being full of risks, it would open up new markets for your own. But instead the opposite happened. These efforts fueled the collapse of their own market.

The struggle over risk definition produces a heightening of risk consciousness. It reinforces the feeling that no authorities, least of all producers who have a direct interest, can be trusted to tell you what's going on. The result here was a market collapse which transcended national boundaries. The national industries of countries who had no direct connection with the production of this particular risk found themselves sharing in the enormous costs.

If, during the height of the BSE crisis, you were wandering through upper Bavaria, and you sat down at an inn and opened up the menu, in all likelihood the first thing you'd see would be a smiling picture of the farmer who owned the place, standing with his whole family and his few remaining loyal cows, and just below a note that said that the beef that you were about to eat came entirely from this locality and had no connection at all with that diabolical British feed chain. This is a perfectly banal example of a person desperately trying to ward off a risk to his livelihood. But what it really evidenced was how unbelievably far these risks had spread, and how deeply they had endangered him even in his mountain fastness. Men like him were trying to combat the banal cosmopolitanism of risks by hoisting the flag of Bavarian localism; they were trying to rebuild trust by relocalizing their products. But in the face of the really existing global circuit of the meat and chemical industries, it was like throwing a straw into the whirlpool of placelessness. It wouldn't save him from drowning.

This brings us back once again to the most peculiar and, to the cynical eye of the sociologist, fascinating quality of risk conflicts: their dynamic of entanglement. The risks of the second modernity have a peculiar tenacity. They seem to move in and make a nest for themselves not only despite but because of our attempts to deny them. This isn't only true of health risks. It also holds when they transform themselves into economic risks, like the collapse of markets and the devalorization of capital, or into political risks, like crises of confidence, the loss of authority, and the erosion of political parties. Second modern risks are, in a word, systemic risks, and they can spread from one system to the next. They are global risks.

I have to admit, one thing that fascinated me about the BSE crisis was how these furious attempts of each nation to blame each other seemed so closely to echo a pattern from centuries ago of how people dealt with syphilis. There too you saw this attempt to blame, this attempt to hoist the national flags, as you put it. The Germans said that when someone had syphilis he had the French disease. The French couldn't take such an insult lying down; they said, "Il a la maladie anglaise." The English refused to accept that they were the culprits and insisted, "He's got the Spanish disease." And the poor Spaniards were left at the end of the blame chain. They couldn't very well say "He's got the German disease." So the Germans had the French disease, and the French had the English disease, and the English had the Spanish disease. Although admittedly that last had at least a grain of truth to it, since syphilis did come from the New World.

Yes, the two cases have similarities. In the case of syphilis, the outbreak of nationalism was also a reaction against the universalization of risk. There the unplaceablity of risk came chiefly from the (at that time) incomprehensible mechanism of bacterial transmission and the shame surrounding the discussion of sex. Nowadays it chiefly comes from the way the industrial and political cosmopolitanization of risks makes them unavoidable. But in both cases, nationalistic scapegoating was the last refuge of the impotent. It was a fantasy idea of imposing a watertight quarantine where it just wasn't structurally possible – in both cases because of the density of transnational intercourse.

I guess the pattern was similar with BSE. By the time all of continental Europe was pointing at Britain, it was already way too late. Everything was already loose within their borders.

Exactly, and that's usually the case. When you see a lot of finger pointing, it's a sign that you have a risk conflict, meaning a frenzied attempt by all parties to avoid the risk, rather than a collective attempt to accept it in common, to take joint measures to reduce it, and to bear the compensation costs together. Finger pointing is a sign that things are beyond the control of politicians and technicians.

However, when nationality is the unit of blame, it means things have broken down on a very fundamental level. We might say that BSE took place near the end of the first modernity while syphilis took place at the beginning. In both cases, the risk was beyond the institutional capacity of the system to cope. In the case of syphilis, the system was eventually after many centuries able to master it, to assign it a causality, and to minimize and absorb the costs until it became an uncontentious thing. But the model it presented in the beginning, of a risk that couldn't be entirely understood, and which was life-threatening, and which seemed to shift its shape and location, is something that is now becoming a rule rather than an exception. So is the risk conflict that goes with it.

There have always been some risks that were really incalculable, and which the risk society of the first modernity misconceived and mishandled by treating them as probabilities. But by and large, the first modernity was a long period during which the model of finite risk management basically worked. A qualitatively new risk society begins with the second modernity, because so many risks escape the model of risk management that the system breaks down.

The main reason for this is that advances in technology and communications (including transportation) have combined to vastly increase the possibility for local risks to mutate into *systemic* risk. Systemic risk always involves what Keynes called radical uncertainty. These are risks that by nature can't be calculated, that can't be reduced to probabilities. Thus they can't be fitted into the old model. In fact using the old model exacerbates them. To misconceive uncertainty as being merely an imperfection in our data is to think that all we need is more information and better knowledge, and then we'll be able to predict and control it just like we used to. But not only can real uncertainties *not* be resolved through more and better knowledge, when we are dealing with what Anthony Giddens calls *manufactured uncertainties*, more knowledge can actually produce more uncertainty.

The technical approach refuses to see that risk definition has always rested on cultural definitions. These definitions were stable for so long because they were stabilized by institutional arrangements. This made them look like they were facts of nature, and made questions of risk behave like mere technical questions. But the fundamental question that risk conflict puts into play – the question of how much risk is acceptable and beyond what limit it is not – is a cultural and political question. Technicians think it is merely a matter of doing tests to determine an objectively safe threshold value. But it is the *process* that legitimates that value. That process is legitimated by a social system. And that social system is legitimated by its ability to assign responsibility and compensation as mechanically and reliably as the technicians assign threshold values. If the back half of the system breaks down, then so does the front half. For that matter, so does the middle, which is the authority and legitimacy of the system as a whole.

Stable cultural definitions once provided frames of reference that made it possible to settle causality, assign responsibility, and divide the risk. When those cultural definitions are set in flux because they lose their institutional underpinnings, then the instruments of technical reason take on a completely different meaning. Statistics and theories of causality become instruments of struggle in a war to ward off costs rather than a means to distribute them justly and efficiently. They fuel risk conflict rather than contributing to its containment.

This conflict then spreads to the underlying cultural values. Cultural stereotypes are reached for precisely because they are simple and stable and seem to offer a way out of this new ambiguity, an old set of certainties that can be rebuilt upon. But because national divisions have a largely illusory relation to current social reality, they are useless for escaping ambiguity. Like disembedded technical procedures, cultural stereotypes just become another instrument of risk struggle, a way of trying to distribute risks by avoiding them, a vain means of trying to win a game of hot potato.

BSE is a textbook case of how this point has still not yet been understood. The European Commission is still trying to settle it by means of a commission of experts, and is still baffled as to why this is not working. They think the technical procedure can work without its social underpinning, that they can produce a decision that the French and Germans must abide by or bear the costs, and that everyone will accept that this is the best way, when obviously they won't. To repeat, the question of how much risk is acceptable is not a technical one. It is a social and political decision. And it is only when that question is settled that technical adjudication can function properly.

Another thing that happens when the technical adjudication process is no longer based in a social and cultural consensus is that it become a means by which competitors try to profit from their rivals' loss by breaking into their market. Unfortunately, if this game is pursued far enough to make a difference, it almost inevitably spirals out of control and ends up collapsing the entire market. It ends up pulling down not only the competitors who thought they were gaining an advantage but innocent bystander-producers in unrelated industries.

The "death of the forests" debate in the late 1970s through early 1980s was an interesting example of this process at work. French companies, which had long ignored environmental questions, interpreted the save-the-forest campaign as a subtle stratagem that the German automobile industry was using in order to force the catalytic converter upon the European market. To a large extent, they were right. There were all kinds of disguised calculations and conflicts going on, which should have surprised no one. This is the rule rather than the exception in environmental struggles, even before they rise to the level of risk conflicts. To pretend that this multi-level game can be flattened out into a merely technical question is naïve. That becomes clear when it enters the patently political phase and people fight over the legislative and regulative details. Any observer can then see that what goes on at the technical level of risk definition is only a surface result of deeper forces clashing beneath. Capital flows and market shares are always being hammered out and speculated on beneath what purport to be neutral assignments of cause and effect and blame and cost.

And yet this unveiling doesn't reveal the truth of the matter either, because this elbows-out jockeying is almost always being conducted on the basis of completely wrong predictions.

There used to be, and still is in some places, a kind of touching faith in wealth as the antidote to risk. It is basically assumed the rich can protect themselves when the poor cannot. It had a certain truth during the first modernity, but it seems less and less true when it comes to the characteristic risks of the second. BSE unveiled how this is no longer true. I suppose during Chernobyl the really rich could say, I'll fly to the Fiji islands and there I'll be far away . . .

. . . although if they stayed there long enough they'd eventually find another long-buried toxin. If their island didn't vanish beneath the waves first thanks to global warming.

So riches are no longer a prophylactic against risk?

In *Risk Society*, I summed this up in a catch phrase that was widely greeted with scorn by my sociological colleagues:

poverty is hierarchical, smog is democratic. Now granted, this shouldn't be overstated. It's impossible to miss the extent to which environmental risks are clearly distributed along the contour map of poverty. Look who lives near the big chemical factories in the third world and you find the poorest of the poor, their lives immediately endangered. But there are global risks which have broken out of this hierarchical class logic of distribution. It is these new kinds of risk, combined with the snowball and contagion effects that derive from their dramatization, that are pushing through a tendency towards felt risk equality. It's also producing a kind of boomerang effect, where the people who are truly responsible for risks – not the direct producers, but the owners and planners and the people who man the institutions of legitimation – now end up suffering real consequences from their decisions. It's possible that this might have the potential for setting up a learning mechanism within risk society.

Often what makes the boomerang effect possible is the way in which health risks are transformed into economic or political risks through their dramatization into risk conflicts. We can see this in the case of corporations who have been treating food with chemicals (and now genetic manipulations) for years without suffering any ill consequences. They were shocked when the situation suddenly changed. When they began production, they mobilized their experts, who told them the risks were negligible, and this became the prevailing opinion. Enormous amounts of capital were invested in plant and equipment in order to build and service a global market on the basis of the assumption that there was no real risk here. Suddenly they found themselves sucked into a risk conflict of competing interpretations. Their experts of course describe it as hysteria, which is always less than useless, because it is precisely the *perception* of risk that leads to the collapse of markets.

The collapse of markets brings this boomerang effect crashing back on the corporations, not only in the form of plummeting stock prices, but in the sudden closing off of vast markets upon whose conquest their initial investment had been based, and without which their projected returns will never be achievable. This is how the consequences of technological risk have come to affect even companies in the USA who previously thought themselves immune. Falling stock prices and soured investments are the kind of things that could stimulate a serious rethink. It's not a certainty; you can't force people to think. But it's certainly a possibility that wasn't there before.

The fact that, in a growing number of cases, risk conflict initiates a dynamic that even the rich and powerful can't escape is a significant feature that distinguishes it from class conflict. Distributional conflicts, when we are fighting over a common pie, permit clear dividing lines to be drawn between the interests of rich and poor. Risk conflicts, by contrast, when they reach a certain level of intensity, get universalized throughout the system, thanks to globalization. The result is a series of degradations and devaluations, not only of health but also of capital, that happen far more rapidly than expectations can adjust. It's these systemic chain reactions that under certain circumstances reach back and strike at those most responsible. It's these secondary consequences that they can't predict or escape or insure themselves against.

These for me are the great dividing lines between the risks of the first and the second modernity: their predictability, their controllability, their evadability, and their insurability. In reality, of course, there are a lot of mixed and transitional cases, and we can argue for a long time over whether this or that particular risk belongs in this or that box. But in broad outlines, the difference between them is exemplified by the difference between traffic accidents and environmental risks.

One thing that really distinguishes second modern risks is that private insurance companies refuse to cover them. Again and again we run into this paradox, where an industry and its experts maintain and even offer to prove that a given risk is negligible, and yet the private insurance industry, which should be making money for jam in that case, reports back that this risk is too enormous for them to cover. Either they refuse to cover it; or they offer cover for premiums that are uneconomically high; or they cover it under conditions that grossly limit their liability, and so which don't really cover the ultimate risks. The second modernity is permeated with this contradiction between the economic rationality of the private insurance industry and the technical rationality of the industries that bring these risks into the world.

Perhaps eventually the insurance business, which has an interest in not being exposed to uncontrollable risks, will come

up with a clear way of distinguishing between risks that are and
are not foreseeable and controllable. An ability to make that
determination clearly would certainly be useful to them as they
sift the globalization of risks for business opportunities. For me,
the key question for any new industry or technology – where
by definition we can't know beforehand all the potential risks
– is: are you able to get private insurance for all your risks or
not? I think it is very revealing that almost all the big new technologies that are controversial in the public arena turn out not
to be privately insured and probably not privately insurable. In
the case of the nuclear power industry the government has
stepped in, but in most cases with cover that is way below the
potential risks. If you ask representatives of the industries who
have recently introduced genetically modified plants into the
world whether they have made any preparations for the even-
tuality that their product might cause illness, you get no answer.

*Or you get the classic answer: progress contains risks, but the fruits
of progress outweigh the possible risks.*

That is the standard answer. But oddly, this answer doesn't fly
when we are talking about the risks of auto accidents. If you
drive a car without insurance, that's punishable. But if you start
up a new business of which no one can clearly say what the
ultimate consequences might be, and where possibly the existence of all humanity could be at stake, no special precautions
are thought to be necessary, and it's considered bad manners to
bring it up. Such a way of going about things has consequences.
It leads to the decay of scientific and governmental authority. It
undermines confidence in industry and in the legitimacy of the
political system.

*Ironically, part of the motivation for denying risks and falsifying
their extent and waging the war of statistics is to try and reverse
this undermining of confidence. What was that famous story about
the case of the "acceptable limits?" How were they set?*

I'm often invited by large corporations to come and explain risk
society in simple terms. So once I was invited by a corporation
in Switzerland, in Basel . . .

We don't want to name names, of course, although as far as I know, there is only one large corporation there now, because the three that used to be there merged.

Right, three companies that we don't want to go into any further detail about. Well anyway, they were very attentive, you had to give them that. They listened very carefully to my exposition and they were very open-minded about it. Then they brought up the specific example of a certain toxin they produced. It was something that was used to increase the yield of certain plants, but which could have possible side effects if it ended up in the drinking water. It was also a relatively unusual situation in that they were the world's sole producer of this chemical, so if it ended up in the drinking water, it would have their name on it. In that respect, the problem didn't exactly fulfill all the main conditions that distinguish global risks. But it was pretty close.

Now their technicians, who had been on top of this problem since the beginning, said that the probability of this chemical ever ending up in the ground water was practically zero. So they decided to set the acceptable tolerance limits extremely low, because they thought this would inspire confidence, and they were sure they could meet those limits. Their initial assumption turned out to be false. After people starting using this protective agent for plants rather intensively, residues of the chemical did start appearing in the local drinking water, with consequences that they were now debating how to solve. Their dominant attitude was, "Oh this is silly, we set the tolerance levels much lower than was necessary in the first place. Unhealthy side effects really only appear above level XYZ, so we'll just reset the acceptable limits higher to what they really ought to have been and that will solve the problem." For them, the problem was completely contained within the limits of technical and medical rationality. It never occurred to them that by adjusting the acceptable limits after the fact . . .

. . . and adjusting them to suit their profit motive . . .

. . . well, certainly not to hurt it – that they were doing the worst thing they could possibly do as far as public confidence was concerned. To reset the limits higher under conditions like this has got cover-up written all over it. Even if scientifically it was justified.

Thus the technical rationality that seduced them into setting these acceptable limits extra low in the first place ended up having exactly the opposite effect from the one intended. Instead of increasing trust, they were actually gambling with it, double or nothing. But trust is actually a vital element for enabling corporations to interact smoothly with their consumers, the neighboring populace, and the general public. It's another one of those preconditions that you only realize the importance of when it suddenly disappears.

So under these conditions, how can responsibility for risks be reasonably assigned? If responsibility can't be clearly assigned, can it be spread out smoothly and distributed efficiently? This seems indispensable if we are to protect jobs from sudden collapse. It would also allow the modernization process as a whole to go forward without being hemmed in. Both jobs and progress are things the state uses to legitimate itself, but as things now stand, it keeps getting drawn into risk conflicts which undermine its legitimacy. Thus it seems the state will have to reach some new kind of modus vivendi *with second modern risks, even if it's just a cosmetic one.*

It certainly has to try. These new kinds of risks, which involve radical uncertainty rather than predictable probability, always raise the responsibility question as a burning issue. But as the examples we've been examining illustrate, rather than getting answered, the responsibility question tends instead to get systematically blocked out. The same instruments which were developed during the first modernity to assign responsibility and accountability and costs, and which performed these tasks so successfully, lead under the conditions of globalized risks to exactly the opposite result, to a kind of *organized irresponsibility*. Under these new conditions, a plaintiff can go from court to court and jurisdiction to jurisdiction only to hear one party after another say, "We didn't have anything to do with that", or "We are only subordinate players in this process."

The problem is that the institutional network which once assigned responsibility univocally and almost mechanically was only designed to operate with risks that could be determined with actuarial precision and certainty. But the risks that arise in the second modernity are characterized by radical uncertainty. Unclarity is inherently part of their nature, concerning both the population they affect and the time span in which they operate. In many cases, the time span alone is so long that prediction is impossible. In the face of risks which by their nature can't be determined precisely, the whole institutional workings of the first modernity seem to get thrown into reverse. Its demand for precision becomes instead a machine for refusing to acknowledge risk. It becomes an apparatus almost designed to allow corporations and government to escape responsibility.

Is there a way out of this impasse? Risk society in its present form is incapable of dealing with the ultimate consequences of civilization. Is there an alternative way to deal with them?

That's a good question. Is there a different way to deal with risk conflicts? A lot of answers have actually been put forth over the last few years, but most of them have been limited to particular risks. For example, the question of how we can avoid the risk of mad cow disease in the future has been answered by determining what conditions make the risk high and seeking to eliminate them. People are also seriously inquiring how we can reverse global warming and other environmental dangers. But as important as these efforts are, they only scratch the surface of the problem, which is that just around the corner will be new risks which will have escaped our present institutional set-up just as completely as these did.

As long as we continue to accept that risks can only be dealt with retroactively, we will never develop a politics that is adequate to them. Their explosive uncertainty can only be incorporated into our institutions if we become future-oriented, if we accept that things like this will happen again and again and by nature can't be predicted. Systemic crashes are now a part of our predictable future, and dealing with them has to become part of our political perspective.

I see no reason why the powerful new technologies of the twenty-first century won't bring new risks in equally powerful measure. As the computer scientist Bill Joy said in his now famous article, "The new Pandora's boxes of genetics, nanotechnology and robotics are almost open, yet we seem hardly

to have noticed." Joy argued that genetic technology, communication technology, and artificial intelligence – three fields
whose speed of development and spread may be hugely accelerated by their interaction – together share three potentially
dangerous features that can make them uncontrollable once
released: they are continuously revolutionizing themselves; they
have an almost infinite range of applications; and, as knowledge-
based technologies, they need only knowledge to get started –
unlike, for example, the building of an atomic bomb, which
requires at the very least some uranium, which can be closely
restricted, and which generates vast amounts of power, which
can be monitored. By contrast, it is perfectly conceivable that a
genetically engineered plague, one designed to have a long
incubation period and to target specific populations, could be
someday produced without its maker encountering much resistance. That would be as awesome a force as an atomic weapon.
And it's only one example.

This is why it is necessary to develop a radical politics in the
sense Marx used the term radical, meaning something that gets
at the root. The root in this case is what I've called *the relations
of definition,* meaning the definition of risks.

We should begin by repeating one more time that risks are
not things. They are social constructs. They are perceived and
established through social mediation: through knowledge;
through publicity; through the participation of experts and
counter-experts; through the ascription and establishment of
causality; through the division and distribution of costs; and
through the assignment and acceptance of responsibility. In
themselves, they may be invisible, they may entirely escape our
sense perception. They are cognitive constructs and are therefore always in a certain sense unsteady. Or rather, they are as
steady as the social relations on which they are based. Risks are
cognitive constructs that are based on relations of power that
are inscribed in a system of science and a system of law. That is
my understanding of the relations of definition.

The concept of the relations of definition is meant to parallel the idea of the relations of production. Marx used the idea
of the relations of production to *unveil* production as a set of
power relations and dependencies between owners and workers.
The relations of definition are meant to make clear the power
relations involved in the definition of risks.

Who decides what counts as a cause and what doesn't, in the face of the complexity and contingency of knowledge, and the difficulty of fully establishing a causality? What norms underlie this process? And what types of causal interpretation does governing opinion accept as valid?

Answering these questions is one way in which the relations of definition are determined. And there is more than one way to answer them. In Japan, for example, they've pulled back from demanding strict causal proof. Now all that's needed is that there be a "statistically significant" correlation, not a 100 percent proof. (Scientifically speaking, the latter has always been unattainable, and the best we've ever been able to have is a very persuasive correlation, but the law books have glossed over this subtlety and left the interpretation to the judge.) In crucial ways, the Japanese approach is even looser than that. Under the currently prevailing Japanese doctrine, if somebody's product plays only a contributory role in a disease, they can still get nailed for it. That is to say, if the prevalence of a disease is aggravated both by naturally occurring chemical X and by man-made chemical Y, the company making Y is still liable. It can't excuse itself by showing that natural background causes are also at fault. It's responsible for its contribution.

Under this system, one doesn't need to be able to prove causality in the individual case through direct evidence. Instead one can use easily calculable correlations according to strict statistical rules. Now, if this principle were to be pushed through in some form worldwide, it would completely change the relations of definition. We already know beforehand that it is virtually certain that some products being introduced today will have negative consequences in the future. Under this scheme, the corporations that make them would have to pay for them – and they would know this was a possibility before they introduced them on the market, so they would incorporate it earlier in their decision-making process. This, I argue, would re-modernize technical logic by making it methodologically reflexive. It would induce a veritable *reformation* in the scientific system (meaning the really existing logic of science's practical usage) by forcing it to take its unforeseeable consequences into account beforehand. And not by predicting them, but rather by accepting the certainty of their unpredictability. (See pp. 204ff.)

Unfortunately, this presumes that corporations will agree to exactly what they have so far strenuously tried to avoid. It was easy to insure yourself against first modern risks. You just made a contract with an insurance company. That approach doesn't work with second modern risks. But if corporations agreed to adopt this Japanese system, they would be agreeing to politicize something that has up until now been quite consciously kept unpolitical.

Yes, this would be a repoliticization, and it would open out onto what Günter Grass, following Theodor Fontane, called "a wide field." But at the same time it would lay the groundwork for a new and sorely needed depoliticization. Because once the perception takes root among the population that certain illnesses *can* be traced back to certain industrial causes, and that this is an objective fact for which they will be compensated, just as for any other kind of industrial accident, it will contribute over the long term to re-establishing a new relation of confidence. The individual will no longer be forced to produce unproduceable evidence. Groups who are affected will no longer have to bear the costs of such illnesses themselves. They will be able to count on a negotiated compensation. And since this compensation would have to be supplied by specific firms, they in turn would be forced to abandon a procedure that privatizes profits and socializes risks. They would be forced instead to take responsibility for the risks they produce. In the end, what we would have would be a new form of insurance contract, but this time mediated by a new kind of politics. It would be determined region by region in accord with a new and more reflexive logic.

Yes, but to get there, we'd first have to go through political conflict.

Which will probably set off other conflicts in a chain reaction.

So I find it hard to imagine it easily happening!

But risk conflict is already producing politicization where it isn't wanted! That's what gives it its intellectual and political explosiveness. Many theorists have bemoaned the loss of the political subject. For me, risk conflicts are one of the answers to that question. Instead of replacing one historical agent with another, risk conflicts force open political space from the inside. Time and time again, we've seen how the effect of such conflicts has been to smash through institutional certainties that moments earlier had seemed set in concrete. This because they have inherent qualities making them difficult to restrain or keep in bounds. It might be through just such a process that the relations of definition will be exposed and remodeled.

Let me try to explain this in terms of risk society theory. Power, money, and truth are all media of communication, in the root sense of both media and communication. Risk might be understood as an unintentional medium of communication. Risk conflict abolishes existing barriers to communication, and puts people into communication who don't want anything to do with each other. It forces obligations and liabilities onto those who have done everything they can to avoid them (and who often have the law on their side). Risk conflicts have a destructive creativity that cuts through existing rules. Consequently, risk crises make it possible to redistribute costs in ways that were considered unthinkable until they occurred.

Another way to put it is that risk conflict overthrows the autonomy, or self-referentiality, of social subsystems like the economy, the political system, and the scientific system. It establishes dialogue and negotiations between subsystems that up until that point were ignorant of, if not actively hostile, to each other. In this way, risk conflict overthrows the existing order of priorities that governs everyday life and business. In a sense, one might say it produces a quasi-revolutionary situation. An inverted picture of the social order is made real momentarily while the mass media attention lasts. And risk publics play the role of the quasi-revolutionary mob.

But this brings us to the next level. Second modern risks are not only ubiquitous but also transnational. So they can't be regulated at the level of the nation-state. Once again, then, we return to the problem of transnational politics. It also returns us to the idea of global risk society, a term you coined. You interchangeably call it world risk society – which, I note, first appeared as the title of a book that is still so far available only in English. What we seem to have here, I would like to note for the record, is a subspecies of self-globalization, which is making itself more and more noticeable as time goes on. I'll be keeping a critical eye on its side effects.

The publisher is a global risk profiteer, no doubt about it!

I'm sure it will all end badly, in a typical Swiss refuge, where the royalties from books in fifteen languages will all end up homogenized into a steady diet of muesli. But back to the point. Second modern risks can no longer be comprehended in nation-state terms. So even if we found a workable national framework, and managed to push it through politically, it would still only be an apparent solution, because the problem is inherently global. We live in a global risk society.

So now I guess is a good time to talk about that. What makes global risk society different from risk society?

Risk society becomes global risk society when it has to process global risks, risks that are systemic, unpredictable, uncertain and infinite.

It's recently struck me that many of what I consider the key ideas in this area were developed by John Dewey in a slightly different but analogous context 70 years ago, in his 1927 book, *The Public and its Consequences*. He was facing the transition from local communities to a national society, and wondering what mediating structures could possibly integrate the latter so that individuals could feel themselves truly represented. He solved it by coming up with an extremely broad conception of the function and the nature of a public. It was far ahead of its time, but for various reasons it's not as far ahead of ours. I think today we are facing a similar transition, this time between national and transnational society.

Dewey's key insight is that the public can serve an integrating function by standing between causes and their consequences, and by giving them a symbolic meaning they wouldn't otherwise have. It is this meaning that makes politics and society possible. In the final analysis, says Dewey, it is not actions but *consequences* that are the soul of politics. It is by giving consequences *meaning* that the public plays its key role in the formation of society.

Dewey wasn't, of course, thinking of global warming, GM foods, nanotechnology, and BSE. But his theory is even more applicable to global risk society than it was to his own. Dewey was asking how society could reconstitute its unity on a new and larger scale for which there were no pre-existing traditions.

His answer was that, theoretically at least, real public discourse could accomplish this task. But to do so, it would have to be interactive, and it would have to cross boundaries. It would have to jump not only geographic boundaries, but even more importantly the boundaries between experts and laymen, and the boundaries between specialists themselves. How could such an integrating public discourse arise? Dewey said it would arise not from consensus but from dissensus, from strong disagreements over the consequences of decisions.

Modern risk crises are constituted by just such controversies over consequences. So where technical thinkers see an overreaction to risk, Dewey would see a reason for hope. He argues that such conflicts serve a vital *enlightenment* function that in their default would never take place. Such conflicts are attempts to bridge the gap between experts and citizens. Global risks have the capacity to knit together publics, and potentially to integrate politics and society on a global level.

The 1992 Rio de Janeiro conference is an excellent example of the capacity of risk conflicts to create new and abiding global social facts. It was at Rio that global warming was first defined as a global problem. It is not an exaggeration to claim it as a turning point in global consciousness, because ever since then, those who don't believe it is a global problem have been the exceptions who prove the rule. They are now the ones who have to justify themselves, where pre-1992 it was the other way round. Furthermore, they now have to justify themselves before a global public. We might in the end be able to date the social construction of global risk society to events like the Rio conference.

Are international conferences what you're mainly thinking of as the formative moments of global politics?

No, in many ways they're the exception, but they're easy to grasp. A more representative example is what happened to Shell in the Brent Spar affair. Shell wanted to dispose of a used drilling platform by sinking it in the North Sea. What's interesting is that the first thing they did was receive the government approval of every country bordering on the North Sea. In other words, the attempt to secure legal permission was still addressed towards nation-states, the same places companies have always turned to in matters of legal protection. It seemed to come off without a hitch. But, as we now know, the consensus worked out among Shell, the UK, Germany, and all the other border states turned out to be no defense at all against the tactics of Greenpeace, who skillfully dramatized the event on an international scale and transformed it into a crime against nature. In the end, the Greenpeace campaign managed to affect the behavior of Shell's customers. Enough of them began to feel that filling up at Aral instead of Shell would be a virtuous act that would contribute to saving the world, and specifically to not sinking this particular oil rig in the North Sea. Shell had to give in, against its will, and despite having secured nation-state permission.

Transnational corporations have achieved their superiority over nation-states through their development of deterritorialized power. (See pp. 47ff.) But to the extent that they have been able to establish transnational markets, they are still dependent upon legal frameworks, and in order to secure these frameworks, they turn to nation-states. In Shell's case, this was in vain.

What this shows is that in the current constellation of global society, nation-states can no longer provide companies with legal security. Beyond that, it's really unclear what the legal situation is in the transnational realm. Currently, the main opponents of transnational corporations are NGOs, nongovernmental organizations like Greenpeace, who act largely independently of both states and corporations. They have not only been able to enter this new transnational power game but to play it with skill.

The central defining fact of the transnational legal arena is that there is no world government. In other instances, transnational corporations have used this fact very effectively to maximize their power position. In the Brent Spar case, it revealed its flipside, which is that there is no ultimate transnational legal protection that can cover all of a company's contingencies. It's actually been quite a while since nation-states have been in a position to provide comprehensive legal protection for global companies. This gap opens up enormous opportunities for applying the mobilized power of a global public. There are many different ways to mobilize that public, and media-savvy consumer movements have taken advantage.

The lack of a transnational governing authority seems to leave transnational corporations free to act as they please. But it also means there is no final legal authority for them to appeal to. It means they have few symbolic defenses that can match the legitimacy enjoyed by global environmental or consumer movements. Ironically, in the Brent Spar affair, it seems Shell was actually right when it asserted that the sinking method would have caused less total environmental damage than towing the platform ashore. But because of its lack of legitimacy, there was literally no place where Shell could make its case. This is the corporations' Achilles heel, and it's where the movements have learned to strike them. If the movements can convince the public that something is a crime, there is no authority on earth that can certify it is not.

So this lack of a transnational legal authority cuts both ways. Transnational corporations have responded to attacks like this with two basic strategies. Sometimes they've taken the path of confrontation. They've attempted to uphold their own definitions of appropriate behavior against the critiques of the new social movements. They've ostentatiously ignored the criticisms and kept on with their old practices. This path runs enormous risks, however, because transnational corporations are operating in a legitimation vacuum into which retail markets can quickly collapse, and environmental or human rights initiatives have the tools to incite those collapses. The alternative strategy is to come to terms with these movements and try to construct a new kind of political protection. But to the extent corporations do this, they are forced to submit to a corresponding surveillance, and to accept as legitimate the environmental or human rights standards of their opponents.

I don't mean to suggest that this dynamic will automatically lead to permanent changes in the relations of definition, or to the universal acceptance of higher environmental and human rights and labor standards on the part of corporations. But I think we should recognize how transnational space is developing its own distinctive dynamic, in which corporate actors who at first sight appeared overwhelmingly powerful are in fact permanently liable to be the object of attack from movements which have much more legitimacy with the public, and who can therefore use this law-free realm to their advantage to compel some remarkable concessions.

But the picture you're drawing shades off in various directions. To take a simple example, if Shell had wanted to sink an oil rig in the Gulf of Guinea, probably hardly anyone would have noticed. I think a large role was played in this case by its location in the North Sea. It didn't just happen in the environment, but in the immediate environment of people with highly sensitized consciousness who react very nervously to environmental threats. When things happen in distant Africa, it doesn't have the same resonance. Take, for example, Nigeria, where oil production has destroyed whole river systems. When the tribes who lived there, mainly by fishing, noticed the fish were becoming inedible, they resisted, and they were literally uprooted. I think "resettlement" was the euphemism used. But that didn't irritate the global consciousness, or the global public, to anywhere near the same degree as the sinking of the Brent Spar. It was publicized (that's why I know about it), and there were calls for a similar boycott. But though it would only have taken the same small effort to not fill up at Shell (or BP, or whoever it is who is engaged in Nigeria), and to fill up at Aral instead, it never caught on in the same way. It never had the same effectiveness. The poor people can't catch fish, and they're beaten to death, and that's terrible, but not enough to cross the street.

So it seems that industry can still find a lot of places on earth to transplant their risk production where they won't disturb people's consciousness in the Northern Hemisphere or its satellites.

That's true but also not true. You are certainly right about the relative effectiveness of the two campaigns. But I don't think the main reason was distance. I think it derived from the grammar of dramatization. I think it has been shown that global risks can be thematized in a way that is location-independent. But events don't generate outrage spontaneously, no matter how horrid they are. They have to be effectively socially constructed.

Some colleagues and I once attempted to set down all the various game plans by which risks have been successfully dramatized so that they led to the desired results. It turns out it's not so easy to say what really works. For the dramaturgy of risk to work, events have to be translated into a culturally relevant symbolism, into a background against which perceptions stand out sharply and clearly. It must be made to seem in a certain way a scandal you experience yourself. There must be something in your behavior that can be construed as contributing directly to this injustice, something you can easily permit or forbid yourself. Lastly, it works best if there is a similarly clear moral choice for the company, something they could do or not do, a simple alternative course.

All these elements were present in the Brent Spar case. I think it was not the North Sea location that made the difference as much as it was the perfect suitability of the materials and the skill with which they were handled. The campaigners managed to convince the public that Shell had a criminal *intent*, for which it could be held fully responsible. They managed to ignite the bad conscience that most of us already have about environmental matters (thanks to the moralization of the problem), but which is usually latent, into a protest movement.

It is true, as you said, that the action required of each member of the public was extremely easy to perform. All they had to do to be virtuous was to fill up at Aral or Esso instead of at Shell. Then they could go off in good conscience whizzing down the autobahn at 200 kilometers an hour. In the event, people not only felt like they were making a contribution to saving the world but they found they could follow it on TV, like a wrestling match between an enormously powerful opponent and a plucky clever little guy. And they could cheer for the gang of Davids, of which they felt a part, as they overpowered the statesmen and multinationals.

It's a series of elements like this that determines whether the dramaturgy of risk will be successful or not. Distance, while important, is only one of many different factors that have to converge for the whole thing to come off. And to be fair, it's not that the Nigerian campaign was so ineffective, but rather that the North Sea campaign was so *extremely* effective. There are many campaigns that only get part way towards success. The method is still in its infancy.

The point is, it is an essential part of risk conflicts that they have the potential to politicize everything they touch, and this potential is in large part based on their independence from place and their abolition of distance. This has become even more apparent with the recent upsurge of resistance to the corporate framing of globalization. For a long time it was assumed it was impossible to politicize globalization because where did it take place? Everywhere and nowhere. There was no place you could bring the conflict to a point. That was the common wisdom before the world media event we now know as Seattle, which showed the opposite is closer to the truth. Globalization can be politicized anywhere. Now wherever the WTO meets, or any of the other organizations which are central to maintaining and expanding the corporate form of globalization, that place immediately becomes the attack point for the next protest. It has taken almost no time for this to become institutionalized, so that in the run-up to the events, the international media expect protests, and this makes them more effective.

The political potential of global risk society is in large part based on the place-independence of risk conflicts. This latent potential need not wait to be released by direct threats to our immediate health. It can be tapped into anytime by people who know how to dramatize it. By heightening the drama, they produce a symbolic substitute for direct threat: they dramatize the interconnection that is global risk society. Such organizers must among other things be first-rate directors of political theater. They must know how to touch cultural nerves, and how to deliver narrative pictures of history to the media.

But global risk society can't attain a reflexive concept of itself until it constitutes itself as a political subject. You've described a process whereby fascination can be transformed into political engagement. But can these individual conflicts be aggregated and institutionalized into a something lasting, into a transformative social movement? And is everyone capable of such politics, or are we only talking about a small number of people who are ultimately politicizable?

This is a key question. Political scientists have repeatedly pointed out that the politicization of risks is usually limited to single issues and is by nature temporary. Such scandals usually have one main theme that catches fire for a short while and becomes the topic of the day. The question is how to make it lasting, and how to connect the dots. There has to be a transnational form of activism that remains in place between events. Furthermore, these forms have to be self-reflexive if they are to produce a political self-consciousness. There has to be a form of political organization that doesn't just appear ad hoc, but which is institutionalized, in order to offer lasting solutions. However, we have to emphasize once again that this institutionalization can and probably will be that of institutionalized individualism.

(See chapter 2.) It can and probably will be the permanence of networks.

For a collective political subject to come into being, there has to arise a political consciousness that isn't simply a reflex of media events, because such events are by nature transient. If we depend on the media alone, it makes it look as if problems disappear of their own accord.

To be replaced by the next toxin of the week.

Exactly. This has its own paradoxical side effect. If there are too many toxins of the week, people start to get blasé. Still, we should note that despite this devaluation effect that the repetition of media events produces, a new impetus is still always breaking out somewhere.

To understand this process, we have to break it down into its individual parts. Instead of just rushing to extrapolate to a possible dead end, we should ask instead, "How *could* a process come into being that was more reflexive, more conscious and more political? What could it look like, and what would be its preconditions?"

The first important fact to note is that while the corporations and the WTO and all the other economic actors in the transnational arena dispose of enormous power, they are almost completely without political legitimacy. So much is this the case, that when you ask them what are the foundations for their action, they are almost speechless. They have the standard economic reply, of course, that they act for everyone's good, but that's often not convincing, and even in the best case, it could only be conditionally convincing. And even in that case, it is essentially the justification of benevolent dictatorship. Real political legitimacy is built in arenas to which these organizations have no access and to which they deny importance.

On the other hand, the transnational movements arrayed against them enjoy a high degree of legitimacy, although it's not because they've been democratically legitimated, because they haven't. It's more because they are seen as Robin Hood organizations. If you ask young people today which political organizations they admire most, most of them rank these movements at the top.

So in the end, we have a *paradoxical inverse relation between power and legitimacy.* Great power and small legitimacy is opposed by small power and great legitimacy. It is an interesting imbalance that will someday finish working itself out. So far we have only seen this dynamic in its infancy. Its consequences are becoming visible by degrees.

This imbalance between power and legitimacy represents an enormous potential for politicization. States have so far taken a relatively neutral role in this conflict, because they are still largely acting as their own self-liquidators. They have so far largely accepted the neoliberal ideology because they believe it's the only way for them to have a presence at all in the transnational power game. But to the extent that states, and the political parties within them, can reconstruct themselves so as to make transnational cooperation among them possible (see pp. 49ff. and 214ff.), it may end up that networks of states will be what finally manages to control transnational corporations. Among these three sorts of actor, it is only states which have any capacity to be democratically legitimated. That gives them a potential the other two don't have. If they realize it through becoming transnational cooperation states, they can win themselves a new position in the transnational power game.

This is the constellation of forces we're starting with. Now comes the question of how the learning process that is bound up with risk conflicts can be translated into institutional structures. I think we should look again at the series of environmental summit conferences that started in 1992 at Rio de Janeiro. It gives an indication of one way, not the only way, but certainly one way, in which this potential power can be actualized in such a way as to constrain the action of individual states. It fits the model put forth by some British theorists of governance that is "governance free."

Rio represented the recognition of environmental problems as global problems. Now of course afterwards the USA can still say, "We think this is all hysteria, and we won't respect the treaties that come out of it," but it means they find themselves on the defensive in every international forum, and will continue to do so into the foreseeable future. In other words, they have lost their legitimacy on these issues. That is something that still shocks political officials, and it's a shock they are forced to relive every time they come to a new conference. This is actually a much bigger effect than anyone expected of Rio, this ability to put powerful countries, even the most powerful, on the moral defensive.

The second surprise was that the Rio series of conferences was able to develop this power despite containing a great plurality of views. Up until this point it was thought that only economic institutions, like those which are forcing through policies of liberalization, would ever be able to exert an independent influence on nation-states. But here was an instance of environmental standards being erected, and held up as norms of behavior which, if enforced, would run counter to narrow national self-interests in the name of a larger and longer-term global good. We shouldn't underestimate the importance of this. It represents a turning away from everything political science presently holds to be true. And we have to remember that this process is really only in its infancy. Its scope for development is still enormous. I think it is more likely that its setbacks are temporary than that the whole process will be reversed.

Of course there is the complaint that nothing has actually happened yet. But that in itself builds a new potential that wasn't there before. There is now an enormous disappointment on the part of the public that nothing is being done. That wasn't there before. And what does it consist of? It's a disappointment that the new standards aren't being lived up to. From conference to conference, the net of findings and regulations grows a little denser, and the attempt to construct multilateral control mechanisms that can work becomes a little more specific and detailed.

What is being constructed here, at least in outline and at least in its beginnings, is a system of regulations that could conceivably exert an appreciable coercive power to compel deviant nation-states to conform to transnational norms. This is one way in which an activated global public can by degrees change the definition of risks by changing the relations of definition. In the clashing and compromising over regulations, this ongoing series of conferences also presents an image of how a political process of reflection can be institutionalized. It's one which is transnational, which has developed an intrinsic forward momentum, and which is trying to gather the power to compel individual states to fall in line with that forward momentum.

It seems that what we have here is something that might once have been called a process of enlightenment. To the extent that people become conscious that there are risks, to that extent people become willing to change their behavior.

Right. If we confine ourselves just to the second modernity, I think we can divide the emergent global risk society into two stages. The first phase is where society persists in defining itself as national industrial society. The dominant faith is still the faith in progress, and it continues to deny that such a thing as incalculable risk can even exist. Risks are defined in terms of probabilities, and if they can't be so defined, it must be because they aren't real. There is an increasing clamor to change this definition of risks, but in the first phase it's largely warded off, even as newer and graver risks are coming into being out of sight. This produces a split consciousness, a kind of institutional schizophrenia. Public perception is still dominated by the industrial society consensus that progress, production, preserving jobs, and producing wealth are society's central goals and that anything that calls these things into question is a threat to be rejected. But denying risks is like fertilizing the soil in which they flourish and bloom. This phase is when the production of global risks is maximized.

The second phase begins when risk consciousness has made enough of a mark for the fundamentalist faith in progress to have been appreciably shaken. Now the position of accusers and accused is, if not reversed, at least substantially altered. In the first phase, the practitioners of the dramaturgy of risk can still be condemned as hysterical. In the second phase, the suspicion has become almost universalized that industry *is* emitting products that can harm us, and is making claims of safety they can't back up. We start to suspect the worst even when they are boasting. The consciousness of risk begins to surround progress like a shadow encircling the light.

In this latter phase, risk consciousness dwells more on risks that haven't yet come into existence than on advantages that might flow from new developments. The establishment retorts by saying we paint everything in the blackest of colors and will end up strangling progress. What is actually happening is that the two sides which are always conceptually present in risk conflicts are being abstracted and expressed as opposites. In reality, neither side has a monopoly on the truth. That is the whole point of the new consciousness, that there is no such monopoly.

It is possible to describe this second phase as the point where risk society starts to become reflexive. This the point where the critical gaze stops being limited to particular cases and begins to look at society as a whole. This is also the point when people we would least expect turn into society's Cassandras. Mainstream politicians start to say that certain kinds of "progress" that we've previously taken for granted actually can't be continued without leading to a disaster. (The case of nuclear power in Germany is a perfect example.) This is a significant turning point. It means one of the central groups in the modernization drama has been won round to the view that sometimes the negative effects of progress really can outweigh the positive. And although the political actors aren't the most powerful ones in this drama when compared with the scientific or economic actors, they are still the ones with the most legitimacy. If they begin to lose their faith in progress, it means the faith that modernization was founded on is decisively waning.

This represents the beginning of the institutionalization of political reflexivity. It is full of ambiguities, and we have to make sure we don't interpret it too positively. The main problem in this second stage is that there is still a complete logjam in our political institutions. Radical reforms are still impossible to pass. This was also made clear by the debate about withdrawing from nuclear power. As soon as we got serious about it, resistance increased exponentially.

The forces of resistance in this case were exactly the same forces as are now preaching the gospel of gene technology and the other future-oriented industries. Once again, they want to charge onwards without setting up any precautionary measures that would be adequate to deal with uncertainty, to deal with the obvious fact that unknown risks can't be calculated. It's as if the experience of nuclear power had never happened. Remember the minuscule probabilities of anything going wrong that were bragged about before Three Mile Island and Chernobyl? If there's one thing we can say with a large probability it's that whatever can go wrong, will go wrong, given a long enough time. And these new technologies have timelines that extend for millennia.

This brings us back to our political starting point. Ignoring the reality of uncertainty simply accelerates the process of political delegitimation. That in turn plays right into the hands of the real pied pipers in the world: not the people who preach uncertainty, but those who preach dangerously simple political certainties.

Conversation 4

Labor Society and the Regime of Risk

JOHANNES WILLMS *Is work as we know it coming to an end? Is that another feature of risk society?*

ULRICH BECK   That's putting it a bit too simply. As I keep trying to emphasize, we aren't leaving one society and entering another. It is rather the creation of a new dynamic while the old one still exists. It is, however, true that the concepts of labor and employment are changing in fundamental ways. The basic certainties that previously defined them are dissolving. It's very interesting to look at this development in historical perspective and then contrast it with the trends we see today.

In the history of western civilization, the concept of labor is probably the one which has undergone the most radical revaluation. It's gone through a complete and dramatic reversal. When western civilization began, if we take it as beginning in ancient Greece, labor was what *excluded* people from society. Those who worked were the non-members of society. Society was understood as political society. Women and slaves, to whom labor was assigned, were external to this society. It constituted them as lacking essential human qualities which only manifested themselves through participation in political life, through life in the *polis*.

We don't want to re-enact the whole process of redefinition, but it is important to note that with the beginning of the first modernity – against the backdrop of the bourgeois revolutions, the rise of market society, and capitalism's rapid take-off – work becomes the central marker of people's social identity, their social position, and their social security. The central importance of work, and the obviousness of this centrality to both individuals and political society, is the end result of a long historical process. It is the naturalization of a set of cultural certainties that developed and reached its perfection with the first modernity.

During this period, the concept of labor was completely transformed. The reason this is so important is because today we are finally experiencing the situation which Hannah Arendt already foresaw in the sixties when she said that we lived in a "labor society that is bidding farewell to labor." She saw this as a huge historical irony, because at the beginning of western civilization labor was considered the lowliest of all activities, and there was a wealth of other activities that were seen as superior, like political action and artistic creation and the exercise of craft. These were considered meaningful activities because they created meaningful objects, while labor was seen as permanently cancelling itself out through the consumption of its own production. Over time western civilization downgraded the importance of these other activities and built a society based entirely on labor, on its production and consumption. In doing so, it completely reversed the scheme of values. But now, Arendt said, because of the increasing rationalization of labor, the kind of labor this society was built upon was vanishing. Hence her irony.

It's important to note that Arendt isn't saying that labor itself is being rationalized out of existence. Rather she's claiming that the core attributes that once enabled labor to give meaning to people's lives and to society are being attenuated. She argues that there were certain attributes that made "labor society" possible. Without them, labor loses its ability to bestow meaning. We then start to return in some ways to the status quo ante, but with the crucial difference that the inhabitants of labor society have by now forgotten that things were ever organized differently. They see no alternatives to labor society. They have completely forgotten its historical alternatives.

The society of paid labor is not running out of things to pay people to labor at. Rather what we are witnessing is the end of classical full employment, which is something that was inscribed in the political cultures of European and OECD countries after World War II as a fundamental principle of politics. The full sense of full employment entails "normal jobs," in which each person learns an occupation and practices it for a lifetime. If people change jobs, it's to another lifelong occupation. This lifelong activity is assumed to be the center of all social existence.

Today, work has been revolutionized away from that model. Work has been "flexibilized," and cut into spatial, temporal, and contractual packets. We see ever greater numbers of so-called independent contractors and temporary workers. We see more and more jobs tailored to avoid regulations; jobs that last limited periods of time; workers working without contracts; workers working in the black or gray markets; people working informally – and this goes on at every level of qualifications, not just at the lowest. All this puts seriously into question the central principle upon which labor society was based, namely the relative security of employment and its long-term predictability. To the extent this is true, the very center of labor society becomes subject to the regime of risk.

What does this dissolution of the traditional, bourgeois concept of work entail? Clearly it fractures the arc of individual biographies. It also has to have consequences at the level of society. How would you describe its effects at each level?

Let's start with society. To begin with, universal participation in the labor market is presupposed by the welfare state. It's the precondition for the solvency of the pension system, for example. Only under the condition that all able-bodied workers continue to be integrated into the workforce under the model of full employment is it possible that the pensions of older generations can be financed by younger ones. To the extent that this precondition is altered in any significant way – for example, because there is a big decline in the birth rate of the younger generation; or because there is a substantial decline in the percentage of employed; or the number of pension years that need to be financed rises considerably because of the lengthening of lifetimes – then the pension system falls into crisis. This is the situation that we in central Europe have been discussing vehemently for several years now without being able to shape a solution.

Work in the traditional middle-class sense is also the precondition for an active democracy. The consequences that the transformation of labor have had in the political realm have not been discussed with anywhere near the same seriousness as the economic shortfall, in my opinion.

The British sociologist T. H. Marshall argued shortly after World War II that social security in the broad sense, which includes the relative predictability of one's career chances, is a necessary precondition for people to take seriously and use the political freedoms that exist on paper. For labor society to work, it has to be filled with citizen workers. Citizen workers are people who secure their financial existence and self-esteem and self-consciousness through participation in the labor market, and then have free time and energy beyond their jobs to pursue other activities like being an active citizen.

On this view, the social welfare state is not only an insurance against the risks of the labor market, it's also the foundation stone of democracy. If people have no jobs and no roofs over their heads, and no source of income, you can't expect them to be active citizens.

The labor market thus distributes essential life chances that ramify throughout society. Work is not just work. Work is something that integrates us into society. It gives us an occupational position and a class position. It determines a great deal of our consumption options: how we dress, how we eat, how we act, how we vote. Our jobs and professions determine our security and participation chances, or our lack of the same. To a great extent, how we live depends on what we do for a living.

But as we have been discussing, these causal chains are getting more and more difficult to construct. Looked at historically, the unity I just described has been progressively eroded. A lot of this has to do with the dissolution of the predictable paths that people used to take through the labor market.

In the end, every aspect of industrial society in its mature form had full employment as its precondition, from the welfare state in its broadest sense to the meaningfulness of parliamentary democracy. This is why politicians have such difficulty entertaining the possibility that the underpinnings of labor society may be growing irreversibly weaker. In order to retain their credibility with the voters, political parties simply have to stick close to the "jobs for everyone" script.

You said that, historically speaking, working for a living hasn't always been the prime desideratum it appears to us. Of course the main reasons people cling to work so tenaciously are more about making money than loving their jobs. But leaving that to one side for the moment, why are we so fixated on the idea of paid labor? Why do we treat it as the only form that serious activity can take? Are we just slaves who would feel lost without our chains? What is the fascination of paid labor that makes it impossible for us to imagine alternatives? Especially when jobs are now being drained of their substance and filled with risks they didn't used to have.

The easiest way to explain the fascination of paid labor is to imagine the problems that would immediately emerge for both society and individuals if we took this foundation away. To start with, it's the primary and tacit legitimation for social inequality. Take away that legitimation, and inequality would become a heated question. There would also be other important things to discuss, like security and status and identity and employment. If you set up a thought experiment, where we had the same economic outcomes we have now, but their distribution was not mediated by how much people got paid for their labor, I think the thing that would strike most people immediately and forcefully would be, "How come on one side there is this small group of rich people who keep getting richer – and whose riches aren't justified by their activity, but are mainly skimmed off the proceeds of capital – and at the other end is this large group of poor people who, scramble though they might, just keep getting poorer, and in extreme cases just drop off the edge of society altogether?"

That is one side of the problem, the material side. There is also the immaterial. A huge social change like that would also destroy what our colleague Dahrendorf once called the ligatures of tradition. It would cut the moral cords that bind us together, what we might call, in old-fashioned Christian terms, the bonds of charity. And that would call the very existence of society into question.

The reason labor has been made into the pillar of civil society is not simply because it allows us to provide people, including poor people, with a certain level of material security. That's important, certainly. But what is just as important is that it counteracts the danger to society from "subjects" who have not been integrated into the pre-existing contexts of meaning and control.

Labor is a means by which the structure of power is internalized through everyday routines, each of which involves the positing of meaning and the submission to control. When every desire to build a life, a biography, an identity, an existence, is forced to be mediated through the labor market, what results is one of the subtlest and most refined systems ever invented for getting people to conform to the societal structure of power. People adapt themselves. They fit themselves in.

This self-activated conformity to rule constitutes the core of labor society. It transforms the control of rulers into self-control. Individuals integrate themselves into the system of labor, they make themselves functional. The net of exploitation that binds them is experienced as self-exploitation, as drive, as something to be proud of. All of this is accomplished by the system of labor. It is the central engine of social control.

This necessarily raises a question. If this system is beginning to dissolve, and if, in many ways, we want it to dissolve, then how can we create an alternative milieu in which individuals who have been fragmented and atomized can be socialized? Where they can experience something like society, and internalize the values of society? What alternative method is there for reweaving these unraveling and self-individualizing individuals back into a fabric of social control? Where they can be assigned the activities and functions that society needs, and convinced that carrying them out is the obvious thing to do, without sacrificing their individual projects?

A full answer to that question might have supplied the necessary second half to Kant's utopian text On Perpetual Peace. *We have finally reached a point in history where perpetual peace, by which he meant a peaceful, prosperous bourgeois society that covered the entire globe, seems entirely within our grasp. But already there is beginning to emerge a new development that Kant didn't foresee, although Hegel arguably did, in a footnote to* The Philosophy of Right, *when he said that perpetual peace wouldn't be desirable in the present state of society, because society would begin to lose its inner firmness and become "swampy." Today we are experi-*

encing some of that swampiness literally, but even more so metaphorically, through the loss of the drive and the certainties that were once provided by real work, upon which were based most of the other certainties of bourgeois society. We are faced with the loss of full employment in the full sense of that term – the loss of real jobs for real wages, whose continuance can be taken for granted over one's lifetime – which in turn calls this whole society into question.

This rhetoric about "welfare state spongers" and "the lazy unemployed" – the reason it gets so inflamed is precisely that it rubs society at this raw point. You can win a lot of political support by denouncing how individuals are abandoning the old work ethic. There is a balm in these negative stereotypes. Uneasy people are quick to unite behind the Us/Them distinctions they represent.

There are, however, a couple of small groups (and it's not yet clear how seriously we should take them) who have declared openly that their unemployment is in a certain sense voluntary. They have proclaimed themselves the pioneers of a new epoch. They also say, perhaps somewhat tongue in cheek, but maybe not entirely so, that they are fulfilling an important social function by being unemployed. For one thing, nobody has to do all the work of providing them with jobs. Or of integrating them into society. They say they are withdrawing from labor society of their own free will because they think they know how to care for themselves.

Such a declaration of voluntary unemployment is of course designed to be provocative. These people are not only rejecting the offer of integration. They are transforming the value of unemployment from something shameful into something valuable, a status worth attaining.

Of course, people are also outraged simply because they want to get paid without working.

Yes, but that's just it. These people have nothing against working. They just don't want paid work, to be paid per hour per task. They want to get enough to live and then decide themselves what work they should do.

Are you referring here to the so-called "self-help networks"?
Where people band together to help each other, either because
they have all fallen off the edge of society, or because they want
to construct an alternative lifestyle?

No, I'm thinking chiefly of a group of activists who actually call
themselves The Voluntary Unemployed. They reject the pre-
given scheme that equates unemployment with immiseration
and loss of identity. They say instead: We unemployed are not
really unemployed. We are fully employed, we have very good
ideas on how to employ ourselves. Of course we need unemployment compensation in order to be able to do these things
that are important to us. To this degree, we are living off the
system, it is supporting us. But we are using this support to
conquer a new realm beyond labor society, simply by doing
what seems important to us. This also makes us the group who
can best provide a critique of, and a new solution to, the problems of work: to its alienation, and to the increasing way it is
being hollowed out and emptied of personal and social meaning.

Their critique of work is simple and to the point. What is so
tempting about the activities that are now on offer as work?
Does anyone get fired up to be a service worker or a secretary
or a manager? To putz about with a computer all day, to be
forced to live out most of your waking hours in a hive of artificial relationships? And accomplishing what, exactly? Most of
us see the activities we do at work as killing time. It's almost a
second job when we go home or out to a party and try to convince other people that what we do is important.

The voluntarily unemployed say: Screw that. We are using
unemployment compensation as a foundation to explore new
forms of existence. We are the pioneers of post-labor society.
We are searching out activities that interest us, that we enjoy.
We want a life where we can switch from one activity to
another, because variety and change in themselves make all
activities more enjoyable. We don't need the control claims of
labor society to organize ourselves. The only work it can offer
us is standardized and commodified labor that is completely
emptied of meaning.

These are interesting ideas. In the twenties and thirties, there was
an economist named Silvio Gesell who thought along similar lines.

Unfortunately, his writings were embraced by the Nazis, so he has been perhaps unfairly forgotten. His idea was that there could be economic networks that could create their own forms of non-state money. His thinking was that we could let the world market continue running on its own, while at the same time building small, self-contained, self-supporting forms of social organization that provided meaningful work, and in which payments of interest played no role, but where instead we exchanged good for good and service for service. He thought this could provide a solution to mass unemployment, which in a different form we are facing again. He thought we only needed to provide a small amount of monetary and cultural support for these new social forms of organization for them to take off and proliferate. The unemployment insurance that provided this support would no longer be regarded as institutionalized alms, but instead as the start-up capital for enterprises of a qualitatively different sort.

There is currently a debate in Europe about the so-called "third sector." This is a sector that is neither paid work nor housework, but rather consists of "initiatives," or citizen action groups. My proposal for *"citizen work"* is an attempt to expand and develop this sector. The idea would be to make available a basic financing that would make all sorts of initiatives possible. I think this is one of the important alternatives that we should be discussing.

Labor society and its totalizing claims are really a very recent phenomenon if we take the long historical view. For most of history, there was a wealth of alternatives. These new initiatives are in a sense an attempt to open that wealth of alternatives back up. Most of them seem to share two characteristics. They have a strong emphasis on self-initiative; and they are activities in which the ends and products are transparent to the people doing it. There is no reason why this sector couldn't include local networks in which a new kind of exchange relation was developed that made use of some kind of currency equivalent or vouchers. We can imagine a world in which it was possible to say, "If you take care of my children or teach a class, then later, when you're old, you can lay claim to services that you'll need, which will then be important for you." Things like this are already being tried out and thought about; one can imagine a real and enduring exchange system growing out of them. But such a thing would only be possible if the theoretical perspective that supported them became dominant and they were provided with institutionalized material support, that is, something like the *"citizen wage."*

This is also connected to the debate about how to reawaken and enliven civil society. The question there is how to create a space in which political activities initiated from below can reconnect people to a society in a way that makes sense to them. If citizen work really took off, it could precipitate out into all kinds of initiatives and organizations. They could stretch from enterprises that bordered on the real economy – for example, attempts to reform our botched-up energy supply system by building small-scale wind and solar power generators and getting them hooked up to the grid with a decent rate structure; or attempts to develop new forms of education that took real advantage of current computer technologies to deepen and broaden people's educational connections – to political initiatives strictly speaking, like aiding and integrating foreigners. Or rediscovering the history of a town or region in order to bring that history alive, to bring it into contemporary political debates, and perhaps as well to lay the basis for a local tourist economy. And so on. The possibilities are endless. But in order for them to flourish they need a space in which to develop, they need material support, and they need social recognition. Conquering this deep-seated conviction that there are no real alternatives to paid labor is an important step in gaining that social recognition. There are attractive alternatives, a wealth of them. But they need to be recognized in order to exist.

This seems even more necessary because of the false consciousness that still sees unemployment as an individual rather than a collective fate. The longer people are unemployed, the more deeply this interpretation seems to get imprinted. That's the way it is experienced in the framework of individualization, but of course it isn't true. It isn't a personal fate to be unemployed in a time of mass unemployment. This brings us to the question of how these societal transformations are working themselves out at the individual and biographical level.

From the individual perspective, labor society is becoming another form of risk society. Full employment society presented the individual with a set of calculable risks. Flexible work is presenting her with a set of uncertainties. It is not clear to what extent this set-up can provide the secure foundations that an individual existence needs to flourish over the middle or long term. There is the potential that we could pass from risk biographies into biographies that are simply fragmented and that can't be fitted together.

But to go back to your question, it's not only our experience but also the reality of unemployment that has changed. Mass unemployment is no longer experienceable as a collective fate in large part because it isn't mass unemployment in the same way it used to be. It is parceled out and individualized. It is distributed in life-phase portions, as it were. In one way, this represents a kind of democratization, because unemployment now becomes an experience that almost everyone shares at one time or another during her lifetime. But viewed from another aspect, this means that even at the center of society, the unpredictability of each individual life is becoming a permanent problem.

This especially affects the formation of families. The capacity of men and women to work together to raise kids is becoming ever more difficult. It is here that two completely different worlds with opposing imperatives meet and clash. In the labor market, flexibility is preached as if it were the highest virtue. Flexibility means the ability to make ever quicker short-term adjustments to changing economic requirements. But the world of living together is characterized by exactly the opposite imperative. In the experimental culture that now constitutes the world of private relationships, people have to be there for each other. They have to build connections they can depend on, they have to be able to grow together. So the demands of healthy relationships, the demands of parenting, and the needs of children are all in clear contradiction to the ever more insistent demand for labor market flexibility.

It's easy to see what happens. If a single mother who is constantly under the demand to adjust her work schedule so as to be optimally available for the labor market gives in and accepts that she has to turn everything in her life upside down from week to week or month to month, she will inescapably become the stereotype of a bad mother. The rhythms of the market will force her to neglect her children. It will be impossible for her to be a good worker and a good mother.

The contractual, spatial, and temporal flexibilization of work all increases the degree of individualization. While this opens up opportunities, it also increases the danger of atomization. As our lives become more parcelized, as the connections between our activities get broken, work steadily loses its capacity to socialize. In addition, work is becoming more independent of place. A necessary consequence is that work is becoming less and less a place of socialization, where social connections are forged and the commonality of a joint situation are established.

Each of the various ways in which work can be flexibilized – contractually, spatially, and temporally – intensifies the extent to which both work *and* everyday life are becoming permeated by risk.

When we consider all these points, it seems impossible to escape the conclusion that society is fundamentally changing in every one of its parts. To take one example at random, all of this seems to make building societies impossible, because it dissolves all the social arrangements that underlie their cooperative financial arrangements. Building societies take as a precondition something that is now becoming very rare, namely that all its members will have a stable career – that all will continue to labor at the same jobs, which will permit them to pay the monthly installments, and that they will continue pursue these jobs in the same place, where their dearly purchased row houses are permanently located. In fact it was originally assumed that when they came to the end of their days, their eyes would be closed by the people who would inherit their homes and the tradition would continue. But all this completely breaks down under current conditions.

It was a pretty idyll while it lasted though, and it's an excellent illustration of just how deeply the idea of labor society permeates our central symbols of identity, and how much it forms an essential part of what society takes for granted. Full employment in the full sense of the term was considered essential to the ideal of owning your own home, because it was essential to the established mechanism of how homes were financed. The symbol of the family home rested on a real foundation. And that foundation was labor society.

It's not only building societies, by the way. All credit institutions have up until now oriented themselves primarily towards the assumption of full employment. From the viewpoint of social utility, none of them makes sufficient provision for the fact that employment has become so much more variable and uncertain, that someone who is employed today can become unemployed tomorrow, and that long-term financial security isn't on offer in the same way as it once was. One consequence of this is that poverty is beginning to break into the lower-salaried groupings and even the middle strata, in part because they are now often suddenly confronted by the impossibility of paying off their accumulated debts.

In fact, indebtedness is one of the central dimensions of the new poverty. Social workers and whole auxiliary service sectors are now active as debt counselors. The ideal of owning one's own home is still strong. But in our increasingly place-independent existence, people are being forced into all kinds of expedients that are changing its essence, like renting out part of it to strangers, or even utilizing their home as a site of production.

There have been some studies that have shown that many women and mothers who spend a lot of time working at home for pay (and currently it is mostly women and mothers who are in this situation), sitting at computers and doing tasks to deadline, end up losing their sense of time. Their daily rhythms come unstuck. They live in a kind of isolation in which they have to supply their own framework. They find they need to go out in the street simply to experience other people and get back in sync. In a highly networked, highly differentiated, and highly flexibilized global society, it's theoretically possible that we could end up with a mass Robinson Crusoe set of life patterns, in which people were globally networked, but lived insular, self-referential lives whose connections with other people were barely real.

Now I freely admit that this is an extreme example of an incipient and perhaps transitory pattern of existence. I'm not claiming it as representative. Rather it is a perfect illustration of how much social reproduction has hitherto coexisted with production, and how completely it is now possible for the two dimensions to diverge. This is not simply Taylorism, which involves the subdivision of the work process. This is a matter of work contracts, work times, and work places. It opens up whole new ways for corporations to organize themselves and, perhaps we shouldn't say this too loudly, to exploit their workers.

Work was once, you might say, the central business district of labor society. Now this society is fragmenting into destandardized labor, into labor that is individualized into previously unforeseen forms whose consequences we are struggling to comprehend even as they continue to mutate. This is why it is increasingly necessary for society and individuals to establish centers of identity outside work, a fact supported by increasing empirical evidence.

To return to something you said earlier, the problem of not having a job is really only the stalking horse for the more profane problem of not having money. Many if not most people know very well how to employ themselves, and are constantly on the lookout for ways to be useful and active. If it were possible to foster and support these activities through a citizen wage, it would solve a lot of problems while creating a wealth of interlocking possibilities. We would no longer feel ourselves trapped. The conviction that there is no other effective system of organizing large-scale social activity besides paid labor seems confirmed by the lacks and limitations that activities on the far side of paid work now come up against. Conversely, if we developed those possibilities, we could develop our ability both to imagine and to create alternative forms of existence. The possibilities and the reality would reinforce each other. Opening up one will help open up the other.

If we can succeed in changing our conception of what is now supplied as unemployment compensation or welfare so that it is no longer thought of as a form of alms, but rather as a kind of start-up capital that can support experimentation with decommodified forms of existence, a huge victory will have been won. It would then finally be possible for an obvious insight to break through which at the moment seems inconceivable even though it's true: that we have finally reached a stage of historical development where the yoke of work doesn't *need* to be borne by all of us in the same measure. A citizen wage will be able to provide a basic material security, independent of paid labor and financed through taxes, once this insight is broadly acknowledged.

There is a second perspective on this that is also extremely important. Our fixation on paid labor has kept us from fully registering that labor society has always included a lot more than paid labor. Labor society has *always* in reality been plural activity society. There has always been a wealth of other activities, unpaid but necessary, without which paid labor could not exist. Paid labor has the monopoly on meaning (that is, for work to be considered significant, it seems it has to be paid for) and it has the monopoly on the means of existence. But these other activities which are always practiced in tandem with it are often more necessary and more highly valued. They form its necessary background, without which it could not exist, and with which it continually has to be reconciled. I am, of course, referring to housework and family work, child care and parent care, and to the wealth of initiatives, honorary offices, services, and networks that run like back alleys through everyday life, supplying society with essential goods and people with identities.

Therefore the first step in effecting change would simply be to make this social reality conscious of itself. We all know about this wealth of necessary employments that are just as important as paid labor. But how can things be arranged so that they are equally valued? I mean imagine, if we had a four-week strike by industrial workers, we'd survive. There'd be lots of difficulties, but somehow in the end we'd get by. But if we had a four-week strike of parents, that would be a disaster. Children would die.

There has to be a way to put these essential shadow activities on an equal footing with paid labor. And a scheme by which they would qualify as legitimate kinds of citizen work would be one way to do it. Under such a scheme, time spent taking care of elderly parents, for example, would be recognized as socially necessary labor. Time would be made available for it, as it already is now in some places. A system of citizen work could be built out of things just like this. It would lengthen and broaden these exceptions and deepen their recognition. It would make it possible for people to withdraw from the labor market for one, two, or even three or four years, and to receive during that time a basic material security, in order to devote themselves to socially useful activities, including useful to themselves. This would be a true "flexibilization" of labor, one that finally benefited workers, and that increased social integration.

There will at first be real resistance to the idea of paid labor losing its monopoly. It will almost be like withdrawal pains. But like all withdrawal pains, it will mark the end of our dependence on one drug for all our satisfactions, and the beginning of being allowed to branch out into a much greater fullness of activity.

That resistance, however, can be expected to come from very powerful groups. It will come from parties and unions and churches, in short, from all the mass organizations that currently claim the right to organize society. Each of these organizations has its own separate objection to what you've just suggested.

Political parties, for example, especially when they are formed along Christian conservative lines, seem to carry the image of the Christian family before them like a monstrance. The father stands there like a carpenter, the mother like a Madonna, and beneath them the little baby Jesus, who will soon be on his way to his well-known bitter end. Labor union proposals, even when they are for shortening the work week, are always founded on the fundamental postulate of full employment, because that's the situation in which they can best push their demands for higher pay and shorter hours. Meanwhile the position of churches nowadays is that anything is possible, just not too much of it. They agree that work time should be limited, but what they mean is that it shouldn't be allowed on Sunday, because Sunday should be the day of Papa in the family and the family in the church.

So all of society's most powerful organizations will put up considerable resistance against recognizing the changes that you've been describing. It seems true that we can't just continue like this because conflicts are building up as the old system unravels. But what can be done to bring these huge opponents on side?

That's one of the toughest questions. When it comes to these mass organizations, we are dealing with the dinosaurs of the first modernity. They all hold fast to their founding ideas while all around social reality is fleeing them, not least in the form of their membership. They are becoming zombie organizations because they deny realities and anathematize them. Maybe the parties, unions, and churches should just join together and put forth a new form of the demand Brecht once suggested to the DDR government: that society should dissolve itself because it is no longer conforming to the fundamental principles of its leading institutions.

There is only one way to break through this crust of denial and that's enlightenment. All we can do is show these organizations through empirical sociology just how much society has changed from their old conceptions and how they'll be left behind if they don't change too.

Another option is that something similar will happen with them as happened with the old DDR. They could end up crumbling from within. For most of them this is still literally unthinkable. But all outside observers know there's a vacuum at the heart of each of these dinosaur organizations. It only takes some specific event to throw this fact into relief, for example, the way the CDU campaign funding scandal revealed how deeply morbid the system of mass political parties is.

There is also the possibility of revolution from within. That is, the essence of these organizations could be transformed behind their initially unchanging façades. There are incipient signs of this already happening. None of these organizations is really as homogeneous as they present themselves to the world. There are splits and movements in all of them. Part of it is new generations bringing in new orientations. But another is simply that their members are increasingly dying off or staying away. That is actually an important aspect of the campaign funding scandal that was largely neglected. The only reason the parties finally came to acquiesce in the system of state funding was that they had reached a point when member financing was producing structural deficits. Individualization has made it possible for members of all of these dinosaur organizations to vote with their feet. More and more are doing do, and on some level it is registering.

There is in the end no pat answer to this question. We have to try all the possibilities. But there is a precedent for why I think the opening up of labor society will go forward despite such opposition.

I think we can compare the end of normal jobs with the end of the normal family. Then too there was a huge outcry at first, until people gradually realized they were all managing more or less fine amidst this multitude of different kinds of family. Back in the seventies there was a dramatic debate over the pluralization of the family (or the breakdown of the family, as it was called then), as well as over the multiplication of sexualities, the crisis of unmarried couples having babies, etc. It was said that all of this would lead to the decline of the West. Conspiracies were darkly hinted at. But now that's all quieted down. Today

it's generally recognized that the side effects of the pluralization of families fall well within the capacity of society's mass
organizations to absorb them. This view is now dominant even
inside the churches and the CDU. I think it will be similar with
the transition from the monopoly of paid labor to an effective
recognition of the really existing plurality of essential activities.
In both cases, pluralization brings these organizations golden
opportunities for renewal. The more individualized society is,
the more non-family and non-work settings are needed for
social integration.

When these institutions accept the demand that non-
paid-labor activities should be given their due and accepted as
equal in status to paid, "real" jobs, that would be exactly the sort
of institutionalized recognition we seek. Personally, I'm willing
to bet that the political party which first inscribes this program
on its banner and finds a way to express it in acceptable terms
will experience an enormous upsurge in membership. Because
the tension of trying to reconcile work and non-work activities
is a central issue in almost everyone's life. Yet no one has been
able to organize around it because it remains unnamed, even as
we all suffer from its effects. It's not just unemployment that's
worrying people. We are all attempting to integrate the very
different activities that make up our lives. We all desire to win
more time for the ones we cherish most. We want flexibilization for the people, as it were.

As I see it, the path forward is to seize on already existing
initiatives, which are enjoyable and productive in their own
right, and build on those which can bear expansion and development until they expand wide enough to present a competing
perspective to the idea that everything is supposed to revolve
around our jobs.

*It's not only the individual content of work that is changing away
from the assumption of lifetime careers, away from the idea of a
calling. It's also the social form of work that's changing in the shape
of the firm. Are there still firms today in the same sense that term
was originally used? Aren't they too dissolving?*

Here once again we're talking about one of the central unities
of the first modernity being put in question. The original justification of the firm is the same as that of the factory. It's that

benefits flow from uniting cooperation and production in one place. Originally it was the only way that complex cooperation was possible. In order to get the firm's product or service to market, people had to be gathered together, and they had to enter more or less into a community with machines.

The factory building stands at the center of the first modernity. The factory was the cauldron in which immiseration was perceived as a collective experience and class destiny was forged out of it. Now, however, this territorial unity of work and production is being dissolved by the new technology and the new economy. Information technology makes it possible to have digital capitalism. We can have direct social cooperation without geographic proximity. Digital networks can connect departments that are spread across continents as closely as those that are concentrated in one place.

So now there's a choice where once there was a given. It's impossible to introduce this geometrically new kind of space, this space without distance, and not have it have an effect on the shape of the firm.

We of course know that there has to be a network of people to parallel these networks of information, that people have to see each other face to face in various places and various times. There have to be meeting places where people can make personal contact in order to clean up the problems that are created by deterritorialized cooperation. Nevertheless, the concrete location is losing its original meaning as the place that unifies the organization of *production* with cooperation. Meeting places can be located far from production.

A second important development is that the internal and external relations that are supposed to define the firm are getting blurred. The classical model of the firm is that hierarchy reigns within and the market without. Today this model is getting inverted by remaking what were once internal departments into stand-alone units, so that competition and market relations more and more characterize the internal relations between parts of the enterprise. Flat organizational forms also contribute to blurring this division.

These two processes taken together not only undermine the unity of the firm but push it towards an organizational metamorphosis. First you have the *deterritorialization of cooperation*, the possibility of organizing cooperation across great distances as if they weren't there, and therefore of dispersing departments geographically and organizing production according to completely new logics. Then in addition you have the *internalization of markets*, the possibility of making subdepartments into independent units so that they are able to enter into market relations with each other. Taken together, this gives us a new system of production.

The nation-state model of the first modernity rested on the territorial unity of production and cooperation. The second modernity "rests" on these new kinds of deterritorialized unities that are still just beginning to emerge. Now that it is no longer necessary for the economic project to be spatially fixed, perhaps it can truly begin to be conceived and organized in terms that span borders. Perhaps it can become transnational as thoroughly as it is becoming trans-sectoral.

We can already see at the level of the firm how this new form of organization introduces a greater flexibility, as projects which are time-dependent, or which need to be modified quickly and in accord with changing demand, can be quickly dismantled and reorganized. The "firm" thus begins to exemplify a fluid organizational structure. It not only abolishes the distance between continents (so that people can work together on a real-time basis with others thousands of miles away) but it also makes possible a functional reorganization so that one person can be active on several different projects in several different places at the same time. In a sense, it allows people to be in more than one place at one time, to be in several different times and places and projects simultaneously. This is the basis for a truly transnational integration.

So there are many possibilities for qualitatively new developments. However, the flipside is that most of our economic knowledge, both as concepts and statistics, is based on the firm just as much as our social knowledge and statistics are based on the family. The unity of the firm is still one of the taken-for-granted foundations of economic thought.

One of the biggest problems with economic statistics today is that they continue to measure everything in terms of the nation-state. Even flows are still framed in terms of place location. And even those who are attempting to draw conclusions about how work and the economy are changing find themselves forced into these old categories of reality. It is a typical chicken and egg problem we find at the beginning of every paradigm change. In order to make an empirical case that a categorical structure is changing, we need data. But the data we really need can only be collected on a convincing scale once large segments of the scientific community are convinced that a categorical change has taken place.

The time-honored macro units of economic analysis, like the national trade deficit and measures of capital flows, take on a completely different meaning when we recognize that world trade is being carried on in large part as *intrafirm trade*. What the national economic perspective falsely registers as the statistics of international world trade, the cosmopolitan perspective uncovers as trade taking place within transnational global corporations. More and more goods and services that cross borders between countries are not in any real sense being bought and sold. They are rather being moved between nominally independent units and branches of the same firm on the basis of internal decisions made by that firm's management. Already in the 1980s it was being estimated that around 80 percent of so-called US imports were actually intrafirm trade. The World Bank estimated that by the beginning of the 1980s 40 percent of all global trade was taking place within transnational corporations.

At the moment we simply don't have a more exact statistic than this hermaphroditic category that combines international trade with intrafirm non-trade. So it's not only in sociology that we are forced by methodological nationalism to tabulate the wrong flyspecks at great expense. It's true everywhere you look. National statistical categories falsify an increasingly cosmopolitan reality. Frozen categories of thought make it impossible to measure how reality is changing.

Here again we see how the transition from the first to the second modernity is taking place on both a macro and a micro level simultaneously. The basic assumptions underlying the organization and control of labor – the concepts and realities of the economy, firm, and market – are all dissolving into something else right in front of us. The process is hard to follow without new categories, but no one knows which categories will finally turn out to be appropriate.

Does this mean that the hierarchical structure that has marked work in the firm since the beginning – the division between masters, skilled, and unskilled labor – is also dissolving? Because now every-one who is active on an economic project is often a kind of sub-entrepreneur, working on his or her own responsibility. Personal responsibility seems to be replacing close supervision as the main guarantee of the quality of the product or service eventually pro-vided to the market.

That's been pretty well documented. Although a more precise way to put it might be to say that alien control is turning into self-control. Subordinate entrepreneurs have to program them-selves, they have to internalize the market's and the firm's demands. Exploitation becomes self-exploitation.

But truthfully this can only go so far. You can't have a firm in the end without there being at least some hierarchy. For years now, people have been championing the de-hierarchized model of business organization as if it were the latest modern dis-covery. The truth is that the world of business fads reflects the reality of business contradictions. For every new model of orga-nization, there is a counter-tendency. For all the talk of empow-erment, there will always have to be restrictions that constrain people. The result is that in trying to rationalize firms accord-ing to these new fluid models, the management class is becom-ing more and more internally contradictory.

On the one hand, management is making its members more and more autonomous through this creation of subentrepre-neurs who can do everything a lot better by themselves than their chiefs can spell it out for them. This is especially true when it comes to knowledge-based industries, where upper-level managers are increasingly incapable of controlling all aspects of an ever more complex reality. On the other hand, it's still their job as upper-level managers to have everything under con-trol. So they have to build in new instruments of control (or at least façades of control, that is, superfluous restrictions) in order to show how important managers like themselves are. Otherwise it would become obvious that their positions were superfluous.

So there is a fundamental tension between differentiation and control. The role conflict of management becomes even more prominent under the neoliberal credo of shareholder value, when boards of directors and shareholders are completely transfixed by the movements of the company's stock price.

True firm rationalizers would be like capitalist Gorbachevs. They would be unwinding the system they were presiding over. The same is true of neoliberals. If they really carried out their ideas, they would become self-executioners. Instead what we end up with is a deeply contradictory process. On the one hand, they are presiding over an unwinding, and on the other, they are trying to build a new dictatorship that can work in the second modernity. They are trying to construct something that will make fluidity controllable again.

Information technology has played and will continue to play a decisive role in both developments. Computer networks in firms make it possible to control action down to the last detail. They also allow a quantum leap in integration because now every individual act in the firm can be instantly visible even to people on the other side of the globe. So this same technology gives the individual parts of the firm, and individuals themselves, the capacity to work more autonomously. The dissolution of place-dependent relations makes it possible to replace hierarchy with self-integration, but this process is going in two very different directions at the same time. And interfering with both developments is the tendency of the flood of information to swamp us in noise.

What kind of practical compromise will grow out of these opposing tendencies is not yet clear. What is clear is that the ideal of perfectible standardization, the Taylorist or Fordist ideal that there is one right way to do everything, these ideals of the first modernity are fading away. The mere multiplication of organizational possibilities seems to be ensuring that.

This brings us back to management fads. One consequence of this wealth of organizational possibilities is that in what is supposed to be the theoretical center of rational action, *rationality is being replaced by fashion.* Today everyone thinks big is beautiful, and tomorrow it's the opposite. Suddenly conglomerates are dinosaurs and everyone wants to be small and nimble. Organizational and management fads rule the executive suites like spring and fall collections, determining what's chic and what's not. And walking the runways like models displaying the latest organizational styles are management consultants.

Of course maybe there's hope in that. Maybe neoliberalism is now the latest fashion but just around the corner we'll see the opposite being propounded and then pushed through.

This picture you describe of centrifugal and centripetal forces certainly seems true when you look at the business world from the outside. On the one hand we've had this huge merger wave that's led to ever more gigantic, and more truly world, corporations. On the other hand we've had a parallel splintering of corporations into subsidiaries that are listed independently on the stock market.

If we tried to sum up our entire argument in an abstract picture it would be something like this. On the one side is the tendency towards globalization which, if carried to its logical conclusion, would ultimately lead to one world firm in the same way it's led to one world market. But this abstract tendency towards globalization (which, when abstracted this far, should probably be called totalization) sets off a parallel process of individualization. People are on the one hand assembled in larger and larger unities, while on the other hand they are ever more thoroughly particularized.

It's at this point that the standard charge leveled against me, that my scenarios of the second modernity are one-sidedly optimistic, just leaves me speechless. The key question I keep coming back to strikes me as extremely daunting, namely how can we create a cosmopolitan form of authority? In addition to keeping order and facilitating negotiation, it will have to be something that is capable of overcoming the private-market protectionism of transnational corporations that are currently institutionalizing the world market to suit their convenience. It will have to be something capable of enforcing regulation on these corporations for the general good against their will. And to make it work, we will in addition have to find some way to create a cosmopolitan economic science. It will have to be an economics that not only takes a global framework as its starting point, but which will be capable of thinking reflexively about the long-term effects of global capitalism. And then we need somehow to incorporate that reflexivity into the core rationality of economic actors. If that's one-sidedly optimistic – well, like I said, I'm speechless.

Conversation 5

Cosmopolitan Society and its Enemies

JOHANNES WILLMS   *Okay, now we'll complete the five horsemen of the apocalypse by taking a look at globalization. I'd like to look at it both in detail and as a whole. What is the essence of this buzz-word and bogeyman that everybody's talking about?*

ULRICH BECK   Often it's less of a word than a fog of meaning. To start with, the meaning of globalization is routinely distorted by a number of elementary misunderstandings that we have already elaborated on. (See p. 56 and p. 58.) Then on top of that it is often treated as if it were a spectre stalking us. Neither the misunderstandings nor the demonization are accidental. It is very important to keep in mind a point we made earlier, which is that many social agents are holding to these misunderstandings on purpose. They want to lead sham battles in order to avoid dealing with the real phenomenon.

The first theoretical problem is that globalization doesn't always mean what it's supposed to mean. It often means *localization*. In a world that is becoming more and more global, a world in which the old coordinates and borders are being overthrown, locality is assuming a new meaning and importance that is central to the whole process. This dialectical understanding of globalization as an interaction between global and local changes has been referred to by some writers as *glocalization*.

Secondly, globalization doesn't only mean that borders are being dissolved. It also means that new ones are being drawn and fortified. It's possible for the super-rich and the very poor to live right next to each other, separated only by narrow security corridors. The result is that both Africa and Europe are becoming so to speak dis-placed. What we are getting more and more instead is a hermaphroditic combination of city and anti-city, of Africa and Europe in the same place.

It is necessary to remember that globalization doesn't just happen by itself. It takes lots of work on the part of the globalizers. This globalization work takes place in specific localities, like the big cities of the metropoles. Here glocalization results in a distinctive 24/7 temporal rhythm, as we can already see in the financial markets. In the land of the globalizers, the sun never sets.

Globalization work presupposes all kinds of local work, especially local services, from the barber to the cleaning and security staffs up through the legal and financial advisers. They all need to be continuously available. As a consequence, a whole network of specialized local activity has come into existence in these places.

The work "place" is gaining a new meaning not only within the firm, as we discussed earlier (see p. 170ff.), but also outside it in the localities that serve as cultural centers, as political centers, and as privileged places where people meet and talk. This last function is becoming more and more important as the world slides more and more completely into abstraction. These globalized globalizers who make globalization possible have to put their feet down somewhere.

So globalization not only de-places but re-places. By superimposing place on place, it creates a new kind of place. And the result is – or should be – a new sociology of place.

Locality must be rediscovered, but not – and this is the next common misunderstanding – in its old form. The old structure of locality was to be encapsulated. Its new form is to exist as a set of superimposed nodes of multiple global networks. The first organizations to understand what needs to be supplied in order to foster such network nodes and make them interesting for people to live and work there gain a leg up on the competition.

There is a way in which globalization pushes all of us and makes us feel inadequate. When the whole world is our background, the always relatively narrow world in which we live seems provincial, and we feel culpable if we don't give ourselves a shove to learn more about what is going on and looming threateningly beyond our borders. So on the one hand, there is no returning to the isolated, homogeneous communities of the past, to societies closed off to the outside. But on the other hand, most of us don't want to. Most of us want *more* opening up.

We also all know that it is only in nostalgic idealizations that localities were ever isolated and complete in themselves. We should now draw out the implication of that realization. It is not an idle fancy that concrete local places can be opened up to the world from the inside. *They always were.* It was always an inadequate simplification to think of them as isolated or separated off. What we are talking about is a matter of a degree, an increase in that openness and a consciousness of it. We need to realize that even if we are high fliers, our fundamental experience of globalization is local. It's a new kind of local experience, although it's not one that should be idealized either. It's a global experience at the same time as it's a local experience.

Another variant of this misunderstanding is the presumption that the national can remain the national under these conditions. What really happens is that everything national is being globalized from within. An internalized globalization is taking place.

The basic idea that nation-states are *containers*, which up until now has governed all our social and political thinking, is false. The revolutions that are sneaking up on us are doing so inside rather than outside these "containers." We've already talked about the banal cosmopolitanism of products, services, and cultural cross-currents. (See p. 36ff.) If you look closely at any contemporary attempt to label some object as national you will quickly understand how mad the idea has become. The London taxi, for example, one of the archetypal symbols of Britishness, is now made in Singapore. Even that's a gross understatement, because no one really knows anymore where all the component parts come from or where they were assembled. That basic fact, that no one knows where they really come from, is now the rule rather than the exception in almost all questions of property, identity, and origin. So the question of what country this belongs to is literally impossible to answer. The firms that have continued to hoist the national flag over their sales campaigns have almost all been cosmopolitanized from within in both their property relations and their relations of production.

What appears to be national, and is described as such, is increasingly transnational or cosmopolitan in reality. For the purposes of sociology, one must carefully distinguish between the *forms of national appearance* (and their statistical fabrication into "social reality") and the *cosmopolitan reality* of capital flows, cultural flows, etc. The fundamental postulate of methodological nationalism, that everything which occurs within the confines of the nation-state can be understood in terms of a national causality, is being continually falsified by this cosmopolitanization from within.

The same thing is happening at the level of the individual biography. Anyone who assumes that native Bavarian speakers and dark-skinned people are mutually exclusive sets are setting themselves up for a rude and embarrassing shock. The old, simple logic of territorial identity, in which a person's birthplace, nationality, mother tongue, and passport could be deduced by looking and listening to him simply doesn't hold anymore.

So it is not an overstatement to say that people today live internationally. They love internationally, marry internationally, and raise their children internationally. Their children speak several languages, and feel themselves comfortably at home in the nowhere of the internet and television. The old idea of nation-states as closed-off social spaces, in which more or less homogeneous collectivities do politics, manage their affairs, are made docile enough to pay their taxes, and occasionally get stirred up enough to sally across their borders to kill the people on the other side – this idea is dissolving from the inside out.

Preliminarily, this is what the heuristic concept of cosmopolitan society stands for: for an existential experience in which all the prerequisites for leading our lives, from nutrition to production, along with their attendant fears and satisfactions, exist globally rather than nationally, whether in the shape of food chains, capital flows, economic or ecological catastrophes, or the Esperanto of pop music. The key question for sociology thus becomes how this transnational space of experience interacts with the national space of experience. To what extent does one dissolve the other? To what extent are the two superimposed on each other? And to what extent are qualitatively new phenomena being obscured because they are construed according to older legal and organizational forms? And older forms of consciousness? Each of these basic questions contains enormous problems for empirical research.

Unfortunately, even where sociology has grasped the importance of globalization, it has usually failed to frame these questions correctly. In the first place, globalization is usually simply thought of as additive. Theorists assume society continues to be organized into nation-states just like before and that globalization is something tacked onto the outside. It's additive rather than substitutive. This means that despite all the dazzling talk of change, globalization is still being treated conceptually as something that happens outside the nation-state rather than as something inducing substantial change within. Because if we can still continue to practice the same old nation-state sociology, then by definition, nothing substantial has changed.

A second and more subtle version of this approach conceives of globalization in terms of what several leading English writers have called *interconnectedness*. Here globalization is conceived of as an increase in the entanglement and interdependence of nation-states. This argument can be developed in very subtle directions, by saying that the thickness, intensity, depth, and speed of this entanglement process is growing, and that it can be observed in culture, information, science, economics, military security, and so forth. To my mind, the finest example of this approach is the book by David Held and his colleagues, *Global Transformations*. I think this is the most sophisticated attempt to conceive of globalization as internationalization, as an increase in international entanglement. But this idea of "interconnectedness" still posits the nation-state as society's container. It does not in the end overcome the methodological nationalism that has up until now governed both sociology and politics.

The third approach is what I've been talking about here and trying to work out in my last few books, namely *cosmopolitanization*. I don't mean the term in its intellectual history sense, which has often with justification been mocked as a bunch of intellectuals talking about what they'd like to have happen. I'm interested in cosmopolitanization as an *empirical hypothesis*, as an attempt to open up the structural analyses of sociology to globalization and the second modernity.

Marx wanted to attain two things simultaneously with his concept of class society. On the one hand, he wanted to produce a theoretically informed description of society. But at the same time he claimed to have revealed the central political dynamic of society, the central political conflict. Cosmopolitanization likewise claims to be both things simultaneously. The concept of "cosmopolitan society" pushes us into a new framework of description and asserts a new dynamic of political conflict. To paraphrase, he who speaks of cosmopolitan society speaks of cosmopolitan society *and its "enemies."*

"Cosmopolitanization" is a weird word. It immediately conjures up the "cosmopolitan," that outsider figure who was traditionally mocked or cursed as a wandering tradesman without a homeland to be loyal to. And the Nazis consistently attached the label "cosmopolitan" to every group they eventually planned to exterminate in the gas chambers, from Jews to gypsies to communists.

You of course mean almost the opposite. What you mean by cosmopolitanization is an internal change in the nature of nation-state. You see every nation turning into a microcosm of world society, and not only at the level of the nation, but also at the level of the region, the locality, the metropoles, and even the bedroom, where catastrophes from all over the world march in and out via the TV. So what is gained by choosing a term that has so much historical baggage?

Interestingly, as soon as you leave the so-called West for the so-called periphery, you get hit with exactly the opposite accusation (and I speak from experience), that the term is too euphemistic. In these countries, the term "cosmopolitanism" is often looked at askance because it is connected in people's minds with the era when bourgeois capitalism unfolded the colonial expansion of its power. For them, cosmopolitanism is strongly associated with the western intellectuals of the past who championed that colonization. And we who use it today are accused of following in that tradition by forging terms that prettify the naked power of global capital.

Such strong resistance from such widely separated quarters should force us to carefully re-examine the intellectual history of this concept. And at first sight it does seem odd that we are using a term which last experienced an apogee in the eighteenth century. Why are we are using a word that was big before nation-states arose to describe a key feature of the second modernity?

During the Enlightenment, European intellectuals heatedly fought over what today would be called two "buzzwords": "citizen of the world" and "cosmopolitanism." Both terms were always discussed in relation to the then still nascent nationalism. What we need to do now is what Walter Benjamin called a "saving critique" of the Enlightenment's distinction between nationalism and cosmopolitanism so we usefully can apply it to twenty-first-century reality.

First off, it's important to emphasize again that there is a crucial difference between cosmopolitanization and *globalism*. (See p. 56 and p. 58.) Cosmopolitanization stands for the recognition of multiplicity and globalism stands for its negation. This is the kernel of what needs to be saved and what needs to be changed in the Enlightenment concept of cosmopolitanism.

To be useful for our purposes, the Enlightenment concept of cosmopolitanism has to be freed from its origins in imperial universalism, such as we find in Kant and many others. It has to be opened up to the recognition of multiplicity. It has to become the core of the concept.

To do this, cosmopolitanism has to lose its fixation on the purely global and be redirected to the interconnection between the global and the local. It has to be pulled down from the heavens of the love of humanity and related to the new meaning of locality. The opposition between cosmopolitans and locals that people reach for so quickly is only an apparent one. It must be overcome through a cosmopolitan ethic, an ethic of localities that are open to the world, the ethic of glocalization. (See also pp. 199–200.)

Kant once said that man was the "crooked timber" out of which human institutions must be built. This picture of humanity as crooked timber, whose beautifully stubborn kinks should not be planed flat (that would be globalism!) but rather preserved, is the foundation for the counter-ideal of *rooted cosmopolitanism*, of a cosmopolitanism that puts down roots in real localities. Our goal should not be to cut everything to the same height, and not to build superstructures and super-institutions that would regulate everything the same way. Our goal is not to keep everything under surveillance and control and normalize everything. *Rather it is exactly in the macro-sphere that we should seek greater independence of the parts.* There isn't *a* capitalism, and we shouldn't be striving for *a* modern way of life (which would quickly become the American way of life). Rather we should seek to foster *many possible capitalisms* and *divergent modernities*.

Pursuing this ideal means opening our eyes and sensitizing ourselves to the uniquenesses of different cultures, characters, and historical landscapes, and concentrating especially on those which point towards local paths to different cosmopolitan futures. If the idea of cosmopolitanism truly comes into its own, we will start talking about cosmopolitanisms in the plural rather than cosmopolitanism in the singular. We have to search out the roots of Islamic cosmopolitanism, Jewish cosmopolitanism, Chinese and African cosmopolitanism, etc. That is the only sound basis on which to build.

A separate but equally important aspect of rooted cosmopolitanism is that it involves the consciousness of crisis, the consciousness of a collectively shared future that is collectively endangered. This is variously expressed in terms of a crisis of the cosmos (that is, of nature), of the polis (that is, of politics), or of western rationality itself. We discussed these various dimensions of global risk society earlier. (See chapter 3.) What is significant about the consciousness of crisis is that it is a consciousness defined by the future. Unlike nation-state society, which is integrated by its shared past, the cosmopolitan society that is coming into being is being integrated in terms of its *endangered future*. If cosmopolitan society is to have a tradition, it will be the *tradition of the future*. Which many would say is an exceptionally fragile future: the future of there possibly not being one.

An important line of inquiry concerns whether there are limits to the cosmopolitanization of national societies. On the one hand, the national space of experience has been denationalized; it has been overlaid by cosmopolitan experiences. On the other hand, social life is still bound into the same national institutions as before regarding education, money, political rights, and language; most institutions of the public sphere; and who is defined as society's enemy. In all these crucial ways, what might be at bottom a cosmopolitan microcosm is still perceived and experienced through the filter of the nation-state. The relation between national structures and transnational realities is thus full of contradiction and contingency.

It is easy to go wrong here in two different directions. In one direction looms the cosmopolitan error, and in the other the national one. The *cosmopolitan error* is to act as though every-thing I've described as "cosmopolitanization" can be directly extrapolated into consciousness and action. In other words, to start from the assumption that this *globalization from within* of nations automatically leads to cosmopolitan sensibilities in people. Looked at realistically, the opposite, the resurgence of national reflexes, is a more probable first reaction. But despite that, everything we've said still remains true. Many crucial things that occur in national space can't be explained in national terms or even really properly located there. There is a split between reality and perception. But because of those appear-ances, and because of nationalist counter-reaction, breaking out of this *national error* is not only difficult, it may be becoming harder.

So how can we examine this idea in empirical terms?

First we have to distinguish variables that can answer the ques-tion to what extent and in what manner national societies are being globalized from within. If we can accomplish that, we can then wrestle with the theoretical question of to what extent cosmopolitanization *in itself* has become cosmopolitanization *for itself*. To what extent it has become reflexive and a political force in society? And lastly, there is the political question of how this tendency can be encouraged.

Our empirical task starts out, as always, by asking basic questions like those examined by Elisabeth Beck-Gernsheim in her book, *Jews, Germans and Other Landscapes of Memory*. For example, how many people marry foreigners? How does Germany compare with France, Great Britain, etc. in this dimension? Which nationalities do they marry? How many children are growing up in a bilingual environment? How many languages are spoken? Then we can move onto higher-level questions like how high is the proportion of the working popu-lation that can be seen as actual or potential winners or losers from globalization? How do they see their situation themselves? Is it true that there are a lot of middle-class professional groups whose jobs haven't been visibly touched by globalization because of the way they are bound up in national peculiarities? So how do they see their future? Do they fear a change might come that will undermine their jobs? Or are they excited because they think globalization is expanding their economic prospects? And what is the reality behind these perceptions?

Another set of questions concerns the extent to which cultural programs and products are being exchanged. What is the proportion of foreign content on TV, on the radio, in the bookstores, etc. in different countries? This of course involves us in the fundamental conceptual problem of how to define "foreign," which is just as hard as defining "national." We can also investigate how telephone conversations are distributed between domestic and foreign calls, and at what rate that distribution is changing. Similar questions can also be examined in connection with tourism. The Germans, as we know, are world champion tourists.

Last but not at all least, we can examine how multicultured or ethnically homogeneous the membership and leadership of each of society's central institutions has become. I'm referring here to central, everyday institutions like the police, the political parties, the schools, the universities, the court systems, and the governments. Ethnically speaking, are they the same as they have ever been with just some surface token changes, or have they really changed their composition? Are they approaching the model of the French national soccer team that won the world cup? Or are most spheres still dominated by one ethnic nationality?

Of course, someone could still say, after we've collected all this data, "Well fine, but what does it matter if Germans travel to a lot of foreign countries, or if the frequency of long-distance calls and international flights is growing exponentially?" Internally, people might be staying the same or even closing themselves off more resolutely than before. The information we have on these data questions is really not bad. We can eventually work out a pretty fair picture of reality. But getting from there to the larger question of what it really means is much trickier. We have to be very careful not to interpret all these changes as if they signified an immediate change of consciousness in a cosmopolitan direction.

So after doing the hard work of determining empirical reality, we then have to do the harder work investigating empirical consciousness. We have to investigate dispositions. To what extent are new cosmopolitan sensibilities and willingnesses in fact coming into being? Is there a growing demand to break out of the monogamy of locality that was the norm when society was territorially fastened down? Many people fall in love with foreign cultures and end up deeply involved with more than one culture or locality at a time. How large a proportion of the population do they represent? And is there an impulsion to defend this attachment as an important part of their identities? Does it change the political debate? Or conversely, is globalization from within mostly seen as a threatening spectre? And if, as is likely, we find that both reactions coexist, what does their mixture look like? How do they inter-react, and how are they trending? In short, how is society reacting, in its self-understanding, in its public debates, and in its institutions?

We want to investigate the degree of cosmopolitanization in all social contexts, from universities to primary schools. Only then can we truly answer the question of whether an underground or background transformation of national experience is really taking place, and address the relation of this new reality to consciousness. And then we can finally ask whether a national frame of reference and experience is being replaced with a cosmopolitan one, or whether the two will continue to be combined in a contradictory reality. Or whether one will target the other as the enemy with explosive results.

In sum, having identified this creeping cosmopolitanization from within, we have to produce frameworks that will allow us to measure how significant it is, and a conceptual terminology that will allow us to accurately describe to what extent it is reflected in the behavior and self-consciousness of people. This is something that has to be investigated separately for each aspect of society, for the economy, for politics, and for the military.

Can you give an example of creeping cosmopolitanization in one of these subsectors?

Perhaps this would be a good time to take a look at a social actor whose "cosmopolitan renewal" has been viewed mostly so far (and for good reasons) with distrust. I'm referring here to the military, and especially to NATO. In Europe today (although also to a surprising extent in the USA) military policy makers have brought about a curious situation in which the institution that most perfectly embodies the ideal of national sovereignty

– national security, the holiest of holies – is becoming transnational in its essential core, in both its internal organization and the tasks it carries out.

In both the composition of its personnel and in its hierarchy of command, the NATO bureaucracy no longer reflects the will of a single nation, not even that of the dominating USA. Decisions about weapons systems and about strategy and tactics are no longer made nationally, but rather transnationally. What I find interesting is the way the transnationalization of weapons production (including tanks, fighters, air transport planes, and information systems) has transformed what was once the most vehemently defended premise of national autarky and made it almost completely into its opposite with so little opposition.

European security and military power are today attainable only through international cooperation. National security is still the end being ultimately served, but the path to attain it long ago passed through its partial suspension and subsumption into a larger cooperative enterprise.

In terms of personnel, NATO's upper echelon has already completely succumbed to the multicultural virus. Most missions are now miniature multinational societies, in which officers and troops from all member countries mix and cooperate even more than in multinational corporations. Large-scale military exercises have become transnational not only in their means but also in their ends. The main objective of most such exercises is to "improve international military coordination and integration," in other words, to foster military transnationalization.

The French withdrawal from NATO in 1964, which was intended to demonstrate and preserve the sovereignty of *la Grande Nation*, ended up in many ways demonstrating the opposite. The only thing that has allowed the clever French to pretend otherwise for so long is that they've managed to turn "strategic consultation" into a functional substitute for membership. The recent Kosovo war displayed how even in the ultimate case of military command, the declaration of war and peace, such a "sovereign" decision can now be made at the new transnational level rather than at the national one.

Kosovo is an interesting case in many ways. I don't mean to downplay the NATO generals' new-found love of human rights, but the absence of the Warsaw Pact has obviously weighed on them heavily. It's an absence as threatening as an enemy. It threatens their jobs and their status. Nevertheless, their decision in this situation to suddenly stop the nationalist rhetoric and start posing as cosmopolitans was remarkable. Although sometimes you can still see the effort it takes the old veterans to swallow their first reaction when they see themselves forced to do international social work.

One thing I find interesting about the military sphere is that it highlights just how short the national phase of social organization has really been when placed in historical perspective. The idea that armies should be national, in the sense of ethnically homogeneous, is something that could never even have been considered by the empire builders of the past. All the great world conquests of western history, from Caesar to Napoleon, were only possible on the basis of multiethnic armies. Empires could only be erected and secured by employing states from beyond one's original borders. In fact, the willingness of Rome to open up its citizenship to an ever increasing circle of military recruits was a major factor in making its victories possible.

When you take this long view of military history, it's not immediately apparent how we managed this transition. Multicultural armies have been history's rule. How did we get to the modern exception, where the ideas of an ethnically homogeneous nation, state, and national army not only dominate our military thinking but seem like unchangeable facts of nature? Against this historical background, the question we really have to ask is what made homogeneous national armies possible. What conditions were necessary for it to occur? And if those conditions no longer obtain, perhaps we should not be surprised if our armies start to revert to the historical rule.

Secondly, we should also keep this historical background in mind when we hear about the army's new "cosmopolitan mission" in a post-national, multiethnic world, or its conversion into the knighthood of a new crusade. Multiethnicity was never incompatible with empire. And the original crusades were not models of tolerance.

So there are good reasons why the transition we are facing in Germany today, from a national duty to serve, to a professional army oriented towards international "peacekeeping missions" – a phrase that would have made Orwell smile – is regarded with ambivalence. This critical attitude is good, and it is the attitude we should take in general towards cosmopolitanization. Cosmopolitanization is not a scenario where everything becomes good. Rather it throws up entirely new kinds of risk. And one of them is the risk that the very concept of "cosmopolitan society" might offer an effective ideological legitimation for the imperial powers of capital and the military.

One of the most influential analyses of the middle class today is that of Pierre Bourdieu. He maintains that there is a fraction of the new middle class that acts as a cultural intermediary for society in the sense that it brokers the advent of new ideas. But the motives that impel these cultural vanguardists are their passions for autonomy, innovation, and fashion. Now if his analysis holds for ideas just as it does for other fashions – if these are the motivations which ultimately determine what passes for a sense of social justice, or what constitutes an imminent threat to the system – isn't it possible that cosmopolitanism might end up just being treated as the latest theoretical fad and then cast aside?

Sure it's possible. Cosmopolitanism could end up being another new idea that had its day and passed, an intellectual pose people adopted and then discarded. But it's important to recognize that the challenges it is responding to are real and will endure. The problems posed by the second modernity are not just an intellectual game. Somehow they have to be solved, and as far as I am concerned, the intellectual component of those solutions will have to take us beyond the nation-state in our thinking. And any attempt to go beyond the nation-state, when every social concept is so closely and surreptitiously bound to it, will always set off counter-reactions and attempts to discredit it. Accusations of "faddishness" will always be part of that.

The bottom line is that while I have no idea whether the word "cosmopolitanism" will survive, I am sure there will sooner or later have to be an intellectual movement that tries to define post-national constellations in new sociological and political terms. A new school of thought has to confront how the new background conditions of the second modernity – the transnational flows of capital, culture, and information – are changing and ultimately transforming the boundaries of container societies, and the lives and identities of the people who are no longer contained within them.

Weber famously defined the state in terms of the monopoly of the means of legitimate violence within a given territory. What is the place of legitimate violence in post-territorial states and societies?

That gets right to the point of what's changed. In cosmopolitan constellations the threat of force is no longer the foundation of sovereignty, as it was for Weber. Empirical examination shows you this clearly. Who has the monopoly over legitimate violence within Bavaria? That is to say, who decides when Bavarian troops go to war? Is it the state of Bavaria? The German Federal state? The European Union? NATO? The US government? The United Nations Security Council? We have already left the world of unambiguous military sovereignty. Instead we now live in a situation of ambiguous overlap. In addition, we now have to consider the possibility of post-national wars, as Mary Kaldor does, and quasi-wars, which of course include terrorism. If on top of that we consider the enormous destructive potential represented by bio- and nano-technology, we might even be looking at the individualization of war.

It seems as if in order to really assimilate this new logic of risks, we will have to construct a series of worst-case scenarios and give them some serious and dispassionate evaluation. Otherwise we will be in danger of committing naïve mistakes, on the one hand, or of making ourselves unnecessarily hysterical, on the other.

The unintended side effects of cosmopolitanization have to be thought through systematically, just like everything else in this age of unintended side effects.

Applying the theory of cosmopolitan society does not mean seeing the world through rose-colored glasses. Applying a cosmopolitan perspective means using a new theoretical apparatus to throw some light into the corners of supposedly closed nation-states in order to illuminate how and where transnational nodes and networks are already in there developing. We need a language that can describe clearly how localities are no longer just localities, but instead have a dual nature. How they are simultaneously a territory *and* a deterritorialized zone where transnational and globalized networks overlap.

This is what my concept of cosmopolitanization is directed towards, towards unearthing and unraveling the secrets of this *inner* world society, this *internalized globalization*. I personally think Friedrich Nietzsche was getting at something very similar in his very subtle discussion of the "Age of Comparison." He argued that globalization (for which he used various different terms) was not mainly about big events taking place external to us and far away. Rather globalization was something that took place locally, in the microcosm of our own lives. Furthermore, he argued, this life of distant-but-near others would demand a hitherto unknown degree of tolerance, because the oppositions we would now have to bear were oppositions of a fundamentally new type. Intellectually and socially, they have a completely new kind of explosive potential. When society was dealing with external enemies, that naturally produced internal unity. But now the problem is the coexistence of what some writers have called *contradictory certainties*. These are certainties that exist simultaneously and yet which are mutually exclusive. By the logic of non-contradiction, it seems impossible even to bring them into relation, never mind to bridge them. And yet society and individuals somehow must.

Globalization as you describe it seems Janus-faced. On the one side there's this open, friendly, all-affirming side, which you've identified with cosmopolitanization. Then on the other side there's this hateful face of globalism. Can the two faces be separated? Can we say one is a misunderstanding and the other is the truth?

No, I don't think the good and bad sides of globalization can ever be cleanly separated like that. But I do think we can make a clear distinction between cosmopolitanization and globalism, and it's important that we do so.

Globalism is the ideology that the world market ought to rule. (See p. 56 and p. 58.) It is the world view that corresponds with neoliberal policy. It equates globalization one-dimensionally with economic globalization precisely because it is trying make the compressed argument that all aspects of social existence should be placed under the diktat of the world market.

So all this talk about the world market is really a political strategy in disguise. What globalism is really about is specific groups and organizations carrying out a specific political program that furthers their particular interests under the aegis of the world market.

Now, to the extent that what people are critiquing is globalism rather than globalization in the broader sense, then it is fair to speak of Americanization and a new imperialism. Globalism very much is the attempt to make everything the same. Its goal is that all economic systems should fit the same norms, like McDonald's.

They haven't attained this goal yet; there is an exaggeration in the charge of McDonaldization. And yet there is something behind that charge that is disturbingly true. Globalism has largely succeeded in recent years in getting the argument accepted that market choice can and should be equated with real choice over one's destiny. As if having a choice between one yogurt and another is the same as having a choice between fundamentally different sets of political policies. The conclusion that follows from this premise is that since market choice is growing, freedom must be growing. But the reality is often the opposite. Market choice can grow while political choice diminishes. The appearance of freedom that comes from being able to choose between 12 kinds of yogurt can silence the question of who determines our lives. The number of these apparent choices that each of us is constantly making can be increasing at the same time as our joint capacity to co-determine our destiny is shrinking. In a phrase, democracy can get replaced by consumerism.

What would you say to the argument that cosmopolitanization is a side effect of globalism?

Banal cosmopolitanization, which plays a central role in the process of globalization from within, certainly is a side effect of globalism. But we have to be very clear what it means for one phenomenon to produce another through the accumulation of unintended side effects. Unintended side effects are just that, unintended. Causality of this sort doesn't make globalism the hidden truth of globalization any more than it makes capitalism the hidden truth of feminism.

When a qualitatively new social dynamic is produced by side effects, it is because several sets of unintended side effects, emanating from several different spheres of society, have all coalesced to produce a result none of them was aiming at, and which they might well have tried to stop if they'd had any inkling. Calvin certainly wasn't trying to produce liberalism when he encouraged people to learn to read.

An interesting example of banal cosmopolitanization as an unintended result is how transnational corporations end up assembling very varied teams of people. I think it's fair to say that without a certain degree of cosmopolitanization, that is, without some recognition of the difference of the other, they probably couldn't function. This is in part a counter-tendency generated by the same corporations which otherwise support full implementation of the neoliberal program. Their working conditions are capable of producing people who are more cosmopolitan, and who have more world awareness.

But while the situation is contradictory we shouldn't make any mistake. The dominant ideology of global capital is still globalism. Global capital is fractious and made up of independently operating and sometimes opposing factions. There may be factions among them who would really like to take environmental standards seriously; or who are seriously interested in the new possibilities of cosmopolitan democratization; or who would honestly like to, how should we say, tame exploitation and make it more humane. But these voices are not dominant yet.

Conversation 6

The Prospects for a Second Enlightenment

JOHANNES WILLMS *Doesn't it seem that what you have defined as global risk society and its side effects will eventually force globalism to open itself up to cosmopolitanization? I mean, it's always possible to shut your eyes for a while to ultimate consequences, and that's a large part of why we've been able to go on poisoning our rivers and cutting down the rain forests the way we have. But eventually these processes will approach their natural end when they become clearly unsustainable. At that point, clearly it will be impossible to say, "Let the market take its course." At that point, things will have to be decided politically.*

The question is, when we reach that point, will it simply be the age-old situation where might makes right? I personally still cherish hopes the world can change sufficiently in the intervening years so that this won't be true, at least not entirely. I'm hopeful that political globalization in some form or another will finally catch up at least part way with the other aspects of globalization. Do you think there is any chance of this? Or is this just a naïve hope?

ULRICH BECK   I'm very happy to see that, now that that we're approaching the end of our conversation, we've exchanged roles. The idea of global risk society clearly seems to have a contagion effect.

That's certainly the risk!

We've already discussed the many ways in which risk society sets in motion both a societal learning process and an involun-

tary process of politicization. This could happen on the global
level; cosmopolitanization could be part of that process. There
is no doubt that I've pursued my theorizing against the background of this hope. But I don't think it's merely a hope. I think
there are reasonable grounds for treating it as a possible future.

Earlier we discussed the progress that's been made on environmental questions, both in consciousness raising, and in
institutionalizing a series of conferences that embody it. (See p.
141ff.). Two things have thus happened that a few years ago
even the most open-minded and optimistic of political scientists would not have thought possible. In the first place, a global
consciousness really has come into being that accepts that there
is an environmental crisis, and that the environment by nature
is a global problem. And secondly, an institutional dynamic has
emerged from this in the form of an ongoing series of negotiations and a growing body of laws and initiatives. This latter
seems to me an excellent example of what some English theorists call a system of "free governance," that is, of regulations that
are promulgated not by a single government, but which are realized instead through the participation of all governments
affected.

This could be an example of a transnational regime in
embryo, that is, something which is not a state, but which is
rather founded on the shared interests of the participating
actors. It may be as weak as an embryo, but with as much of a
future before it. It is definitely something new.

Similar things are also true in the realm of economics. If one
reads the newspapers or listens in at conferences, the spectre of
financial meltdown is always in the background. During each of
the last few economic crises (Asia, Russia, etc.) there were literally thousands of people in London and Wall Street who were
employed to make the incalculable calculable. And yet both the
Asian and Russian crises came out of nowhere and surprised
them.

I think if we took global surveys after these crises we'd find
that most people in the world feel the global economy is an out-
of-control process of organized irresponsibility. To some extent
this feeling has already reached the stage of self-conscious
reflection. Both politically and in terms of economic theory,
globalism has already been put on the defensive. At every conference of the global economic actors, there is now a global

public that is present and watching, represented by reporters, who keep asking the representatives if they're afraid they'll be tracked down in their suites by the anti-globalists, which then promptly happens. The results are observed worldwide not only with sympathetic smiles but with people actively cheering them on.

If someone took a worldwide poll today about globalism, it would probably turn out that only the small minority who profit from it would vote for it.

This kind of change in attitude is precisely the kind of thing that we would expect to be set in motion by the risk dynamic of global society. Only here it's working itself out in the sphere of economics rather than ecology.

The concept of "side effects" is more than a slogan. It is the key difference between this theory and the social theories of the classical era. It is what prevents us from naïvely imitating what Marx did in the nineteenth century and applying it to the beginning of the twenty-first by postulating that a global cosmopolitan subject necessarily has to emerge from global risk society.

We don't have a dialectic of necessity anymore. All we have is the dialectic of unintended side effects. All we can do is to spell them out so that the conditions for movement and counter-movement can be clearly named and examined. We can't predict like they did.

In a world like this, a diagnosis of cosmopolitanization must always necessarily leave open the possibility that it will be the reaction against it that will end up dominating. It is a necessary part of this method of theorizing that we always go out of our way to keep an eye out for exactly the movements that run counter to whatever it is we're describing.

In the case of cosmopolitanization, this refers to things like the reinvigoration of ethnic identities, their reinforcement through new laws of citizenship, and the way they take up arms with every weapon in the modern arsenal. We side-effects thinkers can't wave off such tendencies as atavisms we know are doomed. They might well in the end prevail. In a similar vein, we have to worry about things like the way the military dynamic becomes steadily more independent of states as "normal" war approaches the borders of civil war and terrorism.

Mary Kaldor does an excellent job of tracing how side effects like that are getting played out in the military sphere in her book, *New and Old Wars*.

Now, we can oppose these scenarios with counter-scenarios, and our prognoses themselves will help to activate counter-forces. But only by looking objectively at both sides, at both possibilities – at both cosmopolitan society *and* its enemies – can we fully decipher either of them. This is the only way to make clear what the field of action is.

Collectively, we now have almost all the elements necessary to commence with a new sociology. What we need to do now is convince people who have invested themselves in it that it can capture a public.

It seems as if we are facing two alternatives, world society and world catastrophe. And for world society, the condition of its possibility is perpetual peace.

You know, of course, that perpetual peace was always bound up for Kant with a practical agenda. There are two images that run through that book from beginning to end: the inn and the graveyard. The inn is where philosophers will meet and argue and struggle over the question of perpetual peace and puzzle it out together. Kant tells us in the very first sentence that he originally took this title from a satirical sign on the signboard of a Dutch inn, where it was inscribed above the image of a graveyard, as if the pleasantness of the inn were being compared to eternal rest. And he notes that it was never clear whether the sign referred to the dreams of the philosophers or to the opposite, the final graveyard of perpetual war. Under the false rationality of national rulers, he says, it will surely be the graveyard. But he thought there was an alternative path. The inn full of philosophers, his equivalent of the Deweyan public sphere, could lay the groundwork for a different logic of international relations.

It's a very rich idea, and alarmingly up to date. The only difference today is how much more possible both of those options seem.

Earlier we discussed whether nationalism could be reconciled with cosmopolitanism and combined into a new synthesis. This is another idea that was first put forth two centuries ago. There were actually several people in Kant's time who argued that a nationalism or patriotism that did *not* allow people to be citizens of a particular nation *and* citizens of the world simultaneously would be inherently inflammable.

Remember, this was exactly the moment when modern nationalism was first becoming a force to be reckoned with. Heinrich Heine neatly squared the circle when he said that Germans should champion cosmopolitanism as a matter of national pride. He thought they should look at advanced thinking on cosmopolitanism as one of the essential contributions their country had made to world culture. He also prophetically went on to say that if Germany ever squandered this patrimony, if its pride in cosmopolitanism were someday entirely pushed aside by the noisy and aggressive nationalism he saw around him, it would lead to worldwide catastrophe. Which of course is exactly what happened.

Cosmopolitan nationalism is a specific form of the cosmopolitan localism we earlier discussed as being the true essence of cosmopolitanism. So back when national patriotism was still in its infancy, there were already attempts to do exactly what we now want to do today: to base the nation on openness towards the world; and to combine in a new unity what only on the surface appears to be opposed, namely national and cosmopolitan identities. Like them, we are still wrestling with the question of the possibility of a *cosmopolitan nation*. This is why the search for "native" cosmopolitan traditions is so important.

It is very important here to avoid two mistakes that we've already touched on. The first is the false distinction between *cosmopolitans* and *locals*. When the Americans say "all politics is local," they are hitting a very important nail right on the head. Many things distinguish rooted cosmopolitans, but certainly one of them is their sense of being near to everything in the world now that distance has been abolished. This brings with it an accompanying antagonism towards narrowness and closedness. Cosmopolitans actively want their localities to become more open to the world. The true cosmopolitan is also a true local. She is a cosmopolitan rooted in a particular place, a "glocal." Even so-called "global players," if you ask them their identity, they'll name a place. That place might be many different things, of course. It might be their birthplace, their place of origin, the place they grew up, or the place they live. But in the end, they are all still places.

The second and related error is to suppose that cosmopolitan openness is epitomized by the high-income nomads who live in the no-man's land of airports and hotels and conference centers. On the contrary, people like this live everywhere in the same nowhere and barely come into contact at all with the strangeness of other cultures. Interestingly though, things are pretty much the opposite with poor people who live a modern nomadic existence. The immigrants and illegals who live from hand to mouth are by contrast forced to make connections with different cultures simply in order to survive.

The new cosmopolitan society that the second modernity has made possible will be recognizable, if it arrives, by its *immanent world-openness*. If it continues to develop, more and more "world localities" will come into existence, not in the sense of a few giant cities that contain multitudes, but in this broader sense of localities with a dual nature that are open to the world. The world will flow in and out of these localities, and everything that is fragile or catastrophic at the global level will thus be present in every corner of the globe as a local condition, as a consciousness, and as an a spur to counter-action.

At bottom this sounds like a program for enlightenment. If that's a fair characterization, the worldwide discussion you and other sociologists have been having about globalization could be interpreted as the beginning of a second enlightenment.

A title like that would only be possible after it was all over, and after a quite a few arguments had played themselves out and we knew for sure what they meant. Such a thing can't be declared beforehand. It is no longer possible to announce a grand program like that after the advent of postmodernism.

That of course is exactly what would have to distinguish a second enlightenment. If it is possible at all, it will have to be an enlightenment that can exist without an overarching grand narrative, because that would once again set in motion an imperialist universalism. The universalism where one person sat at a desk and propounded universal truths, that was the first enlightenment. A second enlightenment would have to be one in which grand narratives from various traditions were brought together and we were able to learn from the resulting multi-plicity. By definition, none of them can be either as grand or as narrative as before. But they will have the potential to be both more enlightening and more integrating. I think a second enlightenment in this latter sense is both possible and necessary.

The first task of such a second enlightenment would be to work out a realistic and effective notion of *cosmopolitan democracy*. I think the intellectual efforts that would be necessary to accomplish this are already underway. I'm thinking, for example, of David Held and his group in Great Britain; of Jürgen Habermas; and recently of such theorists as Rainer Schmalz-Bruns, Michael Zürn, Klaus Dieter Wolf, and Edgar Grande.

We need to take a new historical step in our conception of democracy. The original idea of democracy famously took shape in, and took the shape of, the ancient Greek city-states. A territorial image of politics and of political legitimacy was thus integral to democracy from the very beginning. With the Greeks, this territorial image was that of the city-state. In the next stage, millennia later, we got nation-state democracy, which emerged out of the political revolutions that broke down the barriers to capitalism and began the first modernity. This parliamentary or presidential form has retained its status to this day as the only conceivable model of working democracy. But this territorial premise will have to be overcome in the step that lies before us. How can we have democracy without the territorial premise? Real democracy that really legitimates?

The first job for a second enlightenment is to bring forth an image, a concept, an organizational model of a deterritorialized democracy. We have to clearly imagine post-national and cosmopolitan democracy before we can institute it. And after imagining it, we have to subject each such conception to realistic criticism as to the possibility of instituting it.

You speak of realism, and that is certainly called for. The democratic idea is not just loosely coupled with the idea of the nation-state. Rather it seems like an inner necessity. Democracy presupposes trust, especially trust among strangers. Otherwise the redistributions it brings about will not be accepted, and the decisions it reaches will not be politically binding. Furthermore this peculiar trust among strangers has to be continually renewed.

Up until now, the social construction of the "nation" has been the only thing that has successfully provided this democratic underpinning.

That's true. But in the global era, nation-state democracy is trapped in what seems like an inexorable pincer movement. On the one hand, if it is to live up to its claim to be able to shape outcomes, and if it is to continue to make its decisions binding, it has to extend its power beyond the national rim: it must grow non-territorially outwards. On the other hand, the cooperation and reciprocity this process demands progressively undercuts the national legitimacy that nations are trying to preserve. They can only preserve sovereignty by giving it up.

The key to breaking out of this dilemma is the notion of the internalization of globalization. The cosmopolitanization of democracy in the broad sense, as something that includes both a set of political forms *and* its necessary cultural foundations, has to be founded on inner cosmopolitanization. We need to spell out what exactly it would mean to have decision centers that were simultaneously transnational and national. All of this has to be thought through.

We have to come up with political forms that will redefine and redistribute much of the sovereignty that has until now been concentrated at the national level in three directions: inwards towards society; downwards towards the local level; and outwards towards new decision-making networks and political arenas. But when we truly get beyond the container notion of the nation-state, the directional metaphor breaks down completely in the idea of cooperation states which contain the nodes of transnational political networks as an integral part of their own political structure.

Cosmopolitan agents and parties that link up with similar actors in other countries can be developed both in national parliaments and at the local level. I think this is how we should visualize the emergence of what Schmalz-Bruns calls the "experimental democracy of multiple locations." Localities that are open to the world would develop their "local that is also global" cultures, and the networks that already connect them would grow denser and more explicit. Thus when new transnational and deterritorialized decision-making centers come into existence (if they do), they will not be starting from scratch, but will rather be the outgrowth of, and a catalyst towards, an alternative form of society that has already been developing on the local (which means up through the national) level.

So the first problem is how to conceive of and instantiate deterritorialized democracy. The second set of problems that needs a second enlightenment to solve them flows from the nature of global risk society.

People who attack postmodernism in the name of the first modernity think that the main problem with it is its corrosive spirit. They think it destroys all truth, all science, and all values. I couldn't disagree more. When it comes to learning the truth about science and values, I think postmodernism already *has* been an enlightenment. It has wielded a pruning shear and lopped off the overarching and unsustainable claims which the first modernity made for universality. This was a major step towards a second enlightenment.

But pruning is not enough. In German there is the concept of "overcivilization." It may be debatable whether you can have too much civilization. But it is clear that the world changes its nature when it is entirely permeated with civilization. It means, for one thing, that the worst-case scenarios of scientific and technological development can only be understood in terms of scientific and technical categories. In a hypercivilized world, even the critique of scientific and technical rationality from the perspective of a broader lay rationality must avail itself of scientific methods, terminology, and evidence if that critique is ever to be successful.

This is the world of global risk society. It is a situation in which our capacity for self-endangerment is by definition – the definition of uncertainty – beyond our reckoning. When you combine that with the complete permeation of society with the scientific and technological world view, you end up with a world in which it is impossible not to make decisions, and it is impossible not to make them based on scientific reasoning. After postmodernism, it will be impossible for us ever to make these simultaneously scientific and political decisions again with the certainty that characterized the first modernity. But it will also be impossible not to make them. Global risk society puts us in the position of facing more and more decisions on which our long-term survival as a species depends with less and less certainty that we're doing the right thing.

In this situation, a doctrine that says there is no basis for decisions because there is no certain knowledge is no more useful than the preceding attitude that we had certain knowledge. It amounts to saying, "Yep, there's no way out, we leave you to your overcivilized fate." What we need is a process that will yield binding decisions based on *un*certain knowledge and a multiplicity of values. That is what we have to look to a second enlightenment to yield.

An enlightenment is a change in institutionalized ways of thinking. It's not about just lecturing people on values. It would be wrong to base our hopes on an opposition of ethics to technics. It's impossible to even imagine mobilizing an ethical movement that could oppose the global dynamic of unfolding technology. In this context, ethics is like a putting bicycle bell on a 747. You can tinkle warnings all you want and technology will continue roaring ahead on autopilot. The only conceivably effective route is to make the technological process, which is both a scientific and a political process, into a self-reflexive process. We have to turn it on itself. We have to make it reveal, and admit, and adjust itself to its true environment of uncertainty. We have to force it to reshape itself accordingly, both conceptually and institutionally.

So in my opinion, we should not be interrogating postmodernism for its supposed "destructiveness" towards values. Rather we should be questioning its default reliance on ethics to accomplish change, along with the political lethargy that is the logical consequence of most of its theoretical conclusions. I should add, however, that there are many political action movements in the world today which think of themselves as postmodern but which have actually moved far beyond these theoretical conclusions in their practice without ever realizing what a profound break with them they've made.

What would make a responsible science and technology possible?

How would it be possible to get science and technology to take their long-term consequences into account? To take seriously both the uncertainty and the possibly vast extensiveness of those consequences? And to incorporate this awareness into their rationality? That's a good question. We need somehow to open up scientific and technological thought to the idea of the fatefulness of action.

If we rephrased that question in terms of the philosophy of science, it would sound something like this. How can we move from a Popperian logic of research, which asks only how its research program can be falsified, to an integrated logic of research and technological development, which no longer rules the consequences of its actions as outside its domain, but allows those consequences (and the research they should necessitate) to redetermine its research program, its understanding, and the framework for action that is based on it? How can we develop a research program that, admitting the reality of uncertainty, and the possibility of irreversibility (that is, that the consequences of a given action may be beyond our ability to control), makes consideration and anticipation of negative outcomes into a constituent part of its rationality? Caution and preparation for the unexpected is a crucial element of what we consider reasonableness in most other realms of human action. But in the scientific and technological realms it is still mainly stigmatized as pre-scientific.

Up until now there hasn't been an answer to this question. But I'm convinced that the experience of risk society, and the failures of science and technology in the face of it, has been causing a growing split in the ranks of both scientific theorists and technological professionals. There are a growing number of them who want to incorporate the reflexivity of risk society into the logic of scientific research simply based on scientific and technological criteria. They don't want to be proven wrong and they don't want to create things they can't control or that have terrible side effects. It hurts their pride as scientists and technocrats. I think this split will increase as risk society continues to develop.

Risk society forces a fundamental cleavage between the elements that define rational action. We are forced to make more and more far-reaching decisions based on more and more uncertain information. In such a situation, the simple faith in science that defined the first modernity is insufficient. I believe the result, over time, will be a changing world view among scientific and technological personnel, one that is programmatically more uncertain, and which will attempt to deal with that uncertainty by gathering more perspectives, by integrating a wider field of experience. I think the programmatic indifference to the consequences of scientific action that defined the first modernity – something that was enshrined in the ethic of "value freedom" – will be criticized and replaced by a reflexive logic of research and action.

I'm the first to admit that nothing is certain, of course. But such an outcome is not only possible but I would argue probable. And if it comes about, it will be an important foundation stone on which a second enlightenment could be based.

Who would be social agents of this possible second enlightenment? I mean besides a handful of sociologists like Ulrich Beck, Anthony Giddens, Jürgen Habermas, and all the others I don't feel like naming right now. Are there any large-scale historical actors waiting in the wings?

We touched on one actor a moment ago, namely global capital. To me it's not yet settled that, in the future, global capital will be found exclusively on the side of globalism. It's possible that one may find a few cosmopolitans on the side of capital. I actually think the question of to what extent capital can be usefully divided into (potentially) cosmopolitan, neoliberal, and neo-national fractions is an intriguing one. We should return to this question.

The main answer, however, is that central actors of the second modernity will be the same actors already produced by the first modernity. All of them contain the possibility of transforming themselves from a national to a cosmopolitan basis. For example, the union movement could reorient itself in a cosmopolitan direction. Or parliamentary parties could be created, within the national political arena, that were primarily oriented towards transnational action.

Lastly, of course, there is the by now standard answer to this question, namely NGOs, those non-governmental organizations which have already carved out for themselves such a large presence in the emerging pluralistic global society, and whose high legitimacy is still in striking disproportion to their actual power.

It's true that at first sight this looks like just a fuss made by a bunch of sociology-heads who are in part promoting their books. When push comes to shove, these aren't the people who hold the balance of power. But really, the possible forces that could be enlisted on the side of cosmopolitanization include every social agent that was created by the first modernization in addition to every one that is in the process of formation.

Currently, every one of our major social actors has nation-state society inscribed in its conditions of existence. But every one of them could also reinvent itself, and could be motivated to do so purely out of self-interest rightly understood, as well as out of a desire to promote its central defining values. This goes not only for the large, society-defining collectivities like unions and parties, but also for the key smaller collectivities that have been produced by the division of intellectual labor. Professional groupings, from scientists to lawyers to economists, simply as researchers and as experts and as professionals earning a living, are all running into both practical and theoretical problems that might be easier to solve if they globalized themselves from within. And to do so, they will find they need a more cosmopolitan world, in the sense of one characterized by internalized local openness, where there is an easier and more immediate connection between every locality and the world as a whole.

Interestingly, besides these archetypal modern actors, the same rule holds just as true for social actors whose origins precede modernity, like the Catholic church. Ironically perhaps, there are elements of its organizational form, its mission, and its collective memory that seem perfectly suited to a cosmopolitan world precisely because they did form before the nation-state existed and so don't presuppose it as a condition of existence. A similar argument can be made for the other world religions, but let's play it through with the church.

In a certain sense, the Catholic church has been a global player from its beginnings. Unlike political parties or unions, it didn't need nation-state capitalism to come into existence, and it doesn't face the problems they do in overleaping its boundaries. This is also true on a conceptual level, where Catholicism is even less methodologically nationalist than in practice. In principle the Christian faith is completely independent of national and ethnic oppositions. Christian brotherliness is based on a concept of humanity that disregards all national and ethnic boundaries, and to that extent it provides a cosmopolitan foundation for action (even though we all know the brothers have some pretty long-running problems with the sisters.)

But before I start sounding like a convert, I have to point out that this foundational cosmopolitanism has been based on a grave defect ever since the beginning, which is that to be recognized as a brother or sister, you have to be of the faith, you have to be a Christian. One has to be baptized to enter the brotherhood. That means the condition of membership is literally a symbolical transformation, a complete renunciation of previous beliefs. When equality is based on this condition of sameness, you obviously don't have the crucial acceptance of the other as other. Historically speaking, without the symbolical homogenization of baptism, you not only didn't enter the brotherhood, you risked getting killed outside it. This is why when we speak of the church being a "global player" in times gone by, the first things that come to many people's minds are the wars of religion, the violent intolerance of dissenters, and the wake of worldwide devastation that followed the imperialist drive to convert people.

So the Christian concept of humanity has left an ambivalent legacy. It is a transethnic and transnational system of faith that is also not a recognition of the other in his otherness.

Along with this conceptual apparatus is a long institutional experience of existing as part of a global, multiethnic world society. It was out of that history that the church developed its form of organization. It transcends states and borders, and disregards (at least in principle) everything that nation-states regard as central, like borders, and the principle of excluding other nationalities, skin colors, and political persuasions. The church still preserves in its collective memory the idea that "humanity" is not determined by these oppositions, but rather by their overcoming.

So the Catholic church presents a pre-modern answer to the problem of the second modernity. Or more precisely, it *could* present a solution to second modern problems if it drew on its institutionalized collective memory and then transformed it.

The confrontation between individuals and world society seems like it ought to present an opportunity to the church. It looks like individuals will always need intermediate institutions and contexts in which meaning can be molded, experienced, interpreted, and made socially binding. Theoretically at least, a

Catholic faith that reconstructed itself, that distilled out its cosmopolitan essence and made it into a new basis of practice, could provide exactly that. It could provide individuals with a context of action and meaning that made more sense and was more effective than this Robinson Crusoe idea of being self-entrepreneurs trying to survive the war of all against all.

However, when I talk about a cosmopolitan reconstruction, I'm talking about deep structural changes. The church would have to embrace the internal openness that defines cosmopolitan world society. In church terms, that would mean opening its churches to the citizens of *all other religions*. Even the Lutherans!

That's an intriguing train of thought. The first modernity was in large part defined by its opposition to the church. Modernity's champions felt oppressed both by its temporal power and by its claims to define what counted as legitimate values. So it runs counter to our inherited prejudices to even entertain the possibility that the church in the second modernity might end up on the side of tolerance and intellectual innovation. Out of curiosity, is there any sign of this happening?

First off I have to make clear that I am not declaring the church *as it is* to be an agent of the second modernization. Like every other social institution, it could only serve such a role *if* it was fundamentally transformed. The reason I find the theoretical possibility of its transformation so interesting is precisely because it is a limit case. If we can imagine how this sort of internal transformation could happen to the church, which isn't even modern, then surely it's possible to map out a plausible route to cosmopolitanization for every other major social actor.

You are quite right to point out that in its institutionalized collective memory, right along with the idea of a transnational humanity, there is also this idea of the church as the agent of anti-enlightenment. There is also another problem. The timeless way the church has preserved a pre-nation-state world society in its organizational memory may actually be a function of its hierarchy. The doctrine that has contributed most to maintaining its transnational hierarchy for two millennia might ironically be its most explicitly anti-cosmopolitan dogma: the *nulla salus extra ecclesia,* the doctrine that outside the church there is no salvation.

Another thing that bears mentioning is that while the church predated the first modernity, it was also deeply affected by it, in both its ideology and its organizational form. The church now contains many organizational forms that do divide along the lines of nation-states. There have also been other fatal compromises with the ideology of nation-states, as when the church gave its blessing to war, even against other Christians. Many theologians and church fathers like to argue that nihilism is the reason the modern world is full of slaughter. But this is a bad faith way of letting themselves off the hook. Churches not only facilitated most of the first modernity's mass slaughters, they gave them their blessing.

For the church to progress in a cosmopolitan direction, there would have to be a fundamental self-criticism of this mortal sin of entanglement in the nation-state. In order to take advantage of the new transnational possibilities, the church would have to re-evolve an appropriate organizational structure, just like transnational companies had to.

The key question for the church will still remain the key question of cosmopolitanism: "How does one deal with the otherness of the other?" In the case of the church, the others are the members of other religions, including the enormous body of what were once called the "pagans" and now includes the secular. It is this fundamental relation that would have to be changed if the church wanted to adapt itself to the second modernity.

But the church doesn't seem to find the current situation very encouraging from a religious point of view, and I'm not sure I do either. What I see is that when the church loses its monopoly on truth it enters into direct competition with other world religions. The result is that exclusive certainties believed on faith clash with other exclusive certainties believed on faith.

I don't see the situation as that gloomy from the viewpoint of the church's growth. It's really not that fundamentally different from the situation that faced St Paul. When the Christian religion began, of course, it had no monopoly on truth and was in competition with other religions. Also Christianity originated in the context of what you might call imperial Roman pluralism. Instead of the modern norm of one people and one state, there one state included many peoples and many religions intermingled. That context brought out the Christian religion's strength, namely its ability to overleap boundaries between nations, ethnicities, religions, and classes.

If we take the long historical view, the development of the Christian religion and its "one true church" looks like a vast ironic circle. The church had its origins in a tiny sect set in the middle of ancient Roman pluralism. It grew up to become the world-view monopolist of the West – a West originally defined by that world-view monopoly – and it repressed other religions and sects. Now, in the second modernity it's back to the beginning. It is once again one religion among many. The only thing that is lacking is the freshness of its beginning.

The first modernity was defined by a clear opposition between science and religion. In the second modernity, claims to truth are relativized, including even science's monopoly on truth. This is partly the result of enlightenment about the role of science as a legitimating ideology; partly a reaction against the reign of experts; and partly the experience of the cumulative side effects of scientific progress – the experience, in short, of risk society. As you said, much of this is self-critique put forth by scientists themselves. Could the result of this be that in the second modernity the relation between science and religion might be less oppositional? And that this might allow religion in general and the church in particular new space in which to experience a resurgence?

Yes, it could. This is an excellent example of how the second modernity offers new development chances to old institutions. Science has given up its claim to being the sole and absolute ruler in the realm of rationality simply by consistently following its central principle of self-criticism. If the church then takes the crucial cosmopolitan step towards internal openness, which means finding a way to allow in the citizens of other world religions, both institutionally and in terms of a change of consciousness, then it could stand ready to supply services for which there is now a great demand. It could supply out of its collective memory and history a reservoir of meaning and practice that could counteract some of the tendencies that push individualization towards atomization.

One of the biggest showdowns that stand before us is the critique of globalism. The critique of market domination is essentially the condemnation of putting profit above all. On that level it's similar to the church's traditional critique of naked mammonism and the worship of the golden calf. So given its traditions, its membership problems, and the new opportunities to solve them through being a global player, why couldn't a cosmopolitanized church turn into something that could lead the charge against globalism? And why isn't it conceivable that out of such confrontation the church could gain a new persuasiveness, a new attractiveness, and a new membership?

The Catholic church is facing the real danger that it will soon become a zombie institution in Europe, which was once its core. It is halfway there already if one looks at the numbers of church members, or the average age of people who say they regularly attend mass. At the moment, these diminishing trends look set only to continue. And then you have places like Poland, which still counts as one the most Catholic countries in Europe, but whose abortion numbers are Europe's highest. That means that even in countries where people still look to the church to orient them, it is losing its power to influence their behavior.

So facing such a crisis, why wouldn't it be tempting for the church to renew itself with a crusade against globalism? When globalism triumphs in a country, it crushes cultural differences and dismantles the preconditions of democracy. That drains the legitimacy of all national institutions and creates the demand for an opposition. Unions are no longer, or are not yet, suited to lead such opposition. Normal politics has been unsuited for a long time because it is still so tightly bound to the limits of the nation-state. But the church already has a rhetorical arsenal that is purpose-built to make the problem of poverty the world's central problem. So it seems almost perfectly suited to shame globalism before the world, to care for its victims, and to uncover and help the world perceive its bad consequences.

This is all no more than a theoretical possibility, of course. The church would have to go through enormous transformations before it could take on such a role. For one thing, it would have to fight its way through to a real recognition of individualism, in the sense of letting people do things on their own initiative. It would have to reinterpret the idea of people being in the church's care more loosely, and retreat from all this silliness that the church knows better than individuals themselves, and that priests should maintain surveillance over the details of individuals' lives. All of this is completely inappropriate for the wide awake I and the social customs of the second modernity.

But we if we allow ourselves to follow out this thought experiment to the end, then the church offers the image of a social actor that wouldn't have to be entirely invented anew, but rather could put itself in a position to take on many fundamental problems of the second modernity by drawing on the resources of its own institutionalized collective memory. It could position itself as a major center of resistance to the current developmental tendencies of the global market, sharpen its profile, and increase its attractiveness. It's interesting to imagine what kind of situation would be produced if at the next world trade conference priests or theologians were to show up as speakers and declare their intention to continue to do so. Or if such activities and protest forums were to receive support from the Catholic church in the form of a major statement. What kind of attention would that attract, and what kind of possibilities for long-term and large-scale mobilization of people would it open up? And lastly, what kind of growth chances for the future would it yield to this particular world religion? If it were successful, can't we imagine this thought experiment we've been playing out with the Catholic church being carried through by other religions? There could at least theoretically arise a global competition between the different world religions over how to properly define the second modernity and rise to its new challenges, rather than over how best to deny its reality.

As a thought experiment, this point of view is very attractive for its impish subversiveness. But as a plan for action it's all a bit discouraging, isn't it? I mean, it would need a second reformation, on a much greater scale, this time among citizens of the world, for anything like this to happen. And there's little sign of that. We'd have to think in terms of centuries in order to place our hopes in this. Are the possibilities for the reform of normal politics really exhausted? You don't place any hope anymore in politics and the state?

Sure I do. But as always I can imagine two scenarios heading in opposite directions. On the one hand it is possible to imagine state politics escaping from its territorial bondage. We might call this, following Klaus Dieter Wolf, the "politics of a new *raison d'état.*" I spoke earlier about "cooperation states." (See p. 47ff.) Such entities act and create in combination, in networks of multilateral arrangements, which have been steadily knitting themselves together in order to compensate for the loss of the power of single states to determine their own fates. But there is also an opposite tendency in the drive to privatize state functions. Down that road we can see emerging the paradox of a "global privatized state," in which the economy, operating under the direction and authority of its own agents, appropriates the tasks of an international state.

From my point of view the more hopeful possibility is, of course, that of a new *raison d'état.* This is yet another instance where a deterritorialized phenomenon can only properly be appreciated when we realize it is emerging simultaneously on both sides of the old territorial boundaries, not only beyond them but also within them. This can be seen clearly in Europe. The member states of Europe have imposed on their governments a common budget discipline that in many ways ties their hands. But because this international regime of fiscal and economic policy sets narrow boundaries on what governments can do, it also relieves them from some of their legitimation pressures. It shields them from the domestic political resistance they would otherwise face because they can now claim that whoever rejects the regime's budget cuts is being anti-European.

It sounds like Hegel's enlightened bureaucracy, only this time at the transnational level, with the much-abused Brussels setting itself against the various national egoisms.

But think about what the parallel implies. Cooperation states are capable of creating a binding power to which each individual state must continue to submit regardless of whether there is a change in party government. This came out clearly when the red–green coalition in Germany attempted to carry out its promise to abandon atomic energy. That policy choice had been legitimized by majority support in the election. But the Kohl government already had woven a net of international agreements with its nuclear-friendly neighbors Great Britain and France that turned out to be fully and effectively binding on successor governments. These contracts not only stipulated how atomic energy and waste had to be handled, but threatened substantial penalty costs to any party which withdrew from them.

International regimes like this have been increasing in binding force. Michael Zürn describes a similar trend with regard to environmental policy. The fact that their binding force is transterritorial means that when such agreements come into conflict with the sovereign right of elected governments to make their own decisions, it is increasingly national sovereignty that has to give way. What we have here are banal but exemplary instances of collectively binding decisions that are made in transnational space, that are incorporated in laws that are purely regulative, and yet that bind with the force of superior law. That is, they override the law-making force of national sovereign bodies.

Now of course the term "new *raison d'état*" implies a new kind of state, one that reaches across borders, the regulative cooperation state. Cooperation states are embodied in regulations and they purchase their deterritorialized reach at the price of binding themselves. The extension of sovereignty and the renunciation of sovereignty are two sides of the same process.

At the same time, this process allows national governments to gain new political maneuvering room with which to outflank their domestic political opponents. Under certain conditions, the backing of the EU or the World Bank or the IMF allows decisions to be put through for which there is no majority in national parliaments. True, the governing transnational agreements have first to be forged, and national parliaments have to nod their assent. But even this assent is mostly given because the costs to a nation of going it alone are seen as too high.

Of course there is also an enormous downside to this. So far the transnationalization of state control has only increased the de-democratization of politics. Regulative regimes that cross borders give states extra playing room only at the price of removing these decisions from democratic legitimacy and control. It increasingly reduces democracy to a formal ritual where democratically elected governments are only free to communicate their post-hoc consent. Thus far, unfortunately, the transnationalization of the state and the loss of democracy have been two sides of the same coin.

The transition from the national to the regulative cooperation state seems to be following the model of enlightened despotism. It looks like the main agent of the European enlightenment will be the European bureaucracy rather than the national or European parliaments. Whether this means we're about to enter the second enlightenment, or whether this time we'll just get the despotism, is still an open question.

Let's return to the political role played by the economy. Marxists used to start out from the premise that the state had to be conquered and transformed into a dictatorship of the proletariat. Your second scenario seemed in a way to turn that idea on its head, describing a situation where the economy takes over state functions, the state is progressively minimized, and thus conquering the state yields less and less power to effect change. It's as if the capitalist economy could grow its own dictatorship of privatized state functions. Is that true?

A transnationally active economy needs security of contracts beyond what nationally limited states can offer. Ever since it first encountered this barrier, the global economy has been evolving its own institutions and organizational forms, which it now depends on to secure its contracts in transnational space. I'm thinking here of things like IMF letters of agreement or the imprimatur implied by World Bank participation in international loan syndicates. In addition, when an African state or a successor state to the Soviet Union decides that it wants to become a part of the world network, with whom does its government negotiate? With the WTO. WTO entry requires bilateral negotiations with governments, but it just as certainly requires bilateral agreements with market-leading companies. You can't enter the world network without reaching satisfactory agreements with those companies, especially the market leaders in telecommunications and information technology. So these corporations end up in a sense practicing their own private foreign policy. And it doesn't just affect these countries' foreign policy. It affects their vital interests across the board.

Susan Strange and Saskia Sassen have both extensively researched these questions, and they discuss both of these examples at length. I think they've developed a perspective that would give most political scientists hives if they really thought about it because it contradicts the fundamental postulate of political science, which is that state power rests on the monopoly of violence and the monopoly of law. On this view, the economy has neither military force nor the power to make law at its disposal. But this is exactly what is no longer true. You can have a transnational state which is a purely regulative state and which disposes of no military force. The example of the EU shows this clearly. It still doesn't have a military force of its own. But it shows just how much legally binding force can be administered through regulation when it is inscribed in a cooperative network with penalties in the form of lost opportunities for not cooperating.

It is this same binding force of transnational regulation that has been privately appropriated and perfected by the global economy in pursuit of its own administration. It wants to rationalize its legal environment in the same way as it previously rationalized the production of cars and computers.

However, we should not lose sight of the essential difference. The economy has privatized many state functions with great effectiveness. It has created numerous and powerful political facts. But neither effectiveness nor facticity is a basis for legitimacy. And legitimacy is ultimately still necessary for law to have a truly binding force. The bestowal of legitimacy is still reserved for the public and its parliaments. The global economic institutions of the "privatized state" still have lots of public conflict before them. They have yet to pass their hardness test.

So the world economy is carrying out all kind of political tasks but with precarious legitimacy. This bring us deeper into the concept of "politics." What does "politics" mean in connection with economic decisions nowadays? Surely it is not the straightforward merger of decision making we find in state monopoly capital (or "stamocap") theory?

The zone of intersection between politics and economics, between state and market, is broader and grayer than ever. We need to focus our concepts before we can make any sharp distinctions.

The migration of state functions to the economy usually means at first that the state loses some of its power over the economy. A relation between state and economy is replaced by one between economy and economy. There are many kinds of power in transnational space. In this realm the state is merely one actor among many, and one which can be trumped by its economic competitors.

When state functions are transformed into private economic ones, they cease to be *perceived* as political functions. They become perceived as non-political functions, and an economic calculus comes to dominate their decision making. But their essence as political decisions does not change. This is how the administration of the economy becomes "subpoliticized." It is reduced to the side effect of global economic strategies.

When BMW withdraws billions of dollars in investments from some country, as it did from the UK in the Rover affair, it's not only regional labor markets that collapse. It's also the political commitments behind them. In this particular case, the fallout forced Tony Blair to re-justify his idea of a "Third Way" (which places so much faith in business) before a furious public, and it wasn't easy.

Wherever lots of corporations invest, there national economies flourish, and the parties and governments that facilitate that investment grow and blossom. Such governments are living off the political side effects of global corporate investment policies. Conversely, their legitimacy is liable to be uprooted at any moment by strategies conceived and implemented in corporate boardrooms far away. Politicians, governments, and parties are thus forced not only to accept but more and more to justify to a furious public the consequences of decisions which they had little or no hand in making. Mobilizing consensus for decisions taken elsewhere has become in many ways the central task of national politics. This is precisely why it is becoming zombie politics.

If we look at this argument in reverse, it leads to an interesting question. For better or worse, modern nationalism was the creature of national capitalism. Could modern cosmopolitanism be the creature of global capitalism?

We all know the opposite possibility, which is that as world capitalism becomes radicalized, it could end up destroying the sources of cultural multiplicity and the preconditions of democracy and freedom. I don't mean to play that down. But I want to raise the question whether it is conceivable that global capitalism could be impressed into the cosmopolitan renewal of the state the way nineteenth-century capitalism was harnessed to strengthen the nation-state. Is it possible that the subpolitics of investment decisions could be forged into an instrument of power, which on the one hand could be used to enforce rules on the now-unshackled capitalism, and on the other could serve to force nation-states to open themselves up in the broad, cosmopolitan meaning of "opening"? Can we imagine a network of cooperation states which not only learned how to regulate the global economy, but how to turn its power of investment strike into a tool for fostering human rights, democracy, and justice in a way that overcame the dilemmas, and availed itself of the opportunities, offered by the second modernity? Or is this only conjuring up false hopes and false consciousness?

In a sense those questions allow us to return to the beginning. What role is being played by intellectuals in all this? Are they laying the conceptual groundwork for a second enlightenment?

You want to expose me as a pessimist? You want me to end this conversation by painting everything in gloomy colors?

How so?

I think the intellectual landscape today is largely desolate except for a few scattered oases. On the one hand, boundaries which up until very recently had been thought eternal are dissolving before our eyes. It is one of those moments when all that is solid melts into air, in Marx's justly celebrated phrase. And despite now forgotten predictions, it has not been the *Internationale* of labor which has brought us these changes, but the internationalization of capital. And what are the intellectuals doing? As far as I can see, most of them have refused to think anything new.

The theorists of postmodernism, neoliberalism, and system theory (like Luhmann, for example) disagree about almost everything. But they agree on one point. They all proclaim that what we are facing is the end of politics. And then they stop. They seem to have no intention of getting out of their fat armchairs of authority and taking a look. This is paradoxical to the point of being comical. And when these conceptual prisons are displayed with pride as the last redoubts of critical thinking, it makes me beside myself and speechless at the same time.

Don't tell me that you, Ulrich Beck, of all people, are going to end up like so many of your illustrious colleagues – Helmut Schelsky, Friedrich Tenbruck, maybe Jürgen Habermas (although I'm not sure in that case) – by becoming an anti-sociologist?

No. My opponents will go on hoping for that in vain. My goal is still wonderfully unreachable: to think society anew.

Selected Works by Authors Cited in the Text

Albrow, Martin, *The Global Age: State and Society beyond Modernity* (Stanford: Stanford University Press, 1997).

Barker, Eileen, "The Freedom of the Cage," *Society*, 33/3 (Mar./Apr. 1996).

Bauman, Zygmunt, *Liquid Modernity* (Cambridge: Polity, 2000).

Beck-Gernsheim, Elisabeth, *Juden, Deutsche und andere Erinnerungslandschaften. Im Dschungel der ethnischen Kategorien* (Frankfurt am Main: Suhrkamp, 1999).

Habermas, Jürgen, *Die Postnationale Konstellation. Politische Essays* (Frankfurt am Main: Suhrkamp, 1999).

Haraway, Donna, *Simians, Cyborgs and Women: The Reinvention of Nature* (London: Routledge, 1991).

Held, David, et al., *Global Transformations* (Cambridge: Polity, 1999).

Joy, Bill, "Why the Future Doesn't Need Us," *Wired*, Issue, 8/4 (April 2000).

Kaldor, Mary, *New and Old Wars: Organized Violence in the Global Era* (Stanford: Stanford University Press, 1999).

Kaufmann, Jean-Claude, *La Trame conjugal: analyse du couple par son linge* (Paris: Nathan, 2000). (Translated into German as *Schmützige Wäsche*, "Dirty Laundry.")

Leibfried, Stephan and Leisering, Lutz, *Time and Poverty in Western Welfare States: United Germany in Perspective* (Cambridge: Cambridge University Press, 2001).

Sassen, Saskia, *Denationalization: Economy and Polity in a Global Digital Age* (Princeton: Princeton University Press, 2003).

Schmalz-Bruns, Rainer, *Reflexive Demokratie. Die partizipatorische Transformation moderner Politik* (Baden-Baden: Nomos, 1995).

Schroer, Markus, *Das Individuum der Gesellschaft* (Frankfurt am Main: Suhrkamp, 2001).

Strange, Susan, *The Retreat of the State: The Diffusion of Power in the Global Economy* (Cambridge: Cambridge University Press, 1996).

Werckmeister, Otto Karl, *Zitadellenkultur* (Munich: Carl Hanser, 1989).

Wolf, Klaus Dieter, *Civilizing World Politics: Society and Community beyond the State.* Edited with Mathias Albert and Lother Brock (Boulder, Colo.: Rowman and Littlefield, 2000).

Wuthnow, Robert, *Acts of Compassion: Caring for Others and Helping Ourselves* (Princeton: Princeton University Press, 1993).

Zürn, Michael, *Regieren jenseits des Nationalstaats: Globalizierung und Denationalisierung als Chance* (Frankfurt am Main: Suhrkamp, 1999).

Books by the Authors in English

Ulrich Beck

Risk Society: Towards a New Modernity (London: Sage, 1992).
Reflexive Modernization: Politics, Tradition and Aesthetics in the Modern Social Order (with A. Giddens, S. Lash) (Cambridge: Polity, 1994).
Ecological Politics in an Age of Risk (Cambridge: Polity, 1995).
Ecological Enlightenment: Essays on the Politics of the Risk Society (Atlantic Highlands, NJ: Humanities Press, 1995).
The Normal Chaos of Love (with E. Beck-Gernsheim) (Cambridge: Polity, 1995).
The Reinvention of Politics (Cambridge: Polity, 1996).
Democracy without Enemies (Cambridge: Polity, 1997).
World Risk Society (Cambridge: Polity, 1999).
Individualization (with E. Beck-Gernsheim) (London: Sage, 2002).
Power in the Global Age (Cambridge: Polity, forthcoming).
The Cosmopolitan Perspective (Cambridge: Polity, forthcoming).

Johannes Willms

Paris – Capital of Europe: From the Revolution to the Belle Epoque (New York: Holmes & Meier, 1997).

About the Authors

Ulrich Beck teaches sociology at the University of Munich and the London School of Economics. He is the editor of the Second Modernity Series whose books address the new framework from a wide variety of aspects. He is also the director of the Institute for the Study of Reflexive Modernization at the University of Munich, financed by the *Deutsche Forschungsgemeinschaft*.

Johannes Willms is a historian, the author of numerous books, and the editor-in-chief of the *Süddeutsche Zeitung*, a leading German newspaper.

Index

CPSIA information can be obtained
at www.ICGtesting.com
Printed in the USA
BVHW04s2336150818
524084BV00021B/176/P